ASSEMBLY CODES

ASSEMBLY CODES

The Logistics of Media

Edited by Matthew Hockenberry,
Nicole Starosielski, and Susan Zieger

FOREWORD BY JOHN DURHAM PETERS

DUKE UNIVERSITY PRESS DURHAM AND LONDON 2021

© 2021 Duke University Press All rights reserved
Designed by Aimee C. Harrison
Typeset in Portrait Text, IBM Plex Mono, and IBM Plex Sans
Condensed by Westchester Publishing Services

Library of Congress Cataloging-in-Publication Data
Names: Hockenberry, Matthew Curtis, [date] editor. | Starosielski,
Nicole, [date] editor. | Zieger, Susan Marjorie, [date] editor.
Title: Assembly codes : the logistics of media / edited by Matthew
Hockenberry, Nicole Starosielski and Susan Zieger.
Description: Durham : Duke University Press, 2021. | Includes biblio-
graphical references and index.
Identifiers: LCCN 2020052553 (print)
LCCN 2020052554 (ebook)
ISBN 9781478009733 (hardcover)
ISBN 9781478010760 (paperback)
ISBN 9781478013037 (ebook)
Subjects: LCSH: Communication—Social aspects. | Mass media—
Social aspects. | Mass media—Political aspects. | Mass media—
Economic aspects. | Mass media—History. | Technological
innovations—Social aspects. | Communication and technology.
Classification: LCC HM1206.A78 2021 (print) | LCC HM1206 (ebook) |
DDC 302.23—dc23
LC record available at https://lccn.loc.gov/2020052553
LC ebook record available at https://lccn.loc.gov/2020052554

Cover art: (*Center top*) Ezra Stoller, CBS/Columbia Records.
Inspec-tion and packing of injection molded records (7-inch only).
© Ezra Stoller/Esto Photographics. (*Center bottom*) The Macintosh
computer assembly line at the Apple factory in Cupertino, CA,
January 25, 1984. © JP Laffont. (*All other images*) Stills from Stirling
Engineering, "Floppy Disk Assembly Line," video. Courtesy of
StirlingEngineering, San Jose, CA, https://www.stirlingeng.com/.

CONTENTS

Some Assembly Required

ONE OF THE OLDEST STORIES going in the history of technology is what Lewis Mumford called *etherealization*. In this story, innovations progressively liberate us from matter, from our bodies and our jobs, from clocks and desks, from anything dull and ordinary. Nineteenth-century commentators on the telegraph and the railroad, including Karl Marx, made the eighteenth-century poet Alexander Pope's thought about annihilating space and time ubiquitous in reflection about the convulsions of modernity. Charles Horton Cooley, the pioneering sociologist, famously wrote in his 1894 dissertation that "transportation is physical, communication psychical." Daniel Bell, in *The Coming of Post-Industrial Society* (1974), saw the preindustrial extraction of raw materials and the industrial production of goods as giving way to a new service economy in which knowledge was the highest value; he thought mining, for instance, of relatively little relevance to his forecast for coming times. For current examples, we need look no farther than the techno-liberationist talk and sleek products coming out of Silicon Valley. Ether-alized terms such as *cloud computing* and *wireless*, now normal in everyday speech, are perfect examples. What could be more earthy than the cloud or cable-y than Wi-Fi? And how does anyone ever manage to say "fulfillment center" with a straight face?

This book is a refreshing counter-blast to the ethereal narrative. It shows what the university can do at its best, as a place where thinkers can dissent against prevailing powers, analyze the fatuousness of prevailing ideologies, imagine what could be, and pull away from easy frames of reference, even if university life is subject to many of the same dispiriting pressures as other cultural industries. Forget the idea that mining or shipping are no longer relevant; drop the fantasy that your devices come to you immaculately conceived and without labor pains. This book gives voice to new and old histories. Slavery lives on in digital life. Bodies still bleed. Minerals are still pulled from the earth by people under precarious conditions. The sea matters. The earth has not gone away. The material circulation of political economy drives the work of all media. The logistical imagination is alive and well!

Logistics has a long history, and if it was originally defined as the art of assembling and supplying armies, we might think about different sorts of armies. Friedrich Kittler was enamored of the fact that the Greek word *stoikheia*—which featured in the title of Euclid's geometry and was translated as *elements*—also means letters and soldiers, that is, things that are arrayed into lines—as of battle, poetry, or parallelograms. Like Paul Virilio, Kittler deplored—at times with an alarming eagerness for military matters—the civilian orientation of most media history. War is hell, as military people know better than anyone, but war's sheer repulsive awfulness doesn't mean we should turn our gaze away. In battle, representation always tilts into operation; there is no easy separation message and medium. To study war is also, as many have told us, to study capitalism—Marx's famous "bellum omnium contra omnes," the war of all against all. We shouldn't leave logistics to the generals and the captains of industry. It is too important a style of thinking for a moment of such massive planetary turmoil, in part because it shows that media are not just channels for ideology, but that channels are themselves ideological. This volume hacks logistical thought for critical purposes.

Media studies may yearn for the fleshpots of interpreting content—something we generally know how to do well—but this book offers a different invitation: to look at *time, space, and power*. This was a formula fitting the work of Harold Innis—which we might update to *time, space, and energy*. A logistical focus on media history opens up much wisdom about past and present. Writing, the ur-medium, might have been developed to store oral poetry in the exceptional case of the Greek alphabet, but much of the history of scripts has been managerial, executive, and computational. Digital media have their backdrop in ancient bookkeeping—of labor hours, celestial motions, wheat, and beer. Even if the term *logistical media* is of relatively recent coinage, the practices and concerns it indexes have been around since human beings first used stones and baskets, clothing and fire, to shape their worlds and selves.

This volume also invites a refreshing turn in intellectual focus. I remember in the 1980s several hip writers telling us we had to drop the ideas about technology developed in the 1940s and 1950s. Those years gave us too much "mass society" talk, too much worry about the dinosaurs of electrical power generators, nuclear bombs, and cultural industries like film and television! Now we were surrounded by new nimble digital mammals and savvy users equipped to wage semiotic guerrilla warfare against the dinosaurs. We know how that story turned out; Apple used it, in fact, in its famous 1984 Super Bowl ad of the lone brave woman taking down Big Brother, and generations of cultural studies majors, schooled in such doctrine, went on to staff the creative industries. I welcome the return of the big and the raw, along with the small and the refined, at a higher turn on the spiral. Those dinosaurs never went away; they just went out of scholarly sight. They went infrastructural. Extractive economies never vanished. We still depend on oil, timber, coal, and corn, to varying degrees of tragedy. We were once told that unmasking ideology was too crude a method for the subtleties of cultural flows. Peter Sloterdijk, in his *Critique of Cynical Reason* (1983), decisively showed just how hazardous and tired a tool it can be. Unmasking can be crude, and it encourages both an arrogance about knowing better than others and a metaphysically shallow split of appearance and reality. But crude times can call for crude responses. The old-fashioned exposure of lies is still fully relevant! There is plenty of propaganda on the prowl. The task is to figure out how to combine an ontological account of media as infrastructures of being with an epistemological one that allows us to say when being is wrong or bad.

Not that these essays are crude in the least. They are often musical in spirit. It is remarkable how often many of them wax lyrical. There is a yearning for beauty and freedom here that grows out of and alongside the analysis. There is a poetry about matter in motion, and these essays range across its many modes and moods—lyric, tragic, epic, elegiac, satirical, even mock-heroic. I kept thinking of another thinker important for media history, Theodor W. Adorno, who believed a commitment to the aesthetic as a philosophical and political practice of redemption went happily together with a hard-headed analysis of culture industries.

Part of what this book brings is a spirit of copiousness, an abundance of topics, methods, tools, and theorists. I learned some new names and cool moves, and some new words such as *destoolment* and *protocological*. It participates in a florescence of field-defining terms in media studies, as we learn to take metal, seawater, sweat, and wood seriously along with our old standby topics. Media. Means. Infrastructures. Regimes. Technics. Technologies. *Technai.*

Kulturtechniken. Platforms. Containers. Utilities. Standards. Logistics. Materialities. Assemblages. Apparatus. Vessels. Environments. Ecologies. *Umwelten.* Networks. Actor-networks. *Milieux.* Ambiances. Ensembles. Kit. Gear. *Gestell.* Paraphernalia. Tools. Implements. Machines. Equipment. Protocols. Clouds. Elements. Operations. Operative ontologies. Hardware. Software. Wetware. Trappings. Even the term *cargo* might serve, as made famous by Jared Diamond's Papuan friend Yali—why did white people get all the cargo, Yali asked about the stuff of modernity such as steel axes, Coca Cola, medicine, radios. This book adds assembly codes, supply chains, and much more to our analytic repertoire for understanding the heaped-up stuff of modernity.

Assembly, it is sometimes said, is the least appreciated of the five rights specified by the First Amendment to the US Constitution. Assembly, we all know, is political even when it involves things of all kinds, whether they are parliaments or programs, laptops or loaves, and quarantine has only shown us how potent it is to be with others in the same space and time. It is also sometimes said that the three saddest words in the English language are "some assembly required." This volume shows us why that is not sad, but an opportunity. This book reveals, and embodies, the pleasure and pain, the toil and possibility that come when we work together to assemble something better, clearer, or at least more puzzling than what we have already. May this book unmask the illusionists hiding the earth metals and the human cost in our everyday tools, and may it lift us to a better place through the poetry and music of its analysis—or at least to one more nervous and well-informed.

—JOHN DURHAM PETERS

ACKNOWLEDGMENTS

WE WOULD LIKE TO THANK our brilliant contributors, whose insights into the connections between media and logistics have driven this project. Several of our contributors presented at the Supply and Command conference at New York University in 2018, and we would like to thank both the participants and our co-organizers for their work to develop this emerging area of media studies. In developing this collection, we have built not only on their contributions but on the groundbreaking research of scholars of media and logistics who continue to inspire us. And, most importantly, we would like to thank Courtney Berger, Sandra Korn, and the editorial team at Duke University Press, whose careful and creative logistical labor has made this book possible.

Nicole would like to thank Matt and Susan for being fantastic coeditors, and she extends thanks to her colleagues and students at New York University, especially Isra Ali, Arjun Appadurai, Finn Brunton, Alex Galloway, Lisa Gitelman, Erica Robles-Anderson, Natasha Schüll, and Helga Tawil-Souri for conversations that shaped this text over the past several years. Nicole is grateful for the members of the INFRA research group, especially Ian Alexander, Neta Alexander, Mei Ling Chua, Rodrigo Ferreira, Marcha Johnson, Sam Kellogg, Harris Kornstein, Ayesha Omer, Anne Pasek, Colette Perold, and Rory Solomon, whose exchanges informed the early development of this book. Nicole would also like to thank Simon Stern for the invitation to present an iteration of this material at the Grafstein Lecture at the University of Toronto; and Scott Lash and Sophie Haines for the invitation to think through logistics at Oxford in 2020. Last, special thanks to Jamie Skye Bianco, Shannon Mattern, and Lisa Parks for the many logistical visions that shaped this book.

Susan would like to thank Nicole and Matt for being such wonderful coeditors, and she would like to thank the interlocutors currently and formerly in the English Department at UC Riverside, especially Fred Moten, Jennifer Doyle, and Sherryl Vint; colleagues at the Max Planck Institute for the History of Science, especially Jennifer Derr, Wilko Graf von Hardenberg, Mike Pettit, and Lukas Rieppel; colleagues at the Institute for Culture and Society at Western Sydney University, especially Ned Rossiter, Brett Neilson, and Tony Bennett; the Department of Language and Literature at the Norwegian University of Science and Technology, especially Anders Skare Malvik, Frode Lerum Boasson, and Knut Ove Eliassen; and the Department of English at Exeter University, especially John Plunkett and Regenia Gagnier. Thanks also to Tung-Hui Hu and Sina Najafi. For research help and image permissions, thanks go to the staff at the Newport Historical Society, the National Maritime Museum, the London Metropolitan Archives, and the Schomburg Center for Research in Black Culture.

Unsurprisingly, Matt would also like to thank Nicole and Susan for being amazing coeditors. He would also like to thank colleagues at New York University and Fordham University, including Lisa Gitelman, Mara Mills, Mary Poovey, Alex Galloway, Ben Kafka, Carlin Wing, Jason LaRiviere, Kouross Esmaeli, Kavita Kulkarni, Patrick Davison, Tim Wood, Diana Kamin, Xiaochang Li, Ella Kilk, Yoav Halperin, Jacob Gaboury, and Shari Wolk; at the Internationales Kolleg für Kulturtechnikforschung und Medienphilosophie, especially Bernhard Siegert, Lorenz Engell, Orit Halpern, and Bernd Herzogenrath; and from Supply and Command and the critical logistics community, especially Colette Perold, Ingrid Burrington, Martha Poon, Dara Orenstein, Miriam Posner, Patrick Brodie, Niccolò Cuppini, Guillermo León Gómez, Silvia Lindtner, Juan Llamas-Rodriguez, and Deborah Cowen. Finally, he would like to thank his partner, Jing, and son, Nicholas, whose care has become his most complex logistical operation.

MATTHEW HOCKENBERRY,
NICOLE STAROSIELSKI,
AND SUSAN ZIEGER

INTRODUCTION

The Logistics of Media

MEDIA AND LOGISTICS ARE GLOBAL OPERATING SYSTEMS. They set conditions for the circulation of information and culture. They activate inventories of materials and networks of infrastructure. They coordinate interfaces between bodies, objects, and environments. Deployed in ongoing projects of capitalization and exploitation, often in the name of global connection, consumption, and security, they affect the day-to-day lives of people around the world. And they are inextricably entangled with one another. Even the text of this book has been enclosed in packets, transmitted, and reassembled innumerable times—a process guided by logistical principles. The materials that constitute it, whether printed on paper or housed in Amazon's cloud storage, were transmitted via trucks, containers, pallets, and hands, their movement likely managed using logistical software. Logistics—the organization and coordination of resources to manufacture and distribute global commodities—depends not only on software and data infrastructures but on a mass of screens, communications devices, and paperwork.

Assembly Codes is the first collection to critically interrogate the specific points of contact, dependence, and friction between media and logistics. We argue that the fundamental interconnections between these two systems are essential not only to understanding both of their operations but to the contemporary circulation of culture on a global scale. To describe the dynamics of media today—its production and industries, its vast infrastructures, its material forms, and its global movements—a basic conception of the supply chain and the science of coordinating techniques is necessary. For the operations of global logistics, a focus on media, whether in the circulation of internet traffic or on the devices that coordinate their commands, reveals crucial links, choke points, and dependencies. Media and logistics are interoperable systems, and the activities of one hinge on the smooth operation of the other.

This collection builds on an exciting field of logistical study that has emerged over the past several decades. In geography, sociology, cultural studies, anthropology, science and technology studies, and history, among other fields, scholars have documented how logistics has been instrumental to warfare and capitalism, as well as to their attendant imperial projects. The idea of logistics was first articulated in the study of warfare, where its theorization elevated it to the same prominence as that of strategy and tactics, but recent work has focused on its adaptation into commerce, especially the impact of the logistics revolution in the early 1960s that cemented logistical operations as a cornerstone of neoliberal economics and politics.[1] In economics, Peter Drucker famously declared logistics the "last dark continent" for commerce left to conquer, and scholars have documented this transition from the more constrained study of "physical distribution management" to the recognition of logistics as "the most encompassing term that describes the management of firms' acquiring and distributing activities over space."[2] Collectively, this work reveals that, as the science of moving goods, people, and information as efficiently as possible to meet the global demands of capital, logistics has been the engineer of the mid-twentieth century. In the subsequent drama of globalization, in which factories have moved to the Global South to exploit cheap labor, and goods are shipped back to the Global North for consumption, logistics has been the star.

In critical logistics studies—a field that coalesced from these inquiries to describe the conditions of logistics, the abstract structures of the supply chain, and their impact on modern life—media is ever-present, even if often in the background.[3] In *The Deadly Life of Logistics*, Deborah Cowen explains that with the expansion of global supply chains, commodities are not produced in conventional geography, but "across logistics space."[4] Logistics space is mediated in a multitude of ways: through process maps, enterprise resource planning software, worker surveillance, the capture of biometric data, and satellite tracking. Logistics, Sandro Mezzadra and Brett Neilson argue, fundamentally "involves the algorithmic coordination of productive processes in space and time."[5] Analyzing these algorithmic architectures, Ned Rossiter calls for a logistical media theory that grasps these technologies'

Matthew Hockenberry, Nicole Starosielski, and Susan Zieger

primary function: "to extract value by optimizing the efficiency of living labor and supply chain operations."[6] These accounts recognize that media are integral to the conceptualization and spread of logistics. Supply chains are defined as much by their communications networks and media technologies as they are by their containers and pallets.

As logistics has become a topic in media and communications studies, scholars have expanded beyond the domain of supply chain management to address its broader conceptualization as a set of coordinating techniques. Paul Virilio's "logistics of perception" places cinematic sounds and images alongside accounts of weapons, people, and materials.[7] Media scholars, including Ned Rossiter, John Durham Peters, and Judd Case, argue that the study of "logistical media" does not simply involve analysis of the visual and computational dimensions of Walmart's or Amazon's operations but a recognition of media's capacity to process data, coordinate movement, and more widely orient sociality.[8] Logistical media, Peters writes, are the media of "orientation," devices of cognitive, social, and political organization and control. They are clocks, maps, and calendars; positioning technologies such as radar; managerial forms such as lists; and commercial codes such as stamps. Due to their ability to organize storage and transmission, and their capacity to locate, arrange, and distribute, all media possess this logistical dimension. Media, in other words, are not simply conduits through which global logistics emerges but exist "prior to and from the grid" through which such operations can be constituted.[9] They are not logistics' black box. They are the instructions for its assembly.

Assembly Codes enters into this conversation about the techniques of global logistics and the operative logics of media with three specific interventions. First, it describes what we call the *logistical imagination*. Logistical technologies have always been accompanied by new ways of seeing and listening, reading and knowing, thinking and moving—which have themselves catalyzed crucial shifts in our modes of communication. To unpack the logistical imagination is to trace the representational and imaginative modes of logistical activity, as well as the aesthetic and performative practices that have emerged to grapple with logistical transformations. Second, the essays here illustrate what we call *logistical instruments*: the extensive array of media techniques, technologies, and forms that are essential to the operation of global logistics. The collection's essays demonstrate that media's operative logics—their logistical capacity to orient, arrange, and sort—are deeply connected to the ways in which they have been instrumentalized in histories of militarism, commerce, and empire. As a result, the media technologies that hold these projects together necessarily advance the trajectories of capitalism, settler colonialism, and biopolitical management. Logistics invests these linked projects with their own seemingly organic and inevitable sense of life, what Cowen describes as an abstract vitalism, at the expense of the human lives of laborers and migrants, and several of our essays touch on these stakes.[10] Finally, the essays reveal how the industrial processes of traditional media production—from cinema to sound recording—are being reshaped as *supply chain media* by logistical technologies and practices. While the processes of sourcing and assembly have always had a substantial effect on how media is produced, distributed, and consumed, contemporary media are being crafted in relation to what Anna Tsing has named "supply chain capitalism."[11] The elements of supply chain capitalism that Tsing documents—actual precarity, collaboration, nonscalability, and translation—are central concerns many of our essays also take up.[12]

While these interventions build across the collection, we have organized *Assembly Codes* into sections that foreground these three ways of rethinking media: as sites of logistical imagination, as instruments of logistical operations, and as products of global supply chains. In the remainder of the introduction, we chart the stakes, contexts, and future directions of these avenues of inquiry, as well as the ties between individual essays and our shared interventions. The authors assembled draw together a diverse set of objects as well as a range of theoretical and conceptual orientations: Black and Indigenous studies, German media theory and sound studies, and the analysis of media industries and production cultures. Their essays foreground the contiguity of production and distribution, the messy relationship between base and superstructure, and most importantly, the continuities between contemporary and historical forms of logistical mediation. They expose the way economic, political, and social power consolidates in and through logistical operations and acts of assembly. Through their careful analyses, the book reveals how contemporary mediation is haunted by its logistical substructures, from the slave ship to the supply chain.

The Logistical Imagination

How did the imagination of the world change once it expanded to include logistical ways of thinking? When did thoughts of logistical operations begin to hold sway over the details of daily lives? How can one represent the expansive system of global logistics? To answer these questions is to unpack the logistical imagination: the new ways of seeing and imagining the world

Matthew Hockenberry, Nicole Starosielski, and Susan Zieger

brought about by logistics and the new forms of mediation, philosophy, politics, and aesthetics that have emerged to confront it. To analyze the logistical imagination is to understand what it means to see like a supply chain, to comprehend the conditions that make one feel like cargo, or to explore logistics' racialized and gendered aesthetics. It is to document how the subject of Western individualism is, fundamentally, a logistical one, and to interrogate how the historical emergence of logistics in commerce and warfare reshaped everyday life for workers, consumers, and citizens. It is also, we suggest, to imagine how the vast contours of logistical systems elide the faults and friction of their diverse and often divergent operations.[13] To do so involves charting how these underlying instabilities, where "capital hits the ground," may elicit new political potentials and subjective possibilities.[14]

Critiques of capitalism often construe logistics as something simultaneously monumental and microscopic. It is always present but nowhere to be seen. Increasingly automated and algorithmic, it is, like capital itself, an inhuman, unknowable thing.[15] Its representations in texts, photographs, and films are almost always defined by the enormous structures erected in pursuit of global trade. Capable of transporting more than ten thousand containers per trip, megaships, for example, are vessels so massive that they are unable to sail through the expanded Panama Canal locks, their decks unreachable by most North American cranes.[16] The mind-boggling scale of these technologies and of the systems that manage their movements are defined by the dark dreams of the "logistical sublime," where global trade flows are ever more precisely patterned in a nightmare of unending rationalization.[17] Researchers have described how logistics is inextricable from other global phenomena, including the conditions of late capitalism and the politics of neoliberalism. Jasper Bernes has argued that "the totality of the logistics system belongs to capital," and as such, it remains cognitively and materially impregnable by traditional revolutionary means.[18]

While the logistical sublime is the dominant form of the logistical imagination, mobilized by capitalists and critics alike, it is not the only representational possibility. As a means of opening up the analysis of the logistical imagination, the authors in *Assembly Codes* delve into the many ways that humans have engaged with and envisioned logistics. A study of these cases reveals that the logistical imagination is always refractive, embodied in the particular moments and media of their production. This is true when workers slow down or speed up to control the fluctuation of logistical time and speed; when protestors blockade ports to limit the movement of materials across logistical space; and when undocumented migrants and fugitive slaves seize opportunities to travel outside the well-ordered regimes of logistical control. But it is also true when middle-class people use location-based apps to hook up, request a car to the airport, or arrange for a next-day delivery in a single click. The logistical imagination not only drives forces of oppression, it ignites resistance and lubricates banal normativity. Our aim is to understand the specific differences that these representations, aesthetic practices, and modes of thinking make to larger logistical projects.

We are motivated by the recognition that new imaginations can catalyze systemic shifts. Indeed, the contemporary concern with logistics—which has culminated in academia in fields such as critical logistics studies—was sparked by the dissemination of new logistical imaginations and representations. It was in part through media coverage of the impacts of globalization, including its supply chains, workers' rights, and environmental impact, that middle-class people in the Global North began to grapple with logistics. The anti-sweatshop campaigns of the 1990s that stemmed from Nike's disastrous "sweatshop summer" gave rise to a new discourse of ethical consumerism, one that expanded to encompass concerns for human rights and worker welfare, the ethical treatment of animals, environmental contamination, and global climate change.[19] Recent conceptions of corporate social responsibility, the connection between local sourcing and consumption, and assessment methodologies like carbon footprinting all bring to light the journeys commodities make as, driven by logistics, they are assembled and distributed around the world. At the same time, the meteoric rise of private carriers like FedEx, UPS, and DHL made delivery trucks and logistical laborers familiar figures, so much so that the 2000 film *Castaway* could reimagine *Robinson Crusoe* as a narrative about a FedEx logistician stranded on a desert island in the crash of a cargo plane. It is precisely because of logistics' extraordinary scale and apparent unknowability that media play such a critical role in shaping our knowledge of these systems and afford the potential for collective forms of resistance.

An attention to forms of mediation reveals the language and iconography of logistics as a potential site for intervention. Marc Levinson's *The Box* (2006) and Alexander Klose's *The Container Principle* (2009), for example, both figure the container as the emblem of globalization and the originary sign of modern logistics.[20] Carried by cranes between ship holds and truck beds, this intermodal innovation accelerated shipping times, ending the era of arduous and time-consuming break-bulk unloading, and the work of long-shoremen who labored on the docks. By the turn of the century, the box was ubiquitous both in distribution, where the TEU, or twenty-foot equivalent

Matthew Hockenberry, Nicole Starosielski, and Susan Zieger

unit, had become the standard object of operational consideration, and in the public imagination, as developers repurposed it for the architecture of everything from modular housing to shopping malls. Sites like Box Park in London, Tolchok near Odessa, and Common Ground in Seoul reveal a logistical imagination at play, one that places global transportation in a local context of commodity display and retail consumption. The shipping container not only infiltrated the visual and architectural landscape, it was remediated in films (such as Allan Sekula's 2010 *The Forgotten Space*), art installations (such as Gabby Miller's 2015 *Turquoise Wake*), and podcasts (such as Alexis Madrigal's 2017 *Containers*). Alberto Toscano and Jeff Kinkle identify a "poetics of containerization," noting the form's mesmerizing power as an icon of capitalist abstraction, especially to visual artists.[21] Engaging with this form, activists, workers, and scholars have attempted to transform its meaning and leverage the logistical imagination in pursuit of progressive political causes.

Analysis of the logistical imagination is not limited to this most recent moment or to late capitalism. Even in the eighteenth century, Adam Smith found modern man the product of an impossibly global network, one where "all the different parts of his dress and household furniture, the coarse linen shirt which he wears next his skin, the shoes which cover his feet, the bed which he lies on, and all the different parts which compose it, the kitchen-grate at which he prepares his victuals, the coals which he makes use of for that purpose, dug from the bowels of the earth, and brought to him perhaps by a long sea and a long land carriage."[22] During this period, the first overtly political imagination of the supply chain circulated when antislavery activists refused to sweeten their tea with "blood sugar" harvested by slave labor and advocated for more space and ventilation on slave ships. The Atlantic focus of this section indicates the centrality of historical logistics to Black studies, especially its engagement with the Middle Passage, a foundational moment at which ethics and logistics clash.

Such imaginations of supply only multiplied as technologies of acceleration such as the railroad, telegraph, and steamship inaugurated the dromological culture of the nineteenth century, speeding the flow of goods, people, and information throughout the world. Instead of UPS trucks, symbols of earlier logistical imaginations included sights such as the "traveling post offices" of Britain's modernized postal system, where workers sorted mail on moving trains to deliver up to five times a day.[23] As a predecessor of the Amazon interface, the twentieth-century circulation of the Sears mail-order catalog in the United States created a consumer culture based on delivery to far-flung outposts. Even military matters were open to acts of logistical reimagination and critique. In the mid-nineteenth century, the Crimean War was widely criticized for the logistical failings that left its soldiers shoeless and starving.[24]

The essays in the first section of this book delve into historical cases and origin points for the logistical imaginations of today's global trade and supply. They make use of a range of interpretive methods that unpack the ways of seeing, hearing, and sensing that result from logistical operation. Stefano Harney and Fred Moten, offering a deconstruction from the perspective of Black studies, reinterpret the Lockean individual as the simultaneous proprietor and inhabitant of the body-as-container, arguing for a fundamentally logistical understanding of mediation and the relationship between mind and body. Materializing this argument in an analysis of a document responsible for the operationality of modern trade, Susan Zieger follows the history of the bill of lading to demonstrate how the form necessitates an imagination of trade as a process of textual and visual revision, improvisation, and interpretation. Examining Alfred Charles Sam's Pan-African vision for African American remigration, Ebony Coletu broadens the scope of these arguments to consider how logistical plans and identities involve complex reimaginings of settler colonialism. Finally, Shannon Mattern interrogates the soundscapes of the logistical world, from antennae beeps to the shouts of the stevedores, to demonstrate how sounding technologies regiment logistical operations. Together, these essays document how logistics brought about new forms of subjectivity, along with new forms of paperwork, reading, images, and sonic surrounds, as they offer directions for reimagining logistical operations.

Logistical Instruments

The communication historian Harold Innis argued for the critical relationship between logistical operation and the history of media technologies, finding in even the mundane materiality of clay tablets an ancient logistical imperative. Since moisture was necessary, Innis wrote, and "since the tablet dried quickly," it was important "to write with speed and accuracy." In this "economy of effort" and corresponding "reduction in the number of strokes," he found an explanation for how the "remnants of pictorial writing" were exchanged for the logistical efficiency of cuneiform. Observing similar sensibilities in everything from Phoenician script to the "problem of producing quantities of letters with speed," Innis offered a foundational history of

Matthew Hockenberry, Nicole Starosielski, and Susan Zieger

mediation defined in terms of logistical capacities like speed and mobility—one that would be influential to the work of media theorists such as Marshall McLuhan and James Carey.[25] Some mediums, Innis explained, were "heavy and durable." The aqueducts and granaries of the ancient world carved out geographies, creating points of orientation persisting in time. Others were, by contrast, "light and easily transported."[26] Papyrus scrolls, the orders Napoleon issued to his troops, and inventories of slave ships are of this latter sort. These media functioned as a kind of "immutable mobile," Bruno Latour would later suggest, permitting movement of abstract assemblies across geographic constraints by allowing others to order their contents. These mobile forms made more durable infrastructures "soft," accessible to new forms of logistical control.[27]

In the history of communication there have been a multitude of forms that accomplished this sort of logistical remediation: maps, lists, orders, and plans; bills of lading, assembly, and exchange; parts lists and production orders; requisitions and receipts. The logistical software that governs the supply chain, including SAP's enterprise resource planning system, is only the most recent form of this operative control.[28] Logistical media studies involves reconciling how these forms have materialized from a particular set of cultural techniques, generalizing the logic that Innis finds in the construction of cuneiform to not only media objects, but the "operative chains that precede the media concepts they generate."[29] Analyzing logistical instruments is then not merely a question of following technologies such as the container, but—as Klose has suggested—techniques like *containment*.[30] The essays in this collection document the new logistical capacities of correspondingly new media, but they also remind us that "old media," like the printed form, telegraph, and telephone, once introduced "new" mechanisms for coordinating and controlling the distribution of goods, materials, and bodies.

To study *logistical instruments* and the cultural techniques they encode, we argue, requires attention to the ways that operative control is interwoven with trade, militarism, and imperial projects. Logistics, in name if not in practice, finds its origins on the battlefield, in its canonization amid the aftermath of the Napoleonic Wars. Recognition of its instrumental importance came when Napoleon's general Antoine-Henri Jomini divided modern warfare into the art of strategy, tactics, and a "third art," which described the moving, housing, and supplying of soldiers. His name for it suggested the Greek for calculation and accounting, but it came from the Middle French word *logis*, "to lodge," and derived, he explained, "from the title of the *major général des logis.*"[31] Over the course of the nineteenth century, an attention to preparation meant that the foraging of resources—the pillaging, looting, and seizing of housing and provisions from the local inhabitants of a region—was replaced by a centralized effort to furnish an army's needs for food, water, heat, fodder, and weapons. The careful control of supply lines both increased the importance of communication and produced the need for more detailed documentation.[32] As Martin van Creveld argues, "essentially nonmilitary" techniques and technologies like "transport, roads, and maps; timekeepers, standards, trumpets, and the ability to write . . . did as much to shape warfare . . . as did any number of weapons and arms."[33] Modern warfare was not only more dependent on the distribution of supplies, but supply itself had become a means of war. This was nowhere better demonstrated than in the British delivery of smallpox-infected blankets to the Delaware Indians at the height of the French and Indian War.[34]

As a means for the distribution of domination, logistics not only supplied armies, but it reshaped geographies to render them smooth surfaces of supply. In doing so, it produced new territories of logistical space essential to projects of colonization. The age of exploration was indebted not only to new technologies such as the carrack and the astrolabe or to new media such as tables of solar declination and astronomical charts but to correspondingly new techniques of navigation. It was through "documents, devices and drilled people," John Law argues, both navigators and a vessel made "mobile [and] durable," that the Portuguese were able to operate "at a distance" and enact their revolutionary form of "long distance control."[35] Logistical media are pervasive in the history of slavery, as suited to transporting the wealth of distant lands as human bodies bound in servitude along the Middle Passage— the moment Fred Moten and Stefano Harney recognize as the birthplace of modern logistics. As Simone Browne notes, as a means of "accounting for a particular ship's cargo," even instruments like the branding iron functioned as a logistical technology. They too served to "mark out a point," to track and constrain black bodies, limiting their movement in space and time. As these technologies reduced the operation of slavery to geometric units, the ship's hold became a grid where a kind of "stowing process" could be drawn.[36] As Frank Wilderson writes, "something happened to us in the hold."[37] Harney and Moten find in this *logisticality* the other side to Law's "drilled people."[38]

In the twentieth and twenty-first centuries, logistical techniques became increasingly essential to warfare, neocolonial projects, and new systems of racial oppression. The logistical operations of ships and maps were deployed across media forms. Religious texts were distributed as a means of

Matthew Hockenberry, Nicole Starosielski, and Susan Zieger

colonial control. Leaflets were air-dropped to inhabitants of war zones, and new forms of propaganda were carried over airwaves beyond the confines of conventional borders. The media theorist Paul Virilio suggests the critical relationship of "logistics" not only to martial but to mediative measures. Reflecting on World War II, Virilio observes the kind of coordination at work in Joseph Goebbels sending "fifty thousand fascist propaganda records to gramophone-owning households," as he forced theaters to show "ideologically loaded shorts" and raised the price of radio sets to prevent intrusion from broadcasts abroad. After the war, Virilio explains, this same sense of logistical mediation was evident in everything from the control of markets to the dominance of Hollywood—a development attributable, in part, to the enactment of logistical techniques in the new "supply system" the United States pioneered.[39]

"The battlefield has always been a field of perception," Virilio argues, with war and cinema both a "logistics of perception."[40] But this was true only because the techniques that underlay modern warfare were founded on a mediative logistics of mobility and distribution. Virilio's very idea of modernity, Benjamin Bratton writes, "is logistical," the world a "dromocratic" government of "differential motility" always "harnessing and mobilizing, incarcerating and accelerating things and people." This theorization is fitting for not just "a world in motion" but one run on the motor of logistical instrumentality. The world is a crystalline landscape of competing forces of surveillance, fortification, and movement, with everything from architecture to computation comprising logistical media. As these new media technologies "consolidate territory into logistical fields," Bratton argues that they instantiate new regimes governed by "abstracted calculation over omni-directional spaces and surfaces." The result is a new order of operation that structures the vast spaces of "open oceans" and "shared spreadsheets" alike.[41]

It is this wide-ranging remit that enabled logistics to span the global reach of capitalist production. In documenting this process, Sergio Bologna argues that logistics, as the "the art of optimizing flows," necessitates a universalizing understanding. It demands not only the knowledge of "how to make food, medicines, weapons, materials, fuel and correspondence reach an army in movement," but "where to stock them, in what quantities." Above all, "it must know how to transport all of this stuff and in what quantity so that it is sufficient . . . and how to do this for land, sea and air."[42] Through the expansion of global capitalism, territories and populations have been increasingly subject to the instrumental logics of these techniques. Logistical media have been deployed to accelerate and impede the movement of peoples and to enable the documentation and monitoring of workers, migrants, tourists, and local inhabitants. Since, as Mezzadra and Neilson write, the aim of logistics is to coordinate this movement "in the interests of communication, transport, and economic efficiencies," it is not surprising that practices of logistical surveillance are "central to the instances of bordering, connecting, and stretching of heterogeneous spaces."[43] From their origins in the codification of paper passports in the nineteenth century, these practices have multiplied and intensified as governmentality has multiplied "borderscapes."[44]

Mobilized under promises of flexibility and efficiency, logistical techniques offer new methods of movement just as they do new methods for reifying established structures of power. Radio-frequency identification (RFID) tags, which are ubiquitous forms of management along the supply chain, are now implanted in the hands of Swedish citizens hoping to smooth the transition from home to office, opening the doors of the gym or paying for train tickets with a wave.[45] Through a logistics of the self, they feed data back to digital corporations for future use in advertising. Beyond these more obvious manifestations in supply chain management, surveillance, and self-tracking, logistical techniques are pervasive in the myriad algorithms for coordinating connections over time and space, the stockpiling of vast repositories of data, and the spread of fibrous networks around the globe. They not only control the mobility of humans and nonhumans, or identify people, goods, and services, they also problematize privacy rights, the nature of consent, and institutionalized racial and gender discrimination.

In their examination of logistical techniques and their inherent instrumentality, the essays in this section consider operations ranging from automation to surveillance, working to reveal how ideas of optimization, efficiency, and interoperability are entangled with the multitude of technologies and media forms—from the canoe to the camera—that have produced them. Liam Cole Young begins by demonstrating how logistical media such as canoes, compasses, and paperwork shaped the circulation of fur and cod in Canada, "canceling" out the indigenous formations of logistical practice and organization that had preceded them. Matthew Hockenberry historicizes the idea of efficiency in US manufacturing and the shift in meaning it underwent after the popularization of the telephone. The result was an auditory understanding of efficiency that, he argues, altered the future of communication and production alike. Finally, Ned Rossiter proposes a logistical media theory capable of attending to the geopolitics surrounding technologies of automation. Taking as examples several customer management platforms, he describes the geocultural encoding that exists at the heart of

Matthew Hockenberry, Nicole Starosielski, and Susan Zieger

corporate operations. Examining media's fundamental logistical capacity, these contributors show, can reveal unseen forms of power and the production of difference within the very mechanisms of mediation.

Supply Chain Media

Understanding the logistical imagination requires an attention to logistics' representational and conceptual patterns. Studying logistical instruments involves tracking the forms of power latent in its techniques. Our third area of inquiry, the analysis of media's supply chain, focuses on the manufacture and distribution of media objects themselves. This includes an attention to their raw materials, locations of manufacture, and networks of distribution. Significantly, it necessitates an understanding of the ongoing forms of coordination and management that tie resources, production, and distribution together. Why, for example, does the revival of old sound formats depend on negotiations with mail carriers? How are efficiencies in cinematic production achieved through the geographically specific conditioning of bodies and labor? In what ways does sourcing—and the winding paths of media's supply—reflect geopolitical conflicts? How do the resulting media objects affectively relay their racialized processes of manufacturing?

Answering such questions, and tracking the long and sometimes circuitous routes by which media reach the receptive eyes and ears of their audiences, readers, and users, builds on emergent fields that track media's infrastructures and industries. The logistics of media production often involves leveraging "soft" infrastructures, the connective systems of organization and classification that support the movement of information (from contracts to production logs), to produce efficiencies. It unfolds across "hard" infrastructures, not only transportation and power systems but also data centers, network exchanges, broadcast towers, and manufacturing facilities.[46] The choices of what infrastructural pathways to engage have material and ecological effects that form the sites of power plays between competing companies. Logistical decisions are often the result of—or crafted in reaction to—the globalized nature of contemporary media production, the regulatory regimes that structure it, and cultures of labor both above and below.[47] While media infrastructures research describes the sociotechnical systems that support the flow of signal traffic around the world, and the study of media industries orients the field to the various corporations, regulations, and operators responsible for the media's workings, the study of logistics describes how systems of coordination modulate flows across infrastructure, reinforce the dominance of some companies, and connect media production to a multitude of other forms of commodity production. It reveals that media and information, like all modern industries, have not only been reworked according to demands of efficiency and automation, but that the logics governing their operation have been subsumed in service to global supply.

The history of media supply chains extends long before the era of shipping containers and logistical software systems. In the ancient world, the distribution of writing depended on the corresponding distribution of plants like papyrus, mulberry, and hemp. In early modern Europe, it came to rely on an increasingly complex industry that processed old rags into linen paper.[48] Even in the modern world, logistical concerns surrounding the difficulties of harvesting, processing, and moving wood as lumber shaped the development of at least two foundational forms of mass media: the telegraph and the newspaper. In *Wired into Nature*, James Schwoch describes the intense obstacles posed by environmental conditions in the spread of telegraphy through the American west. While the eastern United States had long been established in the timber trade, with sawmills and transportation routes along existing roads and rivers, regions like the Southwest and the Great Plains lacked trees, transportation infrastructure, and expertise. One of the most difficult parts of network construction was found in the procurement of telegraph poles. Harvesting, Schwoch writes, was "killing work for men and oxen."[49] Trees had to be hauled, sometimes by hand, to the telegraph route. This not only increased the cost of the network, it jeopardized long-term stability: poles made of poor wood would fall and require repair.

Effectively organizing the supply chains of their constituent components allowed media and communication systems to scale to the needs of industrial mass production. In turn, the operative techniques that pervade factory work and shipping schedules have become powerful organizing influences on media industries themselves. While early telegraph routes proceeded along routes that offered a ready availability of timber, the maintenance of the telephone network was possible only through dedicated stockpiles and specialists who could supply them. And as Michael Stamm writes in *Dead Tree Media*, the twentieth-century newspaper business reached the "pinnacle of industrial capitalism and mass production" in part due to its careful management of the supply of forest products. "Industrial supply chains," he explains, "connected trees to factories to readers."[50] In his research on the *Chicago Tribune*, Stamm tracks how the company assembled an extensive logistical network that reached from the forests of Quebec to the ships that carried logs to its paper mills in New York and Southern Ontario. The firm's

Matthew Hockenberry, Nicole Starosielski, and Susan Zieger

media production did not operate at the mercy of some distant supply chain: it secured logging rights to forests, hired lumberjacks, and owned its own fleet in a massive, vertically integrated operation. Streamlining logistical operations was essential to commercial success.

Media industries have often depended on materials sourced through the expansive global supply chains that leveraged prior colonial networks. The British success in constructing a global undersea telegraph network, for example, was due in part to the ready availability of gutta-percha from Britain's colonies in Southeast Asia. The emergence of the phonograph industry, Lisa Gitelman writes, "depended on a worldwide trade in materials" that included Indian lac and German chemicals.[51] The lac trade, initially organized by the British East India Company in response to demand for the lac insect's red dyes, underpinned the success of the phonograph in the United States. But like many logistical legacies, Jacob Smith points out, "It was small-scale, lacked precise standardization, and resisted modes of scientific efficiency."[52] As Kyle Devine has documented, the "quality of the supply was uneven" and as a result, "record compositions varied, prices yo-yoed, consumers complained about variable quality, and the industry searched restlessly for a new material."[53] The shift from shellac discs to petroleum-based 45s and LPs was underwritten by a shift in resource regimes and global supply.

Media's supply chains, from the newspaper to sound recording, were transformed with the introduction of mass manufacturing. One of the most obvious examples of this has been in cinematic production, which at the height of the studio system literally functioned as a factory. Cast and crew operated under exclusive contracts to their studios. Designs were done largely in-house, with sets, props, and costumes serving as supplies that could be deployed for productions of surprisingly diverse genres. Films were shipped from one theater to another.[54] As a counter to industrial modes of production, alternative media practices developed alternative logistics. Zines took advantage of reproductive technologies such as photocopiers and were distributed to their audiences through concerts rather than traditional publishing distribution channels. In *A Prehistory of the Cloud*, Tung-Hui Hu describes how the Ant Farm collective devised a "truckstop network," which could move media across the United States without relying on the rigid structures of the television networks. This programming was made possible by media vans driving across interstate highways, with Sony Portapaks enabling the capture of images and radio transmitters broadcasting their signals between nodes. Alternative media often inspire new forms of coordination, "grafting" new networks onto older ones to facilitate new forms of connection.[55]

The essays in this collection focus on the supply chains of contemporary media, examining how they have been influenced by the rise of logistics as a global industry. Many of these media forms, we argue, take the shape of "supply chain media." That is, their manufacturing and distribution adhere closely to Anna Tsing's description of supply-chain capitalism. They are "based on subcontracting, outsourcing, and allied arrangements," where "the autonomy of their component enterprises is legally established even as the enterprises are disciplined within the chain as a whole." These connections make possible mediative processes that span the globe, with the "labor, nature, and capital" that fuels them now "mobilized in fragmented but linked economic niches."[56] The distribution of signals, for example, requires the coordination of "digital supply chains." Logistical networks connecting centralized servers, edge caches, and data centers affect how quickly sites like Netflix load, where they can function in the world, and under what regimes they operate, but they are also composed of numerous digital actors: internet service providers, carriers, data center operators, content providers, and many more, all of which come to constitute the supply chain as a whole. Logistics companies such as Amazon have emerged out of existing forms of networked media distribution, and they have, in turn, directed how new kinds of media technologies circulate.

The chapters in this final section of *Assembly Codes* consider the production of sounds, images, and technologies in the most recent era of supply chain media. Michael Palm documents how new logistical technologies are catalyzing growth in the record industry through old logistical networks like the postal service. For vinyl records, online ordering has not replaced brick-and-mortar record shops any more than the digitization of music has replaced its physical production. In both cases, Palm argues, physical and digital practices remain deeply connected. Kay Dickinson considers the transformation of Hollywood into "supply chain cinema," demonstrating how this new formation not only entails a reorganization of materials and transportation networks but a conscious crafting of logistical subjectivity in workers. Drawing from extensive research on British Leavesden studios, Dickinson emphasizes the role of education in transforming populations into creative resources for media production. The final two essays in this collection follow the construction, production, and supply of digital networks themselves. Nicole Starosielski interrogates the logistics of submarine fiber-optic construction, showing how the cable network that facilitates contemporary supply chain media is actually more closely tied to the imperial legacies of its history than to the logistical networks of the present. In the concluding piece, Tung-Hui Hu traces the logistical transmission of affect, circulated through racialized bodies, commodities, and digital environments. Taking as a starting point artist Yoshua Okón's installation *Canned Laughter* (2009), which depicts a fictitious maquiladora in Juárez producing shiny red cans of laughter destined for sitcoms ("evil laughter," "sexy laughter," and so on), Hu argues that a dystopian world where low-wage workers across the US-Mexico border laugh, cry, or otherwise emote for white audiences is not as far away as we might think.

With these interventions, we highlight the importance of media to the critical study of logistics, as well as the centrality of logistics to our understanding of media. These essays demonstrate how some of the most significant impacts of media and communication technologies have been not only to shape modes of popular perception, but to shape the logistics of global production. Contributors excavate media's fundamental logistical capacities and show how media forms depend on, and are constituted through, logistical regimes. Throughout the collection we have also linked these chapters with a series of short, logistically inspired stories, keywords, and object descriptions. Each of these interstitial pieces offers an evocative description that bridges, refracts, or otherwise mediates the arguments on either side of it. We are inspired by Rossiter's description, in this collection, of the "interval," the space between the zeros and ones that defines digital logic and yet forms their externality. Constructing these sections between contributing essays, we hope to draw attention to the work of assembly and connection, the gaps that remain, and the multitude of starting points for further inquiries into the logistics of media.

NOTES

1. On the military history of logistics, see Martin van Creveld, *Supplying War: Logistics from Wallenstein to Patton* (Cambridge: Cambridge University Press, 1977).

2. W. Bruce Allen, "The Logistics Revolution and Transportation" *Annals of the American Academy of Political and Social Science* 553, no. 1 (1997): 106–16, 109–10.

3. Charmaine Chua, Deborah Cowen, Martyn Danyluk, and Lalel Khalili, "Introduction: Turbulent Circulation: Building a Critical Engagement with Logistics," *Environment and Planning D: Society and Space* 36, no. 4 (2018): 617–29.

4. Deborah Cowen, *The Deadly Life of Logistics: Mapping Violence in Global Trade* (Minneapolis: University of Minnesota Press, 2014), 2.

5. Sandro Mezzadra and Brett Neilson, "Extraction, Logistics, Finance: Global Crisis and the Politics of Operations," *Radical Philosophy*, no. 178 (2013): 8–18, 10.

6. Ned Rossiter, *Software, Infrastructure, Labor: A Media Theory of Logistical Nightmares* (New York: Routledge, 2016), 4.

7. Paul Virilio, *War and Cinema: The Logistics of Perception* (London: Verso, 1989).

8. Ned Rossiter, "Locative Media as Logistical Media: Situating Infrastructure and the Governance of Labor in Supply-Chain Capitalism," in *Locative Media*, ed. Gerard Goggin and Rowan Wilken (New York: Routledge, 2014), 208–23; John Durham Peters, "Calendar, Clock, Tower," in *Deus in Machina: Religion, Technology, and the Things in Between*, ed. Jeremy Stolow (New York: Fordham University Press, 2012), 25–42; Judd Case, "Logistical Media: Fragments from Radar's Prehistory," *Canadian Journal of Communication* 38, no. 3 (2013): 379–95. See also Patrick Brodie, Lisa Han, and Weixian Pan, eds., "Becoming Environmental: Media, Logistics, and Ecological Change," *Synoptique* 8, no. 1 (2019): 6–13.

9. Peters, "Calendar, Clock, Tower," 40; and also Case, "Logistical Media."

10. Cowen, *The Deadly Life of Logistics*, 14–15.

11. Anna Tsing, "Supply Chains and the Human Condition," *Rethinking Marxism* 21, no. 2 (2009): 148–76, 148–49.

12. Anna Tsing, *The Mushroom at the End of the World: On the Possibility of Life in Capitalist Ruins* (Princeton, NJ: Princeton University Press, 2015).

13. Tsing, "Supply Chains"; and Tsing, *Friction: An Ethnography of Global Connection* (Princeton, NJ: Princeton University Press, 2004).

14. Brett Neilson and Sandro Mezzadra, *The Politics of Operations: Excavating Contemporary Capitalism* (Durham, NC: Duke University Press, 2019), 154.

15. See, for example, the Invisible Committee, *The Coming Insurrection* (Cambridge, MA: MIT Press / Semiotext(e), 2009).

16. See Edward Humes, *Door to Door: The Magnificent, Maddening, Mysterious World of Transportation* (New York: HarperCollins, 2016), 221.

17. Sam Halliday, *Science and Technology in the Age of Hawthorne, Melville, Twain, and James* (London: Palgrave Macmillan, 2007).

18. Jasper Bernes, "Logistics, Counterlogistics, and the Communist Prospect," *Endnotes*, no. 3 (September 2013), https://endnotes.org.uk/issues/3/en/jasper-bernes-logistics-counterlogistics-and-the-communist-prospect.

19. For the feature most commonly referenced as beginning the controversy, see Sydney H. Schanberg, "Six Cents an Hour," *Life*, June 1996, 38–48.

20. Marc Levinson, *The Box: How the Shipping Container Made the World Smaller and the World Economy Bigger* (Princeton, NJ: Princeton University Press, 2006); and Alexander Klose, *The Container Principle: How a Box Changes the Way We Think* (Cambridge, MA: MIT Press, 2015).

21. Alberto Toscano and Jeff Kinkle, *Cartographies of the Absolute* (Winchester, UK: Zero Books, 2015), 196.

22. Adam Smith, *The Wealth of Nations*, ed. Jim Manis (State College, PA: Pennsylvania State University Press, 2005), 11–16.

23. Duncan Campbell-Smith, *Masters of the Post: The Authorized History of the Royal Mail* (London: Allen Lane, 2011), 165.

24. See Stefanie Markovits, *The Crimean War in the British Imagination* (Cambridge: Cambridge University Press, 2009), 12–62.

25. Harold Innis, *Empire and Communications* (Oxford: Clarendon, 1950), 47–48, 164. See also Marshall McLuhan, *Understanding Media: The Extensions of Man* (New York: McGraw-Hill, 1964); and James Carey, *Communication as Culture: Essays on Media and Society* (New York: Routledge, 1989).

26. Harold Innis, *The Bias of Communication* (Toronto: University of Toronto Press, 1951), 33.

27. Bruno Latour, *Science in Action: How to Follow Scientists and Engineers through Society* (Cambridge, MA: Harvard University Press, 1988), 227; and Rossiter, *Software, Infrastructure, Labor*, 19–20.

28. See Rossiter, *Software, Infrastructure, Labor*; and Benjamin Bratton, *The Stack: On Software and Sovereignty* (Cambridge, MA: MIT Press, 2016).

29. Bernhard Siegert, "Cultural Techniques; or The End of the Intellectual Postwar Era in German Media Theory," *Theory, Culture and Society* 30, no. 3 (2013): 48–65; Liam Cole Young, "Cultural Techniques and Logistical Media," *M/C Journal* 18, no. 2 (2015), https://doi.org/10.5204/mcj.961.

30. Klose, *Container Principle*.

31. Antoine-Henri Jomini, *The Art of War*, trans. G. H. Mendell (Kingston, ON: Legacy Books, 2008), 200–201.

32. Armand Mattelart, *The Invention of Communication*, translated by Susan Emanuel (Minneapolis: University of Minnesota Press, 1996), 208.

33. Van Creveld, *Technology and War*, 48–49.

34. See Gregory Evans Dowd, *War under Heaven: Pontiac, the Indian Nations, and the British Empire* (Baltimore: Johns Hopkins University Press, 2004), 190.

35. John Law, "On the Methods of Long-Distance Control: Vessels, Navigation, and the Portuguese Route to India," in *Power, Action and Belief: A New Sociology of Knowledge?* ed. John Law (London: Routledge, 1986), 234–63, 254, 257; see also John Law, "On the Social Explanation of Technical Change: The Case of the Portuguese Maritime Expansion," *Technology and Culture* 28, no. 2 (1987): 227–52.

36. Simone Browne, *Dark Matters: On the Surveillance of Blackness* (Durham, NC: Duke University Press, 2015), 42, 47.

37. Frank B. Wilderson III, *Incognegro: A Memoir of Exile and Apartheid* (Durham, NC: Duke University Press, 2008), 489.

38. Stefano Harney, in Niccolo Cuppini and Mattia Frapporti, "Logistics Genealogies: A Dialogue with Stefano Harney," *Social Text* 36, no. 3 (2018): 1–16; see also Stefano Harney and Fred Moten, "Fantasy in the Hold," in *The Undercommons: Fugitive Planning and Black Study* (New York: Minor Compositions, 2013), 89–99.

39. Virilio, *War and Cinema*, 29–30.

40. Virilio, *War and Cinema*, 26.

41. Benjamin Bratton, "Introduction: Logistics of Habitable Circulation," in Paul Virilio, *Speed and Politics*, trans. Mark Polizzotti (Los Angeles: Semiotext(e), 2006 [1977]), 7–25, 7–8.

42. Quoted in and translated by Alberto Toscano, "Logistics and Opposition," *Mute* 3, no. 2 (2011), original text from Sergio Bologna, "L'undicesima tesi," in *Ceti medi senza futuro? Scritti, appunti sul lavoro e altro* (Rome: DeriveApprodi, 2007), 84.

43. Sandro Mezzadra and Brett Neilson, *Border as Method, or, the Multiplication of Labor* (Durham, NC: Duke University Press, 2013), 206.

44. See Andreas Fahrmeir, "Governments and Forgers: Passports in Nineteenth-Century Europe," in *Documenting Individual Identity: The Development of State Practices in the Modern World*, ed. Jane Caplan and John Torpey (Princeton, NJ: Princeton University Press, 2001), 218–34.

45. Alexandra Ma, "Thousands of People in Sweden Are Embedding Microchips under Their Skin to Replace ID Cards," *Business Insider*, May 14, 2018.

46. Lisa Parks and Nicole Starosielski, eds., *Signal Traffic: Critical Studies of Media Infrastructures* (Champaign: University of Illinois Press, 2015).

47. Important critical analyses of the history, theory, and cultures of media industries have been documented in Jennifer Holt and Alisa Perren, eds., *Media Industries: History, Theory, and Method* (Malden, MA: Wiley-Blackwell, 2009); Vicki Mayer, Miranda Banks, and John Thornton Caldwell, eds., *Production Studies: Cultural Studies of Media Industries* (New York: Routledge, 2009); Vicki Mayer, *Below the Line: Producers and Production Studies in the New Television Economy* (Durham, NC: Duke University Press, 2011); and in the *Media Industries Journal*.

48. A process that was happily recounted in it-narratives like 1779's "Adventures of a Quire of Paper," *London Magazine*, August, 355–35; September, 395–98; October, 448–52.

49. James Schwoch, *Wired into Nature: The Telegraph and the North American Frontier* (Champaign: University of Illinois Press, 2018), 31.

50. Michael Stamm, *Dead Tree Media: The Newspaper in Twentieth-Century North America* (Baltimore: Johns Hopkins University Press, 2018), 11.

51. Lisa Gitelman, *Always Already New: Media History and the Data of Culture* (Cambridge, MA: MIT Press, 2006), 16.

52. Jacob Smith, *Eco-Sonic Media* (Oakland: University of California Press, 2015), 21.

53. Kyle Devine, *Decomposed: The Political Ecology of Music* (Cambridge, MA: MIT Press, 2019), 55, 58.

54. This is central to Bill Morrison's film *Dawson City: Frozen Time* (New York: Picture Palace Pictures, 2016), where the eponymous city's media archive speaks directly to its place at the end of this supply chain.

55. Tung-Hui Hu, *A Prehistory of the Cloud* (Cambridge, MA: MIT Press, 2015).

56. Tsing, "Supply Chains," 148–49.

THE LOGISTICAL IMAGINATION

Image, Sound, Subject

PART I

1

Habits of Assembly

for Manolo Callahan

If I were asked to answer the following question: What is slavery? and I should answer in one word, It is murder!, my meaning would be understood at once. No extended argument would be required to show that the power to remove a man's mind, will, and personality, is the power of life and death, and that it makes a man a slave. It is murder. Why, then, to this other question: What is property? may I not likewise answer, It is robbery!, without the certainty of being misunderstood; the second proposition being no other than a transformation of the first?
—PIERRE-JOSEPH PROUDHON, *What Is Property?*

THIS is *Natures nest of Boxes*; The Heavens contain the *Earth*, the *Earth*, *Cities*, *Cities*, *Men*. And all these are *Concentrique*; the common *center* to them all, is *decay*, *ruine*; only that is *Eccentrique*, which was never made; only that place, or garment rather, which we can *imagine*, but not *demonstrate*, That light, which is the very emanation of the light of *God*, in which the *Saints* shall dwell, with which the *Saints* shall be appareld, only that bends not to this *Center*, to *Ruine*; that which was not made of *Nothing*, is not threatned with this annihilation. All other things are; even *Angels*, even our *soules*; they move upon the same *poles*, they bend to the same *Center*; and if they were not made immortall by *preservation*, their *Nature* could not keep them from sinking to this *center*, *Annihilation*.
—JOHN DONNE, "Meditation"

THE FIRST THEFT SHOWS UP AS RIGHTFUL OWNERSHIP. This is the theft of fleshly, earth(l)y life, which is then incarcerated in the body. But the body, it turns out, is just the first principal-agent problem. The body is just an overseer, a factor, a superintendent for the real landlord, the real owner, the individual, in his noxious, heavy-handed conceptuality. The legal term for this principal-agent problem is mind. In this regard, the designation "mind/body problem" is a synecdochal redundancy in abstraction rather than an entanglement, or even an opposition, of *anima* and matter.

There's this formulation that Robert Duncan gets from Erwin Schrödinger that helps a certain disordering along. Schrödinger says, "living matter evades the decay to equilibrium." Well, if Proudhon is right, and slavery, murder, robbery, and property are a unit—if the general regime of private property is most accurately understood as social death—then what if death/private property is that equilibrium of which Schrödinger speaks? What Donne speaks of by way of God's sovereign capacity to preserve is a problem that will have been meant to solve a problem, and when Schrödinger speaks of evading the decay to equilibrium, he isn't saying that all decay is bad. Corruption is our (accursed) share, our anontological practice, our eccentric centering, as M. C. Richards might say. How we evade ownership/equilibrium is given precisely in that refusal to prevent loss that we call sharing, rubbing, empathy, hapticality: the undercommon love of flesh, our essential omni-centric or anacentric eccentricity.

Everything, in the wake of such disordering, is loss prevention. John Locke creates the tabula rasa as a container for properties—properties of the mind, and properties owned by the propertied mind. Self-knowledge is self-possession and self-positioning in Locke. His accumulation process is auto-location, because one can't help but settle for that. From the first moment, which appears to keep happening all the time, all property is posited, beginning with the positing/positioning of a body for locating ownership, and the owned, and a mind for owning. The posit and the deposit inaugurate ownership as incorporation, whose inevitable end, given in continual withdrawal, is loss. This requires the production of a science of loss, which is to say the science of whiteness, or, logistics.

Every acquisition, every improvement, is an ossification of sharing. This ossification is given in and as containment. The first odious vessel produced by and for logistics is not the slave ship, but the body—flesh conceptualized—which bears the individual-in-subjection. A profound viciousness begins with this colonization of the posited body, the appointment of the posited mind, and the manipulation—in various modalities of brutality—of their mutually enveloping redundancy, given in the dead perpetual motion of the will to colonize. This enclosure, this settlement, will be repeated because it must be repeated. Every slave will have been every time the mirror in which the self, in seeing itself, comes into existence in and as itself, which is an omnicidal fantasy.

Locke invents the derivative here, a degraded part of the accursed share that is poised to draw on the power of this share, but only to create more derivatives, to create more zones of dispossession by positing possession, in the denial of loss that prepares for loss. All property is loss because all property is the loss of sharing. In its willfulness, property is theft, but beyond the murderousness that would attend theft-in-acquisition one mind/body at a time, the theft in question here is absolute serial murder, which we survive only insofar as all property remains vulnerable to sharing. This is to say nothing other than that all property is fugitive. It flees from its own positing, runs from being deposited. All (property) jumps bail. Sharing, exhaustion, expending, derivation will have been contained and congealed in the measurable and accountable individual unit of the derivative. But sharing is our means, the earth's means in us, and our means in earth. Logistics would seem to value means over ends—everything is how to get it there, not what it is—but logistics is really the degradation of means, the general devaluation of means through individuation and privatization, which are the same thing. It is the science of lost means advanced with every act of loss prevention.

If Locke invents the derivative, then Kant's innovation is high-frequency trading. And when Kant reverses the fortunes of logistics by announcing that it is the ends (of man) and not the means that are important, the human, the ultimate derivative, is fully logistically installed. The human is held up, not by Kant, but by logistics—a logistics that gives the illusion of a free-standing subject. A human universe appears to Kant, full of what he posits as human properties. Kant walks the docks, traversing the seven bridges of Königsberg, surveying the logistical world from a point of view he never needs to leave. From there, his ships come in, and with each new travel log and ethnographic treatise, he is witness to the humanization of the flesh. Logistics now has a subject, and it is race. The humanization of the flesh is the racialization of the flesh. It is the catastrophe that befalls the species being, one not even Marx can reverse. This is why logistics is the science of whiteness in and as the science of loss.

Such is the peril to flesh/earth by the time of Hegel, as Denise Ferreira da Silva teaches. Surveillance. Access. Transparency. Resilience. The globalized, generalized fear of loss is everywhere that logistics sees the need to straighten out our tangled flesh. And everywhere logistics finds monstrosity, it humanizes it. Now, to be obscure as Saidiya Hartman instructs, is to be entangled; it is to be hunted, to be subject to the subject of the grasp. Sub-subjected thus, how can you say that we are persons? Flesh/Earth is assaulted by global improvement, worldly usufruct. With improvement, Hegel produces the regulatory framework called deregulation. Nothing will get in the way of the development of the race or in the way of the race of developers. Arrayed before and through this is our opacity, given in and as our otium, that anteprogrammatic disorder R. A. Judy speaks of as our speech, arrayed, as Fumi Okiji does and says, with mouths agape, in the curse, the damnation, the incompleteness that we share.

IN ZEN BUDDHIST PHILOSOPHY the goal of the heart doctrine is *ji ji muge*, which can be translated as *no block*. Nothing prevents the path, the way, from flowing. The heart travels freely.

So, what are we to make of the fact that today it is the science of logistics that most seems to have realized the heart doctrine of Zen Buddhism? It is the science of logistics that dreams of flow without blockage and tries to turn these dreams into reality. Hard logistics and soft logistics work together. The yang of the Belt and Road and the yin of the algorithm fantasize together of *no block*.

If this is true, we should be worried. In its origins, and its contemporary mutations, logistics is a regulatory force standing against us, standing against the earth. Logistics begins in loss and emptiness. And it begins in a fundamental misapprehension called space-time. The loss that marks ownership, specifically the ownership of private property, the loss of sharing, the loss of the earth and the consequent making of the world, is simultaneously the misapprehension that what is privatized is empty and will be filled by ownership itself, by properties, by properties placed into it. This emptiness will be filled with an interior. This emptiness is confirmed by logistics, by the mobilization, the colonizing drive, of this interior—where properties are imported into empty space.

This begins, again, with Locke, or at least, we can begin again through him. His concept of the mind as tabula rasa—often portrayed as an Enlightenment move away from predetermination—is a projection of this emptiness that must be owned and filled. For this emptiness to become private property it must be filled with and located in the coordinates of space and time. Space emerges as the delimitation of what is mine, and time begins with the theft and imposition when it became mine. The individual mind and its coming to maturity out of the tabula rasa mark this first conquest. Enlightenment interiority emerged from this *emplotment* of time and space— to borrow from Hayden White—this separation from what is shared. But interiority is only for the owning mind. Because what allows this mind to take possession of itself is its ability to grasp property, which is something it now posits as beyond itself. It takes what it is taken from for what it needs to create itself, and not just needs but compulsively, interminably, voraciously seeks without end. In other words, the emplotment of time and space in the mind takes place through the emplotment of time and space on earth, in a conversion of emptiness into world, and is simultaneously taken as a fulfillment of mind, its interior appointment in and of what can now be conceptualized as body. Is it a leap to say logic and logistics start here inseparably?

This is why there is no separating Locke the enlightenment thinker from Locke the writer on race, the author of the notorious colonial constitution of the Carolinas. Ownership was a feedback loop—the more you own, the more you own yourself. The more logistics you apply, the more logic you acquire; the more logic you deploy, the more logistics you require. As Hortense Spillers says, the transatlantic slave trade was the supply chain of enlightenment. It was never-ending quest and conquest, because ownership is perpetual loss. Gilles Deleuze said that he would rather call power "sad." We might say the same of ownership, where lies the most direct sense of loss of sharing. This feeling of loss translates into a diabolical obsession with loss prevention. Logistics emerges as much as the science of loss prevention as the science of moving property through the emptiness, of making the world as it travels by filling it. This is not making the road as we walk, in the anarchist tradition. This is converting everything in its path into a coordinated time and space for ownership.

Such seizing, such grasping, and such loss prevention is the mode of operation for the wickedness of the Atlantic slave trade, the first massive, diabolic, commercial logistics. Already this feedback loop of ownership experiences amplified loss, the loss of sharing, with each emplotment. But now, in taking up the European heritage of race and slavery that Cedric Robinson identifies as emerging in the class struggle in Europe in the centuries directly before Locke and extending into Locke's own time, a double loss is experienced, an intensification of the ownership feedback loop (and what we call the subject reaction). This evil emplotment of Africans is experienced as the potential loss of property that can flee. It is in this double loss of sharing— given in owning and in the imposition of being-owned—that the most deadly, planet-threatening disease of the species being emerges: whiteness. And it is for this reason that we can say logistics is the white science.

This is what many white people—who are the people, as James Baldwin says, who think they are white or that they ought to be—are doing when you see them walk straight past a queue of people and take a seat, or move to the center of a crowded room, or speak more loudly than those around them, or block a sidewalk while discussing "choices" with their toddler. Making theory out of practice, they are emplotting as they've been taught to do, establishing the space-time of possession and self-possession. Every step they take is a standing of ground, a stomping of the world out of earthly existence and into racial capitalist human being. It grows more pronounced the more it is threatened, consumed by its own feedback loop, and it produces sharper and sharper subject reactions in the face of this threat. This is the new fascism: not the anonymity of following the leader, but the subject reaction to leadership, which can just as easily imagine itself to be liberal dissent from, as supposedly opposed to a lock(e)step repetition of, its call.

In emplotted time and space, the shortest distance between two abstract and dimensionless points—the empty spaces that are conjured to be (ful) filled as world, or worlds, or parts of world—is a straight and dimensionless line. Given imaginary extension, nature's nest of boxes is a supply chain, a partnership of trade, a progress of henchmen in the wake of imaginal sovereignty. The basic building blocks of the science of logistics emerge from this narrow geometry as brutalist geography. The traveling salesman problem is the problem of how to extend this idea—that the shortest distance between two points is a straight line—when there are multiple destinations and stops. Of course, logistics has often found that this empty earth contains blocks and denies access. But the science builds itself up to overcome these blocks and achieve this access. Logistics aims to straighten us out, untangle us, and open us to its usufruct, its improving use; such access to us, in turn, improves the flow line, the straight line. And what logistics takes to be the shortest distance between us requires emplotting us as bodies in space where interiority can be imposed even as the capacity for interiority can be denied, in the constant measure and regulation of flesh and earth.

LET'S TAKE A BRIEF LOOK at how logistics works today by way of a book receiving much attention, *The Age of Surveillance Capitalism* by Shoshana Zuboff. Zuboff's book is a defense of interiority against the predatory economic logic of what she calls surveillance capitalism. Her argument is that information technology makes its money today from gathering massive amounts of data on our everyday behavior, packaging it, and selling it to other companies. Thus, Facebook and Google do not make money by targeting your tastes or behavior with advertisements as is commonly assumed. According to Zuboff, they have no interest in us individually, though that does not mean these tools do not also individuate. Rather, it is the aggregate data that matter because it can be used not to track but to change behavior. She notes, moreover, that intervening in aggregate provides even more valuable aggregate data. Facebook is spying on you only insofar as it is spying on us, according to Zuboff, and if we are its raw material, and its product, then her employment of the concept of primitive accumulation is justified. Problematically, this argument appears to assume capital without labor, labor having been replaced by an algorithm that will carry out itself. But what we learn from the Italian autonomists and from centuries of theorization by Africans experiencing the nightmare of total subsumption that Zuboff's assumption of absent work extends, is that we are raw material, product, and labor, too. Our work makes this economic logic, or any economic logic, work. And what is the nature of our work in surveillance capitalism? Logistics. We bear, in the obsessive self-management of "our" clicks and strokes, the overdetermination logistics lays down. It is both through and as a set of applications we apply—both on and underneath a field of platforms we erect—that our labor further concentrates the means of production, with the goal quite simply and starkly of preventing us from taking care of one another, from looking out for one another, by instead making us look at one another, which is taking care of them.

Indeed, the more we look at Zuboff even on her own terms, the more we notice that the other side of modification is *prevention*. To move a part of a population one way is to prevent it from moving another. Soon this logistics of surveillance capitalism seems to be as much about blockage as flow, something that would, of course, be consistent with us being not just raw material, not just product, but socializing labor, as well. In any case, the blockages of surveillance capitalism, of logistical capitalism more generally, raise a question. If their logistics both assumes and dictates that the shortest distance between two points is a straight line, what if our logisticality, before and against both assumption and dictation, improvises in curve—or not even in curve, but in kink—a shorter distance? Kink is neither curve nor circle, much less line. Indeed, a kink is often said to be a block. And what is a collection of kinks, or a collective of kinks, if not a dread, or jam? Watch me? No, watch meh.

Which brings us to the story of Leonard Percival Howell. As if enslavement, indenture, and domination were not enough, imperialized people were also named. So, Howell preferred to go by the name Gangunguru Maragh, or Gong, for short, or Tuff Gong. Gong came from a place named Clarendon, Jamaica. Not all of Jamaica is good for growing sugar, but this part is. After emancipation the British retained their wicked sweet tooth, and so, as with so many places in the Empire, they redoubled the settlement of Clarendon with displaced people from the Indian subcontinent, who were settled, un-settled, and resettled in, while also being indentured to, coloniality's cold logistics and brutal algorithms. Gong, who had worked with Marcus Gar-vey's organization and traveled the world, was looking for an anticolonial faith, after fighting regularly with the English church in Jamaica. He knew that church—the Church of Logistics, the "Christianity" of surveillance, the true religion of colonial rule—could never bear the faith he sought, the faith he found(ed) when he (re)turned to the insurgent homelessness of his home. It was in the indentured Hindu workers from India that he saw proof that each people had to find their true religion. He spent time with them in Clarendon, observing their tea ceremonies with ganja and their Ital diets. He named himself from their language—Gan or Gyan for wisdom, Gun for faith, Guru for teacher, and Maragh for king. Soon Gangunguru Maragh set about building the true religion of the black man as he saw it.

He never wore dreadlocks, but with his dreadlocked followers he made a village, Pinnacle, which British authorities described as socialist. They tried repeatedly to destroy it, and they confined Gong to their newly opened mental asylum. But Rastafarianism would neither be destroyed nor con-fined, which is something to consider if you are sitting in "Slave Island" in old Colombo, Sri Lanka. The Portuguese brought Africans here in the 1500s, but the coasts of Colombo and those of East Africa have always looked across at each other. As Vijay Prashad teaches us in *Everybody Was Kung-Fu Fighting*, as May Joseph teaches us in *Nomadic Identities*, African maharajahs have sat on thrones in India, and the commerce and cultural exchange between Sri Lanka and East Africa is ancient. And yet it was not this straight distance be-tween two points, this straight journey from South Asia to East Africa, that Gong traveled, or that his indentured companions in the villages of Claren-don traveled, to be with each other. The knot, the tangle, the embrace; the puff, the jam, the kink they came and carried: that's the shorter distance, where "watch meh" means watch with me for one hour, while we gather all together one more time.

The Zen heart travels without block. But we might also say it travels with nothing blocking it. And as we know first from Taoist philosophy, nothing-ness is not emptiness. It is not space. When the Zen heart travels through nothing, nothing is its constant companion. Nothing is the block through which it travels, on which it stands, in which it hangs. The block that makes no block possible. Nothing, naught, knot gives the Zen heart its direction-less directions, its wandering syncopations, its tight-knit open pansyncretic practices, allowing in, compelling us to visit and renew, as Manolo Callahan says, our habits of assembly. The unwatchable place we make when we watch with one another, having refused to watch one another, having refused one and another, is shared, unblocked, unloaded.

Watch meh. The shorter distance. Ji ji muge.

STORAGE SOLUTIONS

The storehouse is the quintessential storage medium, present at the beginning of recorded history just as it is at the contemporary moment. One American Warehousemen's Association tract imagines the first incarnation in the Egypt of the Old Testament, where Joseph, alone among the magicians and mediums of the Egyptian court, had the answer to Pharaoh's troubling dreams. In his ambitious "History of the Warehouse since 2200 B.C.," H. H. Manchester reads Joseph's supernatural semiotics in the context of broader Egyptian cultural practices of conservation. Storage, here, was not the first stop on the supply chain, but an environmental response to the reliable, but irregular, flooding of the Nile. This unpredictable overflow, Harold Innis argued, required coordinated efforts to gather people, tools, and goods into cities and towns. Out of the floods came order. But so did the same logic that organized Gutenberg's workshop at Hof Humbrecht and Amazon's first warehouse in Seattle. In Pharaoh's dreams, we find the beginning of our long logistical nightmare.

Joseph Gathering Corn. Detail of mosaic at St. Mark's Basilica, Venice (c. 1275), showing the Egyptian pyramids as the site of Joseph's granaries, as conceived in the popular medieval imagination.

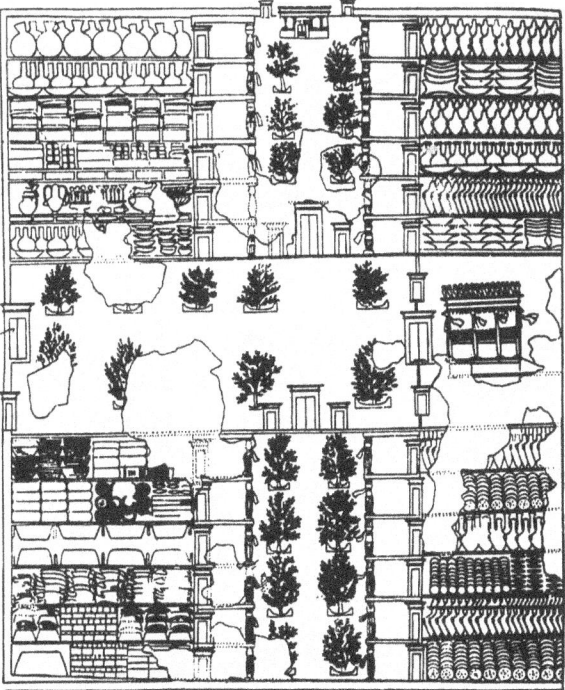

Diagram of Egyptian warehouse at Tel el Amarna, about 1500 BCE.

"Shipped"

Paper, Print, and the Atlantic Slave Trade

LOGISTICAL MEDIA RESIDES at the heart of Black studies. Logistics takes one of its most significant modern forms in the unrivaled inhumanity of the transatlantic slave trade, which transported and packed people like commodities, as efficiently as possible, to turn profits for elites. Treated as human cargo, enslaved people "bled, packed like so many live sardines among the immovable objects."[1] The kidnapping and forced transportation of many millions of people was a project so enormous, it reinvented ancient military and commercial logistics as a science and an art. Logistics thus emerged at the same moment as Blackness and as its antagonist. Pointing to the trade's vast archive as a numerical conjuration of Black death, Katherine McKittrick writes, "This is where we begin, this is where historic blackness comes from: the list, the breathless numbers, the absolutely economic, the mathematics of the unliving."[2] Here, logistics is both a calculative system of abstraction, fueled by finance capital, and its material execution in the mundane paperwork that formed its principal medium. Paper, as medium and material, performed the slave trade's exchanges; like the ships and the chains, it moved millions of people against their will across the Atlantic. Though these handwritten and printed documents aimed for efficiency and supply chain security, they were also flawed and aspirational. Through the lens of Black studies, we can see this paperwork as a dream of documentation, and between its printed and handwritten lines, we glimpse the possibilities for resistance and community, within and against logistics.

Such lists, manifests, bills of lading, and plantation logs now are the ancestors of today's logistical media, the software and algorithms that move cargo, people, and information around the world. Stefano Harney and Fred Moten claim a contiguity between the trade and subsequent shipments of prisoners and mass migrations of industrial workers and indentured slaves: "From the motley crews who followed in the red wakes of these slave ships, to . . . one-way tickets from the Philippines to the Gulf States or Bangladesh to Singapore, logistics was always the transport of slavery, not 'free' labor."[3] So, too, does Christina Sharpe, who links the October 2013 sinking of an unnamed ship overloaded with African migrants bound for Lampedusa to the massacre of enslaved people on the *Zong* in 1781.[4] Revisiting the archive of the Middle Passage and showing how its paper material and print media both facilitated and foiled the efficient counting, packing, and shipping of enslaved people, this chapter suggests the difference this media history makes to the way we conceptualize logistics and freedom now.

Logistics relies on at least two related epistemic procedures: a calculative one that counts, measures, and predicts and a documentary one that tracks and records. The fantastic and hopeful quality of both often goes unacknowledged in critical logistics studies, but we can see and study it when we attend to the material and medium, in this case, paper and print. Global trade, and the transatlantic traffic in enslaved people, depended for much of its history on ephemera: charter parties, indentures, bills of lading, ships' logs, correspondence, and similar documents. As with all modern ephemera, though it was intended to be disposable, it has been preserved.[5] The enormous archive of bills of lading in libraries around the world reflects the paradoxical nature of the paper document as both stable and insubstantial, literal and abstracting.[6] The proof it offers is often partial, contingent, written over, or left blank. It thus simultaneously attests to the reality of logistical violence and to the chimera of absolute logistical control.

Take, for example, the plantation logbooks in which US free labor management practices originated: they controlled enslaved people, yet also revealed their suffering and resistance.[7] Likewise, seventeenth- and eighteenth-century invoices, ledgers, and account books "rationalized efficiency of production" but could not represent "the perceptions of the African captives themselves."[8] Approaching the archive as a trace of an earlier logistical imagination, we rediscover logistics as a lived, human phenomenon, as well as an inhuman regime. Through the methods of Black studies, this rediscovery is not a straightforward mathematical accounting that reinscribes the violence of shipping.[9] Instead, it sees through the archive's pretenses to transparency, to its underlying contradictions, opacities, and interruptions. Here is "a wild and unclaimed richness of *possibility* that is not . . . 'counted' / 'accounted,' or differentiated."[10] To be here is to dwell "in the wake," or "to occupy and to be occupied by the continuous and changing present of slavery's as yet unresolved unfolding."[11] Approaching the archive's historical objects with a supple imagination, Black studies re-poses the contemporary questions about identity, autonomy, and agency that logistics provokes.

Focusing on unstable paper archives and the fractured accounts to which they give rise, this chapter proposes that logistics is a fantasy of rational documentation and calculation. The affordances and limitations of its own medium and the expectations of its genres and idioms complicate, delay, and ultimately prevent its reach for totalization, that is, perfect recording and prediction. Here, the medium has a double identity: it includes print culture, by which scholars mean published, circulating paper text and images, and paperwork, the privately exchanged and circulated handwritten and printed legal documents that performed trades. Circulation is the primary directive of logistics, but the public and private circulation of print and paper can also destabilize their meanings and thwart their social functions. In a bill of lading, an antislavery diagram, and an illustration of a poem, we find the modern origins of a complex, politicized logistical imagination and the contested institution of pernicious, but fallible, logistical techniques. Because logistics is a human activity, it is political; as a modern political activity, it is beholden to its media.

Bills of Lading

Written and rewritten by various hands, and often full of complicated and unverifiable explanations of the mishaps that befell cargo, bills of lading gained a reputation as quasi-fictional. Conversely, long catalog-like fiction resembled the document, as C. L. R. James observed when describing *Moby-Dick* a century after its publication, as "plotted and worked out in order, item after item, almost like a bill of lading."[12] These documents originated in the medieval period, as a book of lading kept by port town officials, to keep a record of goods departing and arriving. In the early modern period, they looked like handwritten letters; in the late eighteenth and nineteenth centuries, they were printed forms to be filled in. What makes these documents so durable is their centrality to the essence of global trade: they are the mechanism whereby the parties to a shipment—the seller, the carrier, the receiver, and their banks—all trust that the goods will be moved and paid for. They are the primary genre of logistics. And through the centuries, their main material, and medium, has been paper.

The first thing one notices about a bill of lading from the eighteenth or nineteenth century is the illuminated *S* in the upper left-hand corner that begins the word *shipped*. The pride of local printers, this visual flourish borrowed the authority of illuminated manuscripts, often portraying ships' hulls, sails, and masts; feminine allegories; scenes of trade; and American eagles within its curls.[13] The word *shipped* meant something quite different then: merely that the goods had been placed on board the ship, not that they had arrived at their destination. This older meaning aligned with the concept of "lading," namely, that the ship had been "loaded" and was now "laden" with goods. The terms indicate the document's function as a contract of carriage. Until this period, the first line of most bills of lading read, "Shipped, by the grace of God, well-conditioned and in good order"; with the rise of maritime insurance and Enlightenment secularism, the clause about God quietly disappeared. Next in the standardized form came a variation on "in and upon the good ship," with blanks in which to record the ship's name and that of its captain. Before the age of steam, merchants considered the reputation of the ship crucial in their calculations: "So far as its owners were concerned, when a ship left port, it disappeared from the face of the earth, until, if fortune favored, it sailed again into its home port."[14] In the mid-nineteenth century, steam navigation made journeys more predictable, which improved logistical calculations, yet the ship's and captain's names were still recorded. When World War I threw transoceanic shipping into disarray and delay, goods often sat at warehouse ports, waiting to be loaded, so bills of lading were revised to say "received for shipment" rather than "shipped." The wartime state of emergency quickly became the standard, because carriers who owned entire shipping lines preferred the flexibility of loading goods on the next available ship: this enhanced the logistical flow. Though the bill of lading as a legal genre has persisted to the present, logistics had already made its key terms quaint more than a century ago.

How did bills of lading attempt to record the transportation of enslaved people? And how can we read between their lines for their stories? The standardized forms left a wide blank for the captain or supercargo to list goods such as hogsheads of rum, iron bars, wax candles, bags of lentils and rice, and almost anything else one can think of in the burgeoning world of

S HIPPED, in good Order and well conditioned, by ~~ *William Einglish* ~~ in and upon the good *Brigantine* ~~ called the *Ann* ~~ ~~ whereof is Maſter, for the preſent Voyage, *Said Einglish* ~~ and now riding at Anchor in the *Road of Anamboe Africa* ~~ and bound for *Port of Kingston in the Iſland Jamaica*—To ſay,

Thirty three men two boys twenty seven women & three girl slaves being the number of slaves purchased with the said Brigantine Anns Cargo ~~

33 men slaves 27 women 2 boys 3 girls

Being marked and numbered as in the Margin ; and are to be delivered in the like good Order and well conditioned, at the aforeſaid Port of *Kingston Jamaica Mortality Excepted* (the Danger of the Seas only excepted) unto *Mr. Thos. Dolbear* ~~

or to *his* Aſſigns, he or they paying Freight for the ſaid Goods *Nothing being the Owners property* ~~ with Primage and Average accuſtomed. In WITNESS whereof the Maſter or Purſer of the ſaid *Brigantine* ~~ hath affirmed unto *three* Bills of Lading, all of this Tenor and Date : One of which *three* Bills being accompliſhed, the other *two* to ſtand void. Dated in *Anamboe Africa July 14. one thouſand ſeven hundred and twenty three* ~~

W. Einglish

2.1 Bill of lading for the voyage of the *Ann*, July 14, 1773. Image provided by the Newport Historical Society.

goods. It is here where kidnapped Africans were enumerated by sex and age, as in this example from a 1773 voyage of the *Ann* (figure 2.1).[15]

After the opening notation that the brigantine *Ann*, captained by William Einglish, is riding at anchor in Anamboe and bound for Kingston, the printed "To say" introduces the handwritten list: "Thirty three men two boys twenty seven women and three girl slaves being the number of slaves purchased with the said brigantine Ann's cargo"—that is, rum, which had its own bill of lading for the outbound journey. Like most of the enslaved in the Middle Passage, these sixty-five people were not recorded by name.[16] If they had been, then the genre would have demanded more recording, to account for their individual injuries, deaths, or other fates, and bills of lading might have become vivid evidence for antislavery arguments. Moreover, their names were of little interest on board, as they were referred to by numbers until they were renamed by their purchasers on the other side.[17] The dehumanizing force of this piece of logistical media is stark and undeniable.

Yet, because its paper affordance reflected the contingency of the voyage and the trade, the bill of lading also opened a space for enslaved agency. For the printed form is interactive, intended to be filled in, and quite often revised. Accordingly, after the cargo list, we read, "Being marked and numbered as in the margin, and are to be delivered in the like good order and well conditioned at the aforesaid port of"—here, Einglish has filled in "Kingston Jamaica." But to the boilerplate "(the Danger of the Seas only excepted)," he has added two words, "mortality insurrection." Einglish, who knew firsthand the volatility of the trade, was covering himself and the shipowners, Jacob Rodriguez Rivera and Aaron Lopez, by anticipating not only the well-known lethal conditions of the Middle Passage, but the possibility that some or all of his sixty-five cargoes might resist their transportation.[18] Though suffering, tortured, and usually bound, enslaved people might nonetheless take matters into their own hands—so "actively expected" an occurrence by the 1780s that insurance companies were factoring it into their calculations.[19] The logistical document anticipates its own failure as it accounts for these other narrative possibilities: the goods may be "shipped," but they might never arrive.

The nondelivery of goods is the indefinite horizon of logistics, which strives for completion but can never fully meet it. Parcels go awry. The goods spoil and break. Supply lines get choked. And even when shipments arrive, they may disappoint. For most of 1773, Einglish was moored on the Ghanaian coast, failing to peddle his rum, awaiting the arrival of kidnapped people, and bemoaning the slackness of the trade in reports to Rivera and Lopez: "Gentlemen, I have but five Slaves on board and God knows when I shall have five more for the Country Trade is so Dull and Slaves Scarce."[20] Later, a drunken mate steals the long boat, which free Africans attack and plunder, delaying the return journey. In this environment of happenstance, random delinquency, and semiorganized violence, paperwork is invested with documentary certainty, and Rivera and Lopez urge Einglish to take pains with it: "You are to be particularly careful, that as soon as you have got your slaves on board, and before you leave the Coast you are to fill up two sets of Bills of lading." They instruct him to send copies of these to them by two different mail boats, "for in case of accident (which God forbid) we have no other way of proving our Interest, than by a bill of lading."[21] The bill of lading assumes critical documentary importance as security against the possibility of failure of nonarrival. As a piece of logistical media, it guarantees that Rivera and Lopez would be repaid by their marine insurer. Its legal recognition furnished financial security to logistical operations.

It is here that the bill of lading's special status as a negotiable document, and as the title to the goods, ameliorates the contingencies and risks of trade by sea. Bills of lading were issued, confusingly, in a set of three "originals"—one retained by the seller, one kept by the ship's captain, and one sent on ahead, by mail boat, to the purchaser, who would present it to lay claim to the goods. That is why all three bills always bore the caveat, "one of which being accomplished, the other two to stand void."[22] In this way, financial interest in the transaction itself would be preserved, because at least one of the parties would realize the value of the exchanged goods. The bill of lading indexed the goods—it described them and attested to their sound condition when placed on the ship—but in doing so, it also secured their financial value while in transit. A bill of lading found in an archive, such as the one in figure 2.1, may not be the one that reflects the events that befall the ship and its cargo, because it may be one of the two voided ones. Only the canceled one might be amended by hand to represent the truth of any changes to the goods en route. And, as I have been arguing, even the accomplished bill of lading, made out accurately, could not faithfully tell the story of the enslaved people whose value it secured. But its nature as a printed, official document that could nonetheless be revised by hand, reflects a double transformation, of free people into commodities in transit, and then into financial securities against risk. Both statuses made them precarious logistical subjects.

Just as parcels go awry and get delayed, so do media transmissions. Before the simultaneous rise of container ships and the deterioration of postal services in the mid-twentieth century, mail or "packet" ships could reliably travel faster than cargo ships, and bills of lading could be sent on ahead to the receiver, who would present them to collect his cargo.[23] Yet Einglish, writing from Mole Saint-Nicolas, Haiti, in January 1774, confesses to his employers that "there was noe opportunity to forward your bills as there was noe vessell being ready to sail for Europe." Einglish eventually found a buyer, though the bill of lading would need to be amended. Einglish "had the misfortune of Buriing Six Slaves on my passage."[24] One of Einglish's worries, "mortality," had come true. The nonaccomplished copy of the *Ann*'s bill of lading, archived and reproduced in figure 2.1, does not represent this grim reality. Nor does its twice-repeated mantra "well-ordered and in good condition" account for the terror, suffering, and death of the enslaved people it carried. This imperfect document suggests instead the ad hoc violence of kidnapping, the misery of disease, the mischances, delays, fiascos, and chaos that characterized the cutting-edge logistical system it organized. Its paper medium attests that in its inaugural modern moment, and in its objectives to record and predict, logistics was not a supremely organized, monolithic, and totalizing system.

The *Brookes* Ship Diagram

If the bill of lading's material, social practices, and generic conventions suggested an excess of abstraction in its imaginative transformation of enslaved people into commodities and securities, this excess could equally underwrite new forms of the logistical imagination and, with them, new politics. In this section, I demonstrate that the British parliamentary debate about ending the horror of the Middle Passage was a crucial turn in the modern logistical imagination. The key piece of logistical media driving it was the *Brookes* ship diagram (figure 2.2).

Marcus Wood has given a comprehensive account of the image's production, instant fame, wide circulation, and reproduction and its enduring meaning as a "memorial to disaster" rather than a descriptive reality.[25] The original diagram showed 294 human figures, individually drawn, packed into four compartments, for girls, women, boys, and men. In truth, before antislavery activists succeeded in passing the Slave Trade Act of 1788 limiting their number, the *Brookes* had carried considerably more enslaved people than were ever depicted in any of the editions of the diagram.[26] By illustrating how many enslaved people could be safely packed into the ship's hold, the diagram enacted a logistical practice, the biopolitical calculation of minimum human needs, as Smallwood puts it, "to manage the depletion of life."[27]

The more publishers reproduced and circulated the image through pamphlets, broadsides, periodicals, and books, the more it varied, expanding the terrain of the logistical imagination. Subsequent reproductions, such as in a children's book (see figure 2.3), make the original's abstracting logic even more apparent. The formalistic version of the diagram reduces the human figures to dashes. Its accompanying prose, beginning as if spelling out a math problem for its young readers, almost normalizes the Middle Passage and undermines its own abolitionist argument: "The captain of a slave ship wishes to carry as many as he can at once; the hold of his vessel is therefore measured and only sixteen inches each, in width, are allowed for men." It ends with the dismal fact, "Nearly half the number have died in the passage across the seas."[28] Logistics emerges as a practice of scientific rationalism in the service of human domination. The diagram and its reproductions owed their visual vocabulary to the cutting-edge discipline of naval architecture, which appeared to the original viewers as scientifically precise.[29] One Scottish aboli-

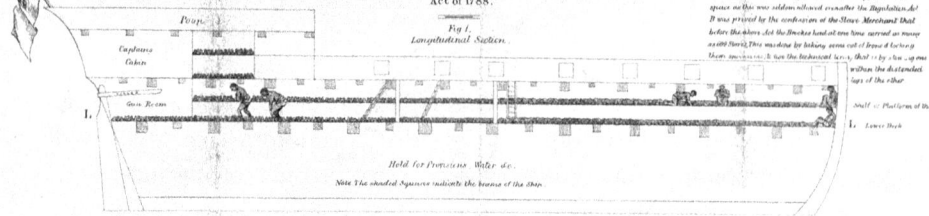

STOWAGE OF THE BRITISH SLAVE SHIP "BROOKES" UNDER THE

REGULATED SLAVE TRADE

Act of 1788.

Fig 1.
Longitudinal Section.

Hold for Provisions Water &c.

Note The shaded Squares indicate the beams of the Ship.

PLAN OF LOWER DECK WITH THE STOWAGE OF 292 SLAVES

130 OF THESE BEING STOWED UNDER THE SHELVES AS SHEWN IN FIGURE 0 & FIGURES.

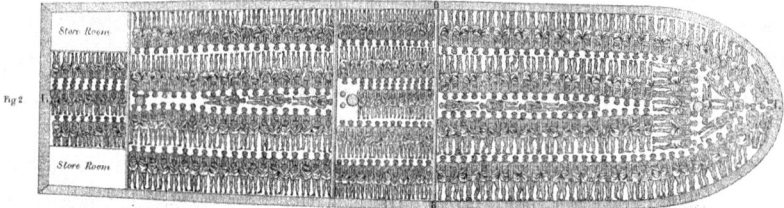

PLAN SHEWING THE STOWAGE OF 130 ADDITIONAL SLAVES ROUND THE WINGS OR SIDES OF THE LOWER DECK BY MEANS OF PLATFORMS OR SHELVES
(IN THE MANNER OF GALLERIES IN A CHURCH) THE SLAVES STOWED ON THE SHELVES AND BELOW THEM HAVE ONLY A HEIGHT OF 2 FEET 7 INCHES
BETWEEN THE BEAMS. AND FAR LESS UNDER THE BEAMS . See Fig 1.

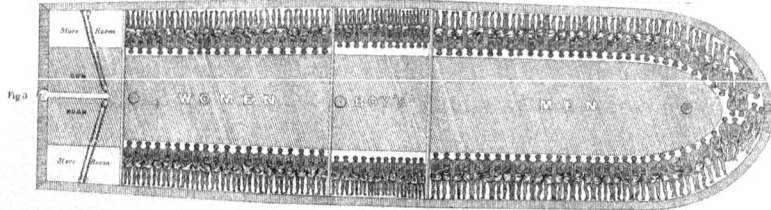

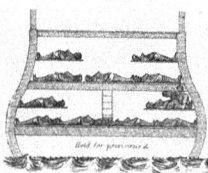

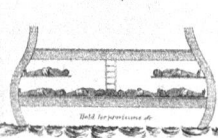

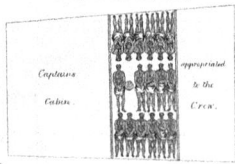

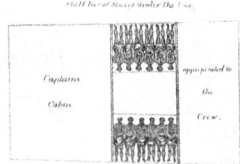

2.2 *The Brookes Ship* (1788). Plymouth Chapter of the Society for Effecting the Abolition of the Slave Trade.

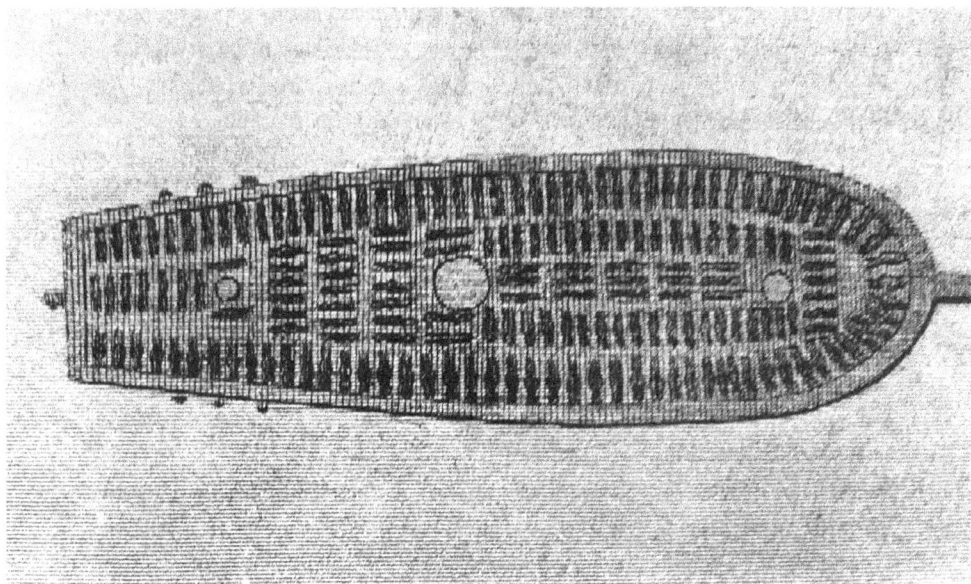

2.3 *Plan of a Slave Ship* From Isaac Taylor, *Scenes in Africa for the Amusement and Instruction of Little Tarry at Home Travellers* (London: Harris and Son, 1827).

tionist remarked on its "rigorous economy": "no place capable of holding a single person, from one end of the vessel to the other, is left unoccupied."[30] The image thus drew its authority and influence from its genre as a technical diagram; it achieved its circulation through print culture.

As Wood argues, the diagram's formalism generated a dialectical horror as viewers imagined the suffering of the enslaved people it reduced to schematic bits of visual information. Its consumers imagined not only the misery of being immobilized in too small a space, but the wretchedness of being too close to others. The Philadelphia version, commissioned by the Pennsylvania Anti-Slavery Society and widely distributed throughout the northeast United States, lamented "one of the most horrid spectacles—a number of human creatures, side by side, almost like herrings in a barrel."[31] This dread of being packed as cargo resounded through parliamentary testimony: the ship's doctor, Thomas Trotter, described enslaved people packed belowdecks as "locked spoonways."[32] Ex–slave ship captain John Newton portrayed them as "close to each other, like books upon a shelf."[33] William Roscoe, in the poem "The Wrongs of Africa," published in two parts and later translated into German, described enslaved people "in numbers pil'd, / And closely wedg'd within the scanty breadth / Of calculated inches."[34] The phrase "numbers pil'd" almost fantasizes the failure of the diagram's mathematical abstraction as the heap of human material begins to overwhelm the possibility of counting.

The diagram, its reprints, and its discourse deployed a "semiotic shock tactic," by using a technical engraving to conjure "a mass of black human flesh."[35] The dread it inspired was double-edged: it recoiled from both the loss of countable individuals and the resulting reformulation of humanity as conjoined in blackness. Ideologically, it simultaneously attempted to lend humanity to figuratively passive, inert enslaved people and withheld it from them as an undifferentiated mass. Underlying the fear is a European Romantic ideology of individualized freedom as wandering: unfettered mobility, self-expansion, spontaneity, and imperviousness to earthly and commercial calculation.[36] This modernizing, liberalizing logistical imagination, primed by print culture, forms in a white abolitionist revulsion at cold, rational calculation and constrained mobility. For the Black enslaved people who endured it, the Middle Passage's logistics was a matter less of the imagination than of their own lives and deaths.

Reading the *Brookes* ship diagram as a piece of logistical media was, and remains, an act of power that has racial dimensions. This power is embedded in the God's-eye view that has figuratively penetrated the hull of the ship and takes in all its inhabitants in a single, sweeping glance. Simone Browne, reading the London Society for Effecting the Abolition of the Slave Trade's 1789 version of the image, describes an active looking that might temper a purely white, dominating, aerial gaze. In this view, "The tiny black figures are not replicas of each other; rather, some have variously crossed arms, different gestures, or seem to turn to face one another, while some stare and look back"; thus, the image depicts "the trauma of the Middle Passage as multiply experienced and survived."[37] Such a mode of consuming the reproduced image requires the imagination. The *Brookes* ship diagram is an example of a logistical image that mobilizes a "critical humanism"; it demonstrates that not all logistical images are "shorn of the subjective, reflective, contemplative features usually ascribed to an artistic representation."[38] The circulated image was, and must be, read for its most subtle affordance, the hint or suggestion of what it cannot show: Black difference, suffering, and resistance.

This affordance of printed visual culture lies in its appeal to different senses, in this case, the tactile, the haptic, and the proprioceptive. The eighteenth-century antislavery audience interacted with these features when it felt the Romantic and Gothic claustrophobic dread of being packed too closely. Contemporary Black studies scholars reimagine that closeness as an alternative mode of Black political subjectivity and agency. Spillers notes the paradox whereby captive bodies become sites of "irresistible, destructive sensuality" at the same time that they are reduced to things.[39] Harney and Moten develop this enigma: "To have been shipped is to have been moved by others, with others. It is to feel at home with the homeless, at ease with the fugitive, at peace with the pursued, at rest with the ones who consent not to be one." Yet, this mode of "hapticality" is neither individual nor collective; it is "a way of feeling through others, a feel for feeling others feeling you."[40] This "consent not to be a single being" stands against the addictive "logistics and logic of racial capitalism and its ends" savored by "the sovereign junkie"—that is, a figure devoted to, and dependent on, individualism, rationalism, and self-governance.[41] Though it could never approach the reality, the *Brookes* ship diagram—reproduced, altered, and circulated within print culture—stimulated in its viewers a new imagination and feel for the logistics of enslaved transportation. A reformist rather than a revolutionary document, it conceded considerable ground to its proslavery interlocutors as it negotiated for incremental changes in naval architecture. Nonetheless, it unleashed new affects and ideas about what constituted the human. These culminated politically in the abolition of the trade in 1807—the humanizing effect of its printed circulation and consumption that imaginatively grew to counteract its evident dehumanizing gesture.

Conclusion

One last piece of print media joins these discussions of the *Ann*'s bill of lading and the *Brookes* ship diagram. It is an engraving by George Cooke that illustrated the 1793 edition of Thomas Day and John Bicknell's popular 1773 antislavery poem "The Dying Negro" (figure 2.4). The poem was inspired by an account, in the *Morning Chronicle and London Advertiser*, of a Black British man who, affianced to a white British woman, was illegally kidnapped and sent to a plantation in the colonies. Separated from his love and refusing to become enslaved, he shot himself.[42] The poem, which combined sentimentality with the trope of noble savagery, went through numerous editions; it was accompanied by an "advertisement" containing the original news item and prompted "sympathetic poetic responses."[43] The poem and illustration were part of a dynamic print culture that shaped the imagination of slavery—and commented on logistical media. For the image transforms the poem's world, of romantic love thwarted by injustice, to a scene of trade: one ship's hand carries cargo; another adjusts some rigging. Boxes with arrows indicating their correct stowage occupy the left foreground. The figure's chains echo the rigging, the ropes around the mast, and the cords on the packages, accentuating his commodification. Most crucially, the artist has placed an inkpot, quill pen, and an unrolling piece of paper atop one of the crates on the left. The flow of the paper mirrors the white loincloth swaddling the Roman figure in democratic nobility. Is this paper his bill of lading? The incongruous placement of inkpot and paper on deck emphasizes paper's role as a technique or instrument of supply chain securitization, as a legal document weighty as the crate and as controlling as the iron chains.

Yet, like Einglish's bills of lading, and like the *Brookes* ship diagram, this paper has already failed to secure the cargo: its human figure lives in a moment of his own decision, searching himself for a response to the brutalizing force of logistics. If we detach the engraving from the poem—a common eighteenth- and nineteenth-century practice for such visual ephemera—its image of defiance can resemble insurrection as much as it models suicide. It stops well short of Harney and Moten's "fantasy in the hold": striving for sovereign individuality, this is no figure of hapticality. Yet, emerging from white abolitionist discourse and the culture of print that supported it, it also participated in a new cultural and political formation of the logistical imagination. It suspended its viewers in the contingency and possibility opened up by the Middle Passage.

I have been demonstrating that the material of paper, the medium of print, and the genre of the bill of lading, far from achieving total logistical control over the Middle Passage, instead reflected its messy, open, and contested aspects. They drew together different threads of the logistical imagination: a sovereign fantasy of control through calculation and recording; a white horror of black bodies packed tight into a mass; a Romantic dream of individual freedom through mobility; the possibilities of cargo lost to disease and rebellion. The aspirational quality of paper documents, and the imperfect archive they now constitute, are neither the failings of old or low technology, nor the foibles of "dead" media that have been superseded by superior, more vital ones. Recent Marxist geography has developed the logistical imagination while maintaining its core dichotomy between inhuman logistical procedures and the humans who suffer by them, be they victims of human trafficking, exploited workers, or middle-class media consumers whose privacy is routinely compromised.[44] Such visions rightly critique the opacity of proprietary software, the fragmentation and de-skilling of labor, and the erosion of privacy that logistical media effects in our neoliberal era.[45]

2.4 A 1793 illustration published by George Cooke. Courtesy of the National Maritime Museum, London.

Yet, accounts that ascribe enormous, often totalizing sovereign power to twenty-first-century logistical media may overstate their case. My examples of imperfect paper and print—the cutting-edge logistical media of the late eighteenth and early nineteenth centuries—frame the sovereignty of logistical media differently. The technological affordances of present-day logistical media do not compromise human rights; rather it is capital, an ongoing, complex assemblage of human agreements, actions, and performances, that does so.

Paper may be flawed, but it remains the universally required medium of bills of lading, even in 2021. As of this writing, no one has invented an electronic system that replicates the affordance of the "three originals" of the paper bill of lading, as electronic copies cannot be uniquely physically possessed and exchanged for goods.[46] Moreover, global trade, driven by numerous diverse software systems, dependent on differential infrastructure throughout the developing world, and hampered by difficult-to-revise international maritime law, proves resistant to totalizing unification. Much-hyped solutions such as blockchain have not yet proven effective.[47] As Ned Rossiter notes in this volume, digital systems are vulnerable to a variety of contingencies that take place in the intervals of its decision-making. Ultimately neither paper nor digital media can reform, through their technological affordances, the world of global exchange in which legal and illegal transactions are inextricably mingled. That would require the kind of moral, political, and economic consensus that outlawed the Atlantic slave trade in 1807. In 2021, it would require a balance between the imagination of new logistical techniques and a critical humanist imagination of the full range of logistical lives.

NOTES

1. Hortense J. Spillers, "Mama's Baby, Papa's Maybe: An American Grammar Book," *Diacritics* 17, no. 2 (1987): 64–81, 69–70.

2. Katherine McKittrick, "Mathematics Black Life," *Black Scholar* 44, no. 2 (2014): 16–28, 17.

3. Stefano Harney and Fred Moten, *The Undercommons: Fugitive Planning and Black Study* (Brooklyn, NY: Autonomedia, 2014), 92.

4. Christina Sharpe, *In the Wake: On Blackness and Being* (Durham, NC: Duke University Press, 2016), 53.

5. I discuss this paradox at length in *The Mediated Mind: Affect, Ephemera, and Consumerism in the Nineteenth Century* (New York: Fordham University Press, 2018).

6. Lisa Gitelman, *Paper Knowledge: Toward a Media History of Documents* (Durham, NC: Duke University Press, 2014), 3.

7. Caitlin Rosenthal, *Accounting for Slavery: Masters and Management* (Cambridge, MA: Harvard University Press, 2018), 82.

8. Stephanie Smallwood, *Saltwater Slavery: A Middle Passage from African to American Diaspora* (Cambridge, MA: Harvard University Press, 2007), 100.

9. On the avoidance of the violence of re-inscription, see Saidiya Hartman, "Venus in Two Acts," *Small Axe*, no. 26 (2008): 1–14.

10. Spillers, "Mama's Baby," 72; original emphasis.

11. Sharpe, *In the Wake*, 13–14.

12. C. L. R. James, *Mariners, Renegades, and Castaways: Herman Melville and the World We Live in Now* (Hanover, NH: University Press of New England, 2001 [1953]), 122.

13. See Tom Cottrell and Robert Dalton Harris, "American Illuminated Bills of Lading (pre War of 1812)," *Ephemera News* 13, no. 1 (1994): 22–23; Robert Dalton Harris, "American Illuminated Bills of Lading (pre War of 1812): Supplement to Article in *Ephemera News* Vol. 13 no. 1," *Ephemera News* 13, no. 2 (1995): 22–23; and Robert Dalton Harris, "American Shipping Bills of Lading (post War of 1812)," *Ephemera News* 13, no. 3 (1995): 14–15.

14. Chester McLaughlin Jr., "The Evolution of the Ocean Bill of Lading," *Yale Law Journal* 35, no. 5 (1926): 548–70, 562. The description of the changing functions of bills of lading in this paragraph is indebted to this comprehensive article.

15. A century previously, a captain's private logbook, not a printed form, would have been used to record such facts. See Smallwood, *Saltwater Slavery*.

16. By contrast with documents related to the Middle Passage, names of enslaved people typically appear on nineteenth-century invoices, bills of lading, and manifests for interstate sale in the United States. The largest archive is the collection of New Orleans slave ship manifests from 1807 to 1860, held by the U.S. National Archives, viewable at https://www.archives.gov/research/african-americans/slave-ship-manifests.html. These are the subject of Ralph Clayton's *Cash for Blood: The Baltimore to New Orleans Domestic Slave Trade* (Bowie, MD: Heritage Books, 2002).

17. Marcus Rediker, *The Slave Ship: A Human History* (New York: Penguin, 2007), 11.

18. For a fuller account of Einglish's voyage on behalf of Rivera and Lopez, see Roderick Terry, "Some Old Papers Relating to the Slave Trade," *Bulletin of the Newport Historical Society* 62 (1927): 10–35.

19. Anita Rupprecht, "Excessive Memories: Slavery, Insurance, Resistance," *History Workshop Journal* 64 (2007): 6–28, 21.

20. Terry, "Some Old Papers Relating to the Slave Trade," 19. Ian Baucom describes this hurry-up-and-wait aspect of logistics with respect to the *Zong* in *Spectres of the Atlantic: Finance Capital, Slavery, and the Philosophy of History* (Durham, NC: Duke University Press, 2005), 14.

21. Terry, "Some Old Papers Relating to the Slave Trade," 15, 16.

22. The bill of lading's customary status as title would be formally recognized in the mid-nineteenth century. See Kurt Grönfors, *Towards Sea Waybills and Electronic Documents* (Göteborg: Gothenburg Maritime Law Association, 1991), 7–24.

23. Grönfors, *Towards Sea Waybills*, 19.

24. Terry, "Some Old Papers Relating to the Slave Trade," 26, 24.

25. Marcus Wood, *Blind Memory: Visual Representations of Slavery in England and America, 1780–1865* (New York: Routledge, 2000), 14–77, 32.

26. Rediker, *The Slave Ship*, 311.

27. Smallwood, *Saltwater Slavery*, 36.

28. Isaac Taylor, *Scenes in Africa for the Amusement and Instruction of Little Tarry at Home Travellers* (London: Harris and Son, 1827), 63.

29. Rediker, *Slave Ship*, 55–56.

30. *Address to the Inhabitants of Glasgow, Paisley, and the Neighbourhood, Concerning the African Trade* (Glasgow: Alex Adam, 1791), 8.

31. "Remarks on the Slave Trade" (Philadelphia: Pennsylvania Antislavery Society, 1789).

32. *Abstract of the Evidence Delivered Before a Select Committee of the House of Commons in the Years 1790 and 1791* (London: James Phillips, 1791), 34.

33. John Newton, *The Posthumous Works of the Late Reverend John Newton* (Philadelphia: Woodward, 1809), 248.

34. William Roscoe, *The Wrongs of Africa: A Poem* (Philadelphia: Joseph James, 1788), 20. On the publication and translation, see Henry Roscoe, *The Life of William Roscoe* (London: T. Caddel, 1833), 1:82–83.

35. Wood, *Blind Memory*, 27.

36. William Wordsworth is the touchstone for this ideology, which is described in Rebecca Solnit, *Wanderlust: A History of Walking* (London: Penguin, 2001); and Celeste Langan, *Romantic Vagrancy: William Wordsworth and the Simulation of Freedom* (Cambridge: Cambridge University Press, 2006). For an important contribution that links this sense of personal automobility to Enlightenment rather than Romanticism, see Sarah Cervenak, *Wandering: Philosophical Performances of Racial and Sexual Freedom* (Durham, NC: Duke University Press, 2014).

37. Simone Browne, *Dark Matters: On the Surveillance of Blackness* (Durham, NC: Duke University Press, 2015), 50.

38. Alberto Toscano, "The Mirror of Circulation: Allan Sekula and the Logistical Image," *Environment and Planning D: Society and Space*, July 31, 2018, https://societyandspace.org/2018/07/30/the-mirror-of-circulation-allan-sekula-and-the-logistical-image/.

39. Spillers, "Mama's Baby," 67.

40. Moten and Harney, *The Undercommons*, 98.

41. Fred Moten, *Stolen Life* (Durham, NC: Duke University Press, 2018), 194.

42. Brycchan Carey, *British Abolitionism and the Rhetoric of Sensibility: Writing, Sentiment, and Slavery, 1760–1807* (London: Palgrave, 2005), 75.

43. Vincent Carretta, *Phillis Wheatley: Biography of a Genius in Bondage* (Athens: University of Georgia Press, 2014), 129.

44. See, for example, Deborah Cowen, *The Deadly Life of Logistics: Mapping Violence in Global Trade* (Minneapolis: University of Minnesota Press, 2014).

45. See Ned Rossiter, *Software, Infrastructure, Labor: A Media Theory of Logistical Nightmares* (London: Routledge, 2016).

46. On the challenges facing the adoption of electronic bills of lading, see Marek Dubovec, "The Problems and Possibilities for Using Electronic Bills of Lading as Collateral," *Arizona Journal of International and Comparative Law* 23, no. 2 (2005): 437–66.

47. See Sanne Wass, "essDocs to Launch Blockchain Solution in Early 2019," *Global Trade Review*, December, 12, 2018, https://www.gtreview.com/news/fintech/essdocs-to-launch-blockchain-solution-in-early-2019; and David Saive, "Blockchain Documents of Title—Negotiable Electronic Bills of Lading under German Law," *Social Science Research Network*, February 7, 2019, https://papers.ssrn.com/sol3/papers.cfm?abstract_id=3321368.

LOGISTICAL MAGIC

In 1849, an enslaved Virginia man hatches a plan to transport himself to Philadelphia in a box. Assisted by accomplices, he constructs a crate with small gaps so he can breathe; the five-foot-eight, two-hundred-pound man squeezes himself into this 3-by-2-by-2.5-foot box. Enduring incorrect loading upside down on a steamboat, and careless unloading, which causes his box to roll down a small hill, the man arrives at the offices of the Anti-Slavery Society almost twenty-four hours later. His recipients cut away the box's hickory loops and pry off the lid with hatchet and saw.

The man, now free, stands up and sings a little song that he has prepared for the occasion. For decades afterward, he sells engravings depicting this moment, as well as song lyric sheets; he also performs his spring from the box, as an escapologist and illusionist. His novel mode of fugitivity shapes African American stage magic, as performers thrill audiences with daring escapes from sealed boxes and elaborate chains. In the early twentieth century, Harry Houdini appropriates this tradition and becomes its most famous icon. An enduring set piece of American entertainment originates in enslaved fugitivity. Its spectacle of claiming freedom for oneself rehearses the magic of logistics. Deliverance becomes delivery. The first logistician, as fugitive and as magician, is Henry Box Brown.

Samuel Rowse, *The Resurrection of Henry Box Brown at Philadelphia* (1850).

3

Pan-African Logistics

IN AUGUST 1958, nearly a thousand people crowded around the Hotel Theresa in Harlem to celebrate the arrival of President Kwame Nkrumah in New York and a year of Ghanaian independence. A short parade, followed by remarks from politicians and business leaders reinforced support for Ghana, while Nkrumah's speech formalized what had already taken place through direct invitations. He called on the African diaspora in the United States to "come and help" build up "our country." The appeal targeted black professionals—lawyers, doctors, and engineers, who might have sufficient experience and ambition to reimagine the remnants of colonial infrastructure and materialize the daily work of Pan-African institution building. In response, a generation of artists, movement leaders, intellectuals, social workers, and teachers made the journey back to Africa to test the promise of welcome in the "land of their forefathers."[1] Maya Angelou, Malcolm X, W. E. B. Du Bois, Pauli Murray, St. Clair Drake, and Adelaide Cromwell all dedicate considerable space in their memoirs and interviews to the experience, sedimenting a narrative about the first movement of African Americans to Ghana and their relevance to Pan-African nationalism.[2]

Half a dozen years after Nkrumah's appeal and on the cusp of a coup that would send many African Americans back to the United States, a book titled *The Longest Way Home* introduced a startling new tale of a migration movement that brought African Americans to the Gold Coast forty years earlier.[3] Sociologists William Bittle and Gilbert Geis chronicled efforts to repatriate African Americans under the leadership of Chief Alfred Charles Sam in 1914. The authors described thousands who were guided by the same spirit of diasporic upbuilding in Africa to buy stock in Sam's company for the purchase of a ship, christened the SS *Liberia*, which would eventually ferry a delegation to the Gold Coast on the eve of World War I. For Bittle and Geis, the movement foreshadowed Marcus Garvey's Universal Negro Improvement Association (UNIA) movement and flirted with fraud. They questioned Sam's claim to chieftaincy and his ability to make good on the promise of mutual benefit through diasporic return. According to US media accounts at the time, the movement collapsed a year after setting sail, with the penniless return of migrants who were unable to claim land, burdened by the difficulty of finding work and food during a war, and abandoned by Chief Sam.

A few years after the book was published, a coup overthrew Nkrumah, resulting in the gradual departure of the "Afros," as African Americans had come to be known. These developments cast the book in a new light. A flurry of inquiry by scholars of African and diasporic studies initiated an analysis of the little-known 1914 back-to-Africa movement launched during the colonial period, now understood as precedent for Nkrumah's invitation and an early test for Pan-African projects. Gambian historian J. Ayo Langley revisited colonial correspondence in London, which complicated the story, exposing efforts by British officials to dissolve Alfred C. Sam's chieftaincy before he could fulfill his plan to adopt returnees and form a village on the land purchased for their settlement.[4] Langley argued that despite Sam's insistence on flying the British imperial flag during the return voyage, the movement posed a political threat to the colonial regime.

Langley suggested that the movement's fundraising and arrival pragmatically sharpened the political and economic claims of Pan-Africanism as a global movement converging in Africa.[5] By contrast with his mentor George Shepperson, Langley concluded that Sam's initiative was not a failed scheme, transient and disconnected from a broader movement. Instead, he maintained that the African Movement was an imminent influence on Marcus Garvey's efforts a few years later, fomenting racial solidarity in West Africa. The movement's legacy was not in the success of mass migration or the shipping line Sam hoped to launch with diasporic capital but in the audacity of practical planning, which stimulated the Pan-African imagination by consolidating spiritual and material commitments between Africans and African Americans.

In response to the book, Langley's provocative research, and the traces of Sam in Garvey's archive, Robert Hill, historian and curator of the Marcus Garvey papers, organized a research partnership in the late 1970s to recover African memories of this immigration experiment.[6] Sam's influence on Garvey appeared obvious. Their business plans overlapped in rhetoric and scale. They both had offices in Harlem, a mere ten blocks apart, tapping similar networks for support. Nevertheless, Garvey rarely mentioned Sam. Hill set out to reconstruct Pan-African appeal and the steps taken to materialize his offer, particularly the moment when migrants landed on African soil. He commissioned James K. Anquandah, the first Ghanaian archaeologist, to interview living witnesses of the ship's arrival in Saltpond, Ghana. Anquandah was eager to conduct oral histories that acknowledged a precedent for both Garvey's and Nkrumah's visions of diasporic reunion and development. He traveled to Saltpond in 1977, beginning a four-year research process to verify the arrival of African Americans in 1915 and document the places where they lived in the Gold Coast. The result of those interviews, combined with archival research, led Hill to write "Before Garvey," in *Pan-African Biography*.[7] What follows is an account culled from my efforts to trace Hill's footnotes through Anquandah's notes, as well as my own interviews and archival research in Ghana. In this essay I argue that the logistical challenges of diasporic return help explain how the first generation of African Americans in Ghana "disappeared."[8]

The Logistics of Diasporic Return

The sixteen-year-old chief of Saltpond, Nana Kurantsi III, was newly enstooled when he heard that a ship carrying a resident of Saltpond and migrants from the United States would arrive in January 1915. Joseph Drybauld Taylor, a close friend to Alfred C. Sam who was also from the neighboring town of Anomabo, made preparations for home stays and food, and oversaw the rapid construction of the AME Zion Church in Saltpond, an institution founded by African Americans to Africanize Methodism in response to segregation. That month, more than one hundred passengers and crew docked their ship in the harbor at Abandze beach, boarding canoes that sailed against the choppy waters to deliver returned kin rather than commodities.[9] Bringing closure to the narrative of departure, the return event staged a reckoning with mass abduction in the form of an emigration and trade corporation. According to Anquandah's interview with the chief, the passengers who gathered ashore identified as "stockholders" consolidating their resources to reverse the historical loss of Africans to slavery by purchasing stock in a Pan-African trade and emigration company.

The journey had taken six months, with planned stops in several U.S. states for passengers, then docking in Cuba, Barbados, and Cape Verde for trade. Testing the potential of a commercial partnership to remedy the systematic separation of families, the Akim Trading Company Ltd. was aimed at "restoring our people to their natural home."[10] But the process was marred by setbacks. Sam defended himself in two fraud trials prior to leaving the United States. The German-made ship was then searched by the British Navy in Cape Verde, resulting in a martial trial in Sierra Leone, and a forced stop at Cape Coast required passengers to pay a new head tax before arriving in Saltpond.[11] These were not mere delays or unfactored costs. The attempt at mass return exposed logistical challenges that evolved in response to the movement. Much of what remains are trial and tax records, receipts for deeds, and media accounts, forming what Neil Rossiter, Judd Case, and others call "logistical media." Logistical media steer action. The arrival of mail, filing of paperwork, and court martial orders all coordinate responses to information across space and time. Media coverage steered readers toward support or critique, while the stock certificate marked a symbolic promise as well as a practical investment of capital. The variety of documents affecting the movement's progress formed a continuum of tools working toward different goals (derailment, on one end, and fulfillment of the migration scheme, one the other). The logistical residue of the African Movement in scattered archives challenges the tidy story of fraud with a more complex account of instruments turned toward liberatory ends—with uneven results and outsize opposition.

What then does it mean to probe for logistical challenges in a back-to-Africa movement? Can obstacles experienced in the path of return be placed on par with transnational infrastructures that secure the flow of commerce? Or are difficulties evidence of narrow competence and overly ambitious goals? Logistics attracts a wide range of definitions, from the sparest abstraction of "orientation and coordination" to a formalized field of calculation that integrates commerce, labor, transportation, and war through superficially apolitical interest in functioning supply chains.[12] In *The Deadly Life of Logistics*, Deborah Cowen argues that "mapping spaces of circulation" at the seams of business and war reveals the "profoundly political" production of logistical space, which has been shielded from political scrutiny under the sign of technical efficiency.[13] Laleh Khalili renders granular what we generically call shipping in stories that trace its various dependencies on racialized labor, migration, and sequestered infusions of capital in ports that conceal much of its operations.[14] The granularity of logistics is another way to grasp the political as a bid for control over time, space, movement, and capital. Mapping efficiencies that enable the circulation of some goods and some people, while limiting others, does partially explain the difficulties encountered on the SS *Liberia*'s route. However, understanding the trace infrastructure of colonialism and slavery that fueled the growth of global capitalism enables a better account of the coordinated resistance to diasporic return.

Logistics generically describes the mechanics of war-induced trade, profit, and reinvestment, but it must explicitly include slavery and colonization as a prompt for the reorganization of global commerce.[15] This approach not only acknowledges a multiplicity of origin stories for logistics. It also addresses how legacy institutions develop afterlives at the level of technical affordances and constraints. By specifying the relevance of slavery and colonialism for logistical analysis, we can understand migration experiments that reverse itineraries against the tide of racial capitalism as highly technical operations that reorient political alliances.

The sum of techniques employed by the African Movement responded to imminent problems while moving toward an idealistic vision of racial solidarity and modernization, which can be called Pan-African logistics. Solving for questions of transport, income, and land purchased from a distance, Pan-African logistics operates within a long-term horizon of mutual benefit for Africa and the diaspora, even against odds. The organization of capital, networks, technology, media, political support, and labor required for African Americans to resettle in African communities relies on determined effort even as large-scale plans can be easily undermined from multiple angles. Pan-African logistics can also repurpose the mechanisms responsible for separation, mobility, and reunion, sailing on shipping routes that produced the collective trauma of forced dispersal while attempting to steer it toward liberatory ends.[16]

The leader of the African Movement, Alfred Charles Sam, was oriented toward shipping through the seminary. Born and educated in the Gold Coast, his religious training proceeded in tandem with a business apprenticeship in the Basel Mission.[17] He was a product of his time, as churches in the colony largely supported themselves and expected catechists to staff factories and oversee shipments. Sam later started a cocoa farming and export business with his first wife, Efua Kuma. Eventually he boarded ships himself to the Caribbean, Europe, and the United States, managing transactions for produce, timber, rubber, and cocoa, the commodity trade that replaced the traffic in humans. After two years successfully navigating the commercial circuit, Sam began to question the long arc of his efforts and the legacy he would leave behind.

A religious experience in Brooklyn, New York, answered the question. Reverend Joseph Drybauld Taylor, who facilitated Sam's first contacts in the United States, had introduced him to members of an evangelical community based in Maine. Representatives of the Holy Ghost and Us Society traveled to Brooklyn and prayed with him according to a prophecy that predicted an African king would influence the future of the community. Led by Frank Sandford, the society was an Anglo-Zionist millenarian community guided by prophecy. Members regularly traveled to England and Palestine for missionary work. Owning a ship for trade and evangelism appealed to Sam. Soon after the first meeting he learned that his uncle had died, placing him in the direct line of succession as king of a small village in the Gold Coast. The convergence of prophecy and the call to return home urged him to think collaboratively. Sandford's racially proscriptive Zionism predicted a return to Jerusalem for Anglo-Israelites, while he encouraged Sam to develop his own church in Africa. However, Sandford was unwilling to send missionaries to the Gold Coast, and Sam began to think through potential partnerships in the United States that could expand trade into a financially sustainable Christian community.[18]

Echoing Sandford's short, prophetic messages, Sam reported that he had taken up the matter of his own future in prayer and received a single-word prophecy: "Liberia." A compressed symbol for diasporic return guided by religious convictions, the prophecy redirected his life path toward organized migration. Diasporic return would fortify trade, expand the Gold Coast with returnees from the United States, and invite new collaborations for building a church that reflected the joint commitments of African Christians and those in the diaspora. He spent the next eighteen months fundraising in the United States, delivering rousing speeches about the African homeland as a refuge from US racial violence and Jim Crow, promising land for an African city networked through trade, and envisioning factories, colleges, bathhouses, and restaurants, designed and supported by diasporic capital and natural wealth in Africa.

With nearly $100,000 from the sale of corporate stock, Sam contracted a white agent in January 1914 to purchase a German-made ship from Cuba, merging trade and migration in a single transaction.[19] Sam's initiative used business as an interface for diasporic return well before the development logic of tourism took hold in Ghana in the 1990s.[20] And yet we are limited by time-bound narratives of neoliberalism and the timeless narrative of fraud to explain the motivation for a religious African merchant to organize along these lines, losing what might be the most significant insight into the corporate mediation of diasporic return. The Akim Trading Company invited capital investments from the surviving descendants of enslaved Africans in exchange for land and inclusion in African polities.

Driven by faith as much as by a business plan, Sam pointed out the mutual "obligations and responsibilities" of a Pan-African enterprise for African Americans and Africans, should they partner successfully to move people and goods against the grain of slavery.[21] The novelty of the movement did not rest on the promise of return. For as long as Africans have been forcibly removed from the continent, return has been an aspiration and a hard-won reality. Returnees from Brazil and the Caribbean had long navigated the route using personal capital without need for an invitation.[22] What Sam offered was a corporate vehicle—a company that incentivized African interest in modernization by inviting diasporic investment and matching that investment with an offer of land.

When the delegation of migrants disembarked from the SS *Liberia* in 1915, Sam indicated they were only "a small part" of thousands who had purchased stock in Sam's Akim Trading Company Ltd. the previous year, all hoping to set sail on this or subsequent journeys.[23] Sam's speech adopted the air of declaration, accentuating the triumph of arrival but also suggesting a dilemma at the heart of diasporic return: "These Negroes are not strangers and should not be considered strangers. They and their forebears were taken away by force from home and they are now some of them anxious to return home. The land is as much theirs as yours. God has preserved you to take care of the land until their return."[24] Yoking land to kinship and loss, Sam translated the migrant's arrival into an Akan ritual of recognition for ancestors buried in the land, justifying the transfer of land as a transfer to kin rather than to foreign ownership. He delivered similar remarks to audiences who gathered to greet the migrants en route to the land purchased for their settlement, emphasizing the necessity of recognizing relatedness as a condition of shared ownership.

By offering to manage the logistics of return, Sam did not simply organize transit across the Atlantic. He attempted to reorganize the interface between different regimes of authority in the United States and the Gold Coast to support a process of *making Africans from distant kin separated by slavery*. In addition to claiming an African ancestral identity for returnees, Sam's proposal to pair diasporic return with African development balanced a fragile proposition taken for granted in Pan-African rhetoric. In contemporary terms, "diasporic Africans" describes a dispersed population of Africans living outside of the continent, whether by forced or voluntary migration. But during the African Movement, the right of return was tethered to the expectation that migrants would become part of an indigenous polity through technical means of adoption, land transfer, and development, leaving their American identities behind.

The logistics of return to the Gold Coast reveals that the invitation to "come home" involved the transformation of identity, a plan to formally convert "foreigners" into kin who could own land, backed by investment in regional development, all complex exchanges rhetorically rendered seamless in the call for racial solidarity (i.e., Africa for the Africans). Sam's enterprise calls attention to the way corporate features navigated questions of kinship, land, and rights under colonialism, a rough terrain whose success was aspirational rather than guaranteed. Modeled after Liberia with critical modifications, Sam's adjustments prioritized indigenous political structures in order to avoid replicating a colonial hierarchy that marginalized indigenous Africans.

The features of corporate kinship activated by stock purchase and tethered to an emigration movement encourage closer scrutiny about the ways we study the business of social movements. While the designation of business failure typically indicates a short-lived influence, I suggest along with Langley that the Akim Trading Company Ltd. forged a template for diasporic return that continued into the next century. The fragile proposition of family incorporation and investment for development remains the organizing logic of return—from President Nana Akufo-Addo's declaration of 2019 as the Year of Return to corporate philanthropies promoting tourism in Ghana.[25] Yet policy mechanisms still struggle to fulfill the open-door promise of welcome for "distant kin." Instead of lodging a charge of bad faith or economic exploitation only, logistical challenges can map the moving parts of diasporic return. The nature of difficulties encountered by migrants can help pose the critical questions: through what practical means do diasporic and indigenous Africans consider mass return a mutual benefit, and what technical instruments are used to fulfill the spiritual and material promise of welcome?

Reunion and Development

Retracing the terms of this corporate proposal requires unsettling common assumptions about African immobility—stuckness in place and time contrasted to diasporic mobility. Alfred C. Sam traveled up and down the West African coast for business, assessing the changing terms of trade and the possibility for expansion early in the twentieth century. Immediately following his prophecy, Sam visited Monrovia in 1912 to meet Reverend Taylor.

Edward W. Blyden, a leading Pan-Africanist and institution builder in Liberia, had died in Sierra Leone that year, reanimating many of his ideas about diasporic return. Taylor, a Fante minister trained in the United States at Livingstone College, had recently taken charge of the AME Zion Church in Brewerville, Liberia. The church had a predominantly American Liberian congregation and was seated at the tip of Monrovia's peninsula. Taylor was the first indigenous African to lead the institution after rescuing the first AME Church in Keta, Gold Coast, from disrepair some years before. Taylor and Sam discussed how Sam might put his pending chieftaincy to highest use given his access to land, including a range of crops from rubber and fruit trees to timber and cocoa, as well as to a trading company recently organized in New York City. As Sam toured the United States to sell stock in the company, emigration aroused enthusiasm from Kentucky to Pennsylvania, leading Sam to expand the mission of the company against the will of the Akim Trading Company's board, which included several African American members. The board roundly denounced the plan—considering migration the death knell of a profitable business. Sam parted ways with the original company, reconstituting the board with mostly African members as the Akim Trading Company. He then solicited ten Akan chiefs for consultation to determine how the controlled allocation of land to African Americans could happen without overturning indigenous sovereignty. In turn, Taylor tapped his church community for contacts to find potential investors, leading Sam to place an ad in an emigrationist paper that was published in Liberia and Mississippi.

The *African League* regularly advertised requests for chartered ships or couriers sailing to Liberia, trade and missionary opportunities, as well as information about land for sale. Tasked with informing African Americans about the logistics of relocation, the *African League*'s circulation held together a loose network of emigrationists, sustaining a communication infrastructure in spite of the American Colonization Society's decline. The Society had relocated more than fifteen thousand African Americans in the first fifty years after emancipation, but with increasingly vocal critique of sponsored emigration, conflict with indigenous Africans on the Liberian coast, and limited funds to charter ships, volunteers dwindled, leaving emigrationist papers to vet queries and advertise options as they became available. Sam used the ad to invite land queries, promising fecund crops secured by the authority of his chieftaincy. The resulting correspondence, initially with P. J. Dorman, who wrote on behalf of prospective migrants in Oklahoma, raised the question of foreign ownership, which allowed Sam to share his solution.

For $25 African Americans could buy stock in a company that would organize mass migration to the Gold Coast.[26] Migrants would be given land to cultivate crops and build factories with the support of Akan chiefs. Sam, who was director of the Akim Trading Company, was scheduled to become chief of a small village within the year. He would coordinate the journey and acquire the land, then adopt migrants under his chieftaincy powers to work around the prohibition on foreign land ownership. Those who responded to the ad would construct a supply chain to the coast for multiple crops and manufactured goods, with plans for a railway and colleges, simultaneously building up capital for a fleet of ships called the Ethiopian Steamship Line.[27] Scaffolding an ambitious infrastructural plan from land queries and a stock offering, Sam offered a logistical workaround to mutual benefit: diasporic reunion in support of African development.

Chief Sam's African Movement stimulated intrigue and enthusiastic fundraising in the United States once word spread, yielding nearly two hundred emigration clubs across the country, from urban centers like Boston and Chicago, to all-black towns in Oklahoma and Florida, raising the money for a ship in less than two years. Within five years, however, thousands of stockholders would hold only their stock certificate as a memento of what might have been.[28] Though it was not considered a lasting success, Sam's initiative persistently argued the practical interdependence of diasporic reunion and African development. The prophetic call propelled Sam and his followers through relentless obstacles in pursuit of a long-term vision of diasporic capital fused with natural wealth in the Gold Coast. Anthropologist Jane Guyer observes that prophecy is uniquely logistical precisely because the end-game appears implausible to others but requires immediate implementation on divine authority, a tendency shared with long-term economic forecasting.[29] Sam responded to his single-word prophecy by immediately restructuring his company's goals, even without board consensus, to raise money and secure agreement from local chiefs, then launching a multistate tour advertising ready crops and markets for potential migrants to sustain themselves.

Penning a critique in the *Crisis*, W. E. B. Du Bois called the plan "an unrealizable fantasy."[30] Even as Du Bois invested in similar Pan-African business ventures that failed in the early decades of the twentieth century, he condemned Sam specifically for rallying emigrationist hope in untested territory. British colonial rule expanded its reach in Sam's lifetime, with no guarantee for control over transnational resettlement and limited consensus among Gold Coast elites about the desirability of African American immigration.[31]

With little support from Du Bois and a sharp denunciation by Duse Mohamed Ali, a Pan-African journalist and businessman who was Garvey's employer at the time in London, Sam's project was described in the press as a confidence scheme.[32]

Making Africans

The Longest Way Home, by Bittle and Geis, emphasizes this line of interpretation. Largely based on the testimony of people who did not travel, and those who returned to Oklahoma specifically, Bittle and Geis framed the movement as a story of flawed investment, punctuated by speculations about fraud based on promises that Sam could not keep. Fraud is a compelling explanatory framework for a failed venture with a narrow chance of success in the first place, but it also obscures motive and minimizes achievements. Once the ship arrived in Galveston, Texas, christened as the SS *Liberia*, participants noted that Sam had already surpassed earlier efforts that could not materialize transport.[33] Historian Kendra Field, whose ancestors participated in the movement as founding funders, interviewed descendants fifty years after *The Longest Way Home* was published. Her book *Growing Up with the Country* substantially revises the media story of failed migration, which depicted investors as gullible and desperate victims of an elaborate swindle. Instead she traces the transnational orientation of black settlers in Indian Territory. Trailed by racial violence that devalued their property investments and narrowed the possibility for justice post-emancipation, migration to Africa was an easily rekindled proposal. On the one hand, it capitalized on a colonization impulse aimed at Liberia, and on the other, all-black towns tipped a black nationalist enterprise into a more robust articulation of Pan-Africanism.[34]

For Bittle and Geis, the outlandish projection of an African city networked to the rest of the world could only exploit the vulnerable hopes of poor African American farmers (a misrepresentation of a cross-class movement) by presenting an unrealistic cost relative to stated benefits. Combined with the return of fifteen migrants a year later, early critics appeared to be vindicated. Though not all the migrants returned.

After learning of descendants who remained in Ghana about three years ago, I began to argue that we should shift the timeline for African American migration *back forty years* because the reasons for the "disappearance" of most migrants illuminates the terms on which indigenous Africans absorbed African Americans as partners in development. This was a fortunate convergence because "the African personality," championed by Edward W. Blyden and later J. E. Casely Hayford, was actively concretized into a shared identity that cut across colonial lines during World War I, and migration tested the strength of rights and capacities attributed to African identity.[35] Though Sam's proposal failed as a conduit for making Africans via mass adoption, those who remained effectively became African within a generation through language acquisition, marriage, and birth, all facilitating options for long-term settlement and income with little incentive to advertise their birth and upbringing in America.

Because indigeneity and Africanness emerged at the end of the nineteenth century to protest colonial land grabs and reassert customary law (which happened much earlier in South Africa), indigeneity operated a political claim, arguing a relationship between identity, land, and caretaking that places limits on sale and extractive profiteering relative to future generations. The Gold Coast Aborigines Rights Protection Society was formed to rally political opposition with these relationships in mind. A group of African barristers and merchants working in concert with chiefs challenged the proposal to absorb fallow land into the category of "public lands" governed by the British. By then a classic "empty land" strategy, it was tested in South Africa to claim everyone was a migrant and land was only acquired by force or farming. The proposal was immediately understood as a means of dispossession in the Gold Coast. J. E. Casely Hayford, a barrister who researched customary land laws for the society's counterproposal that eventually defeated the land bill, insisted on the importance of African solidarity to match the scope of colonial aggression on the continent.[36] As leader of the Aborigines Rights Protection Society in 1912, his writing also invoked literary narrative as a tool for political imagination. In his novel of ideas, *Ethiopia Unbound*, he wrote: "We don't want Afro-Americans so much as we want Africans."[37] Precisely to fortify African as an elective counter-category to "native," he emphasized the political choice to become African, distinct from a naturalized condition of relatedness via blackness. A friend to Casely Hayford, Sam presented a process for diasporic returnees to become indigenous Africans again. But even without the success of a technical strategy, the implications for movement organizing would soon become clear in a commonplace chant among Garveyites: "Africa for the Africans."

Significantly, Sam's commitment to Pan-African business and diasporic migration was not based on the prospect of escape from racism in the United States alone. His proposal emerged as government policies also installed the color line in the Gold Coast, segregating access to housing, employment, licensing, and trade contracts, employing the "native" category to racialize resources and protect European assets.[38] Rather than a claim of origins, indigeneity operated as a way to *make relatives* among those with distinct identities, migrant itineraries, and ambitions, prompting reflection on the practical manner of building shared futures while working with or around generic categories originally designed for racialized control.[39] To this end, "indigenous African" marked a process of "making someone African" that applied to nascent forms of Pan-Africanism on the continent as well as ongoing debates about how diasporic subjects could "belong" without dispossession. Debates about the relative merits of diasporic return during a period of colonial entrenchment are relevant to contemporary questions about diasporic citizenship because they demonstrate recurring tensions. What can we learn by exploring continuities and divergent expectations on both sides? What practical obstacles did Sam and the returnees encounter, and how many of those obstacles persist today?

In the Gold Coast, elite Akan merchants and traders read reports on the African Movement with mixed interest. In editorial columns they challenged the viability of ambitious plans laid out on paper, as earlier proposals collapsed without funding or sufficient knowledge for implementation. The Gold Coast Aborigines Rights Protection Society formally debated the merits of diasporic settlement and trade. Should skin color preauthorize migration? Was blackness enough to enter a contract? What was the basis for discerning the interests of foreigners and their impact on regional development? Returnees from Brazil in the nineteenth century had negotiated land and trade agreements with local chiefs, maintaining distinct visibility as a sign of political coherence that established precedent for successful settlement.[40] As colonialism encroached on settled land claims, the Tabon migrants also "became African" by merging political interests with the Ga community in greater Accra.[41] Ato Quayson, writing about Ga ethnogenesis, says the Tabon as Ga indexes a merger of political identity and migrant incorporation in ways that "assimilation" doesn't fully capture.[42]

When the SS *Liberia* docked in 1915, the Aborigines Rights Protection Society rallied to support the migrants in a radical reversal of earlier critique.[43] Consensus congealed only after colonial officials passed a punitive head tax intended to disincentivize their settlement. The tax and subsequent efforts to repossess the ship unified early critics in a letter-writing campaign to protest discriminatory treatment, forging solidarity and calls to protect the right of return. The tax on arrival was crucial to consolidating support among Gold Coasters because the tax enacted the first immigration policy in the colony, which was rushed through the legislature as news of the ship's departure from Texas reached lawmakers.[44] Caught at the seams of war, trade, and the novel recruitment of African Americans to a new settlement, Sam's delegation was "harassed and hounded" for payment of the immigration head tax.[45] Their food reserves diminished, and the lack of coal during the war blocked plans to sail onward to Liberia in their ship. Though the war functioned as an alibi for reorganizing immigration control, the plan to block African American migration preceded World War I and only accelerated with additional motives once the war began.[46]

Blocking routes to fuel and trade effectively stalled the movement. But another blockade stalled the process of "making Africans." Although Sam was scheduled to become chief of Brofoyedru that year, wired correspondence between London and Accra indicates an active effort to prevent his enstoolment.[47] Further, a wave of Akan destoolments in the first decade of the twentieth century served as justification of the need to check chieftaincy power with regard to land allocations—as some sold and oversold land or granted extractive concessions to increase stool assets while dispossessing families in the village of their rights to use the land.[48] Distinct from popular protest of official abuses, the acting governor, A. R. Slater, pressured a reversal of Sam's appointment. We know little about how this was achieved, but the blank line in the chief's roll during the years of the movement suggests the campaign succeeded. Blocking Sam's appointment also limited his powers of adoption, though had he proceeded there may have been objections to integration via subordinate status, since customary law accommodated adoption outside of one's ethnic group only to claim the formerly enslaved as kin.[49] These workaround strategies to transfer land deeds to kin did not guarantee rights, but instead proposed routes to possible ownership that could be contested. Understanding the Pan-African imagination in this light reveals a contingent set of experimental propositions exploring the fit between distinct spheres of law.

In 1999, when the paramount chief of Akyem Bosome was newly appointed, he assumed authority over the village where Sam was born (Apaaso), where the migrants intended to live (Asuboi), where some lived temporarily (Apoli), and where the land transaction was certified (Aduasa). Early in his tenure, the paramount chief received a visitor named Chief Biney, head of village about the size of Brofoyedru. He claimed to be a descendent of Chief Sam (and was likely the son or nephew of Sam's first wife, Efua Kuma, regarding Sam as a relative by marriage). Presenting his concern, Chief Biney asked that the land purchased for the settlement of African Americans be recognized as properly owned by Chief Sam and intended for transfer to the migrants, putting to rest nearly a century of false accusations about who owned the deed. Unfortunately, Biney died soon after, and the ninety-nine-year lease expired. The land itself was located in the Birim Forest Reserve, now unavailable for farming.[50] Biney's impulse to repair the misrecognition of the deed was intended to recuperate Sam's legacy while also acknowledging the imaginative terms in which African American ownership of land was locally negotiated.

Moving Kin

The understanding of diasporic Africans as distant kin with contested claims to land merits more research in logistical terms to capture what public rhetoric overstates or prematurely claims. After the ownership of the land deed and leasing rights were challenged in court, some migrants moved on to Liberia, which meant the movement was motivated not by attachment to the Gold Coast but by the prospect of choosing where one can flourish. Others moved to Nigeria in a burgeoning returnee community that settled in Lagos. However, the majority remained in Ghana, each making use of Sam's family and business contacts to facilitate settlement. What concealed the reality of majority settlement was the amplification of testimony from fifteen migrants who returned to the United States, followed by the influenza pandemic of 1918, which killed a number of those who remained.[51] The number of migrants buried during the flu pandemic strained Chief Sam's marriage to Lucille Garrett, a migrant herself. During this period of "decline," surviving migrants spread out, claiming the region as a potential home in their passports, noting the purpose of travel was "speculating" or "prospecting," as they moved around West Africa.

For example, Webster and Peggy Langhorn, early funders of the movement, traveled to the Gold Coast, Nigeria, Liberia, and Sierra Leone over the course of six years. In Webster Langhorn's passport the purpose of travel is noted as "prospecting"—traveling to find a place where he might establish a business and own land.[52] He joined thirteen other petitioners late in 1915 to ask the chief of Anomabo to accept them as loyal citizens who would share profits with the chief in exchange for discharging the ship's debt. Without coal, exorbitant amounts of wood powered the ship three miles down the coast to Anomabo to underscore this appeal to the chief. In this sense, logistics not only refers to the commercially coordinated movement of people and goods. It can also reveal how plans of action are creatively reworked when problems arise. Another response was the refusal by some migrants to identify themselves to colonial officials who sought to collect a newly instituted head tax that only applied to the new arrivals. The disappearance of the migrants happened in multiple ways. Some returned to the United States. Others relocated to Nigeria, Liberia, and Sierra Leone. Some remained in the Gold Coast, marrying locally and setting up businesses that were recalled readily in oral histories collected by James Anquandah in the 1970s but nowhere documented in the colonial records for the head tax.

As passports became mandatory during the war, the migrants moved in and out of view, telling the story of black mobility long after the movement was presumed to have failed. Passport itineraries retrace the grooves of the African Movement, inviting further study of black travel circuits beyond the question of who stayed and who returned.[53] Hence, we find that Chief Sam's proposal to make African Americans into kin negotiates competing logistical requirements that ultimately enlarged and tested the Pan-African imagination.

NOTES

1. "We're Brothers—Nkrumah," *New York Amsterdam News*, August 2, 1958.

2. Kevin Gaines, *African Americans in Ghana: Black Expatriates and the Civil Rights Era* (Chapel Hill: University of North Carolina Press, 2006), 89; and Penny Von Eschen, *Race against Empire* (Ithaca, NY: Cornell University Press, 1997). This essay focuses on African American returnees specifically, because migrants from Brazil, the Caribbean, and other parts of West Africa had long resettled in the Gold Coast. By contrast, African American migration to Ghana is marked by four distinct waves in the twentieth century, enabled by anticolonial movements, Africans educated in the United States, and increased opportunities for travel and business. See Samuel Boadi-Siaw, "Black Diaspora Expatriates in Ghana before Independence," *Transactions of the Historical Society of Ghana*, n.s., no. 15 (2013): 115–35; and Steven J. L. Taylor, *Exiles, Entrepreneurs, and Educators: African Americans in Ghana* (Albany: SUNY Press, 2019).

3. William Bittle and Gilbert Geis, *The Longest Way Home: Chief Alfred C. Sam's Back-to-Africa Movement* (Detroit, MI: Wayne State University Press, 1964).

4. J. Ayo Langley, "Chief Sam's African Movement and Race Consciousness in West Africa," *Phylon* 32, no. 2 (1971): 164–78.

5. Langley, "Chief Sam's African Movement."

6. George Shepperson, who mentored Langley and wrote extensively about Pan-Africanism, addressed Chief Sam in passing, but Langley was the first to claim the movement's legacy for Pan-Africanism.

7. Robert A. Hill, "Before Garvey," in *Pan-African Biography*, edited by Robert A. Hill (Los Angeles: Crossroads Press and UCLA African Studies Center, 1987), 57–77.

8. I have written more about the role Anquandah's interviews played in this new narrative of the African Movement in "Descendant Epistemology," *Ghana Studies* 22, no. 1 (2019): 150–72.

9. A. R. Slater, acting governor, "Report on the S.S. Liberia and Immigration of Negroes," June 21, 1915, MP 1104/15, Public Records and Archives Administration Department, Accra, Ghana.

10. Chief Sam, quoted in a speech delivered at Akim Swedru in February 1915. Orishatukeh Faduma, "The African Movement," *African Mail* (March 1915).

11. James Anquandah, "Interview with Nana Kurantsi III," Chief Sam Research 1977–1980 (private collection); and Hill, "Before Garvey."

12. Ned Rossiter and Kenneth Tay, "Uneven Distribution: An Interview with Ned Rossiter on Logistics and Mediated Environments," *Public Seminar*, May 31, 2019, https://publicseminar.org/2019/05/uneven-distribution-an-interview-with-ned-rossiter/.

13. Deborah Cowen, *The Deadly Life of Logistics: Mapping Violence in Global Trade* (Minneapolis: University of Minnesota Press, 2014), 4.

14. Laleh Khalili, *Sinews of War and Trade: Shipping and Capitalism in the Arabian Peninsula* (London: Verso, 2020), 192.

15. Stefano Harney and Fred Moten reinforce this point in *The Undercommons*. "Modern logistics is founded on the first great movement of commodities, the ones that could speak," which marks the doubled role of the commodity as a technology to accelerate colonial expansion and that which needs to be moved across long distances to maximize profit. Harney and Moten, *The Undercommons: Fugitive Planning and Black Study* (Wivenhoe, UK: Minor Compositions, 2013), 92.

16. Adelaide Cromwell Hill and Martin Kilson, *Apropos of Africa* (London: Frank Cass, 1969).

17. Robert Hill, "Before Garvey." See also Jon Miller, *Missionary Zeal and Institutional Control: Organizational Contradictions in the Basel Mission of the Gold Coast, 1828–1917* (London: Routledge, 2003).

18. Alfred Charles Sam, "Letter to Shiloh," 1911, in Frank Sandford Correspondence, Shiloh Chapel Archives, Durham, Maine.

19. Bittle and Geis, *Longest Way Home*.

20. Kwaku Nti, "From Politics to Tourism: Pan-African Connections, Development and Experiences of the Historic African Diaspora in Ghana," *Current Politics and Economics of Africa* 8, no. 2 (2015): 123–40.

21. "The Akim Trading Company," *Sierra Leone Guardian*, May 10, 1912, 7.

22. Boadi-Siaw, "Black Diaspora Expatriates."

23. Faduma, "The African Movement."

24. Faduma, "The African Movement."

25. "Beyond the Year of Return and Birthright to Institutionalize," GhanaWeb, December 14, 2019, https://www.ghanaweb.com/GhanaHomePage/NewsArchive/Beyond-the-Year-of-Return-and-Birthright-to-institutionalize-Year-of-Return-Nana-Addo-815662. See also "Birthright Journeys," Adinkra Group, accessed April 30, 2020, https://www.birthrightjourney.com/yearofreturn. The Adinkra Group offers a small number of "birthright tours" to Ghana modeled after Zionist tours to Israel for Jewish youth. Both initiatives, the Year of Return and Birthright Tours frame the right of return through tourism and spending predictions aimed at boosting the national economy, with the potential to convert residency into citizenship. The government has also advertised right of abode and diasporic paths to citizenship, though to date only 126 members of the historic African diaspora have been granted Ghanaian passports (the number is greater for the immediate African diaspora with one or more parents born in Ghana).

26. Joseph Ephraim Casely Hayford, *Ethiopia Unbound: Studies in Race Emancipation: Studies in Race Emancipation* (London: Routledge, 2012).

27. New York Secretary of State, prospectus for the Akim Trading Company, 1911; and South Dakota Secretary of State, "Articles of Incorporation: Akim Trading Company Ltd.," 1913.

28. Kendra Field and Ebony Coletu, "The Chief Sam Movement, a Century Later," *Transition: An International Review* 114 (2014): 108–30.

29. Jane Guyer, "Prophecy and the Near Future: Thoughts on Macroeconomic, Evangelical, and Punctuated Time," in *Legacies, Logics, Logistics: Essays in the Anthropology of the Platform Economy* (Chicago: University of Chicago Press, 2016), 89–109.

30. W. E. B. Du Bois, "Migration," *Crisis*, February 1914.

31. Carina E. Ray, *Crossing the Color Line: Race, Sex, and the Contested Politics of Colonialism in Ghana* (Athens: Ohio University Press, 2015).

32. Dusé Mohamed Ali, "Afro-Americans and the Gold Coast," *African Times and Orient Review*, April 21, 1914 (Nendeln, Liechtenstein: Kraus Reprint, 1973), 99–100. https://babel.hathitrust.org/cgi/pt?id=uc1.b3352516&view=1up&seq=108.

33. Kendra Taira Field, *Growing Up with the Country: Family, Race, and Nation after the Civil War* (New Haven, CT: Yale University Press, 2018).

34. See Field, *Growing Up with the Country*, especially chapters 3–4.

35. Field and Coletu, "The Chief Sam Movement."

36. J. E. Casely Hayford, *Truth about the West African Land Question* (London: Routledge, 2012).

37. Hayford, *Ethiopia Unbound*, 173.

38. Ray, *Crossing the Color Line*, 56–78.

39. Susan A. Miller offers this definition of indigeneity as a way of making relatives—which connects land to obligations that extend across generations. Thanks to Nick Estes for suggesting this connection in an American Studies Association conference panel on transnational solidarities (November 8, 2018). See Susan A. Miller, *Native Historians Write Back: Decolonizing American Indian History* (Lubbock: Texas Tech University Press, 2011).

40. Kwame Essien, *Brazilian-African Diaspora in Ghana: The Tabom, Slavery, Dissonance of Memory, Identity, and Locating Home* (East Lansing: Michigan State University Press, 2016).

41. Ato Quayson, *Oxford Street, Accra: City Life and the Itineraries of Transnationalism* (Durham, NC: Duke University Press, 2014).

42. Ato Quayson, "'Still It Makes Me Laugh, No Time to Die': A Response," *PMLA* 131, no. 2 (2016): 528–39.

43. "At Last!" *Gold Coast Leader*, January 23, 1915.

44. Langley, "Chief Sam's African Movement."

45. Faduma, "The African Movement."

46. Cowen, *Deadly Life of Logistics*.

47. Spring-Rice to John B. Moore, February 21, 1914, Correspondence of Governor Lee Cruce, British National Archives.

48. Sara Berry, *Chiefs Know Their Boundaries: Essays on Property, Power, and the Past in Asante, 1896–1996* (Cape Town: Heinemann, 2000).

49. Stefano Boni, "Indigenous Blood and Foreign Labour: The 'Ancestralization' of Land Rights in Sefwi (Ghana)," in *Land and the Politics of Belonging in West Africa*, ed. Richard Kuba and Carola Lentz (Leiden: Brill, 2006), 161–85.

50. Interview with Okotwaasuo Kantamanto Oworae-Agyekum III, paramount chief of Akyem Bosome, October 2013.

51. Coletu, "Descendant Epistemology"; and James Anquandah, "Interview with Joseph Kwamena Baffoe," Chief Sam Research 1977–1980 (private collection).

52. Webster Langhorn, emergency passport application, October 27, 1919, Monrovia Consular Affairs, National Archives and Records Administration.

53. Louis Takács drew my attention to emergency passports issued by the consular office in Liberia, which noted participants in "Chief Sam's Movement" as well as return journeys by some of the same migrants, challenging the narrative closure of failed migration. Louis Takács, "Let Me Get There: Visualizing Immigrants, Transnational Migrations and U.S. Citizens Abroad, 1914–1925," Alliance for Networking Visual Culture, accessed April 30, 2020, https://scalar.usc.edu/works/let-me-get-there.

THE MARCH OF DATA

Flow is the object of logistical desire. To maximize profit, to ensure victory on the battlefield, goods and supplies must move continuously. But people—especially soldiers and immigrants—also move in waves, surges, and floods, a distinctly more controversial kind of mobility. Historians credit Charles Minard with inventing the "flow map" in the mid-nineteenth century; his most famous flow map details Napoleon's assault on, and retreat from, Russia in 1812. It is a logistical image that epitomizes the ideal of graphical efficiency: to convey the most information in the least amount of time and in the smallest possible space. The top band depicts the forward march; the bottom one, the devastating return from Moscow to Kaunas. The width illustrates the number of troops.

The logistically minded Minard made maps depicting trade flows, port traffic, and military campaigns. His sole immigration map, "Migrants of the Globe in 1858" (1862), with his signature pastel bands, omits Madagascar, for which there was no data, and enlarges the tiny islands of Mauritius and Réunion, whose numbers were better known. Contemporary depictions favor animated digital graphics, pulsing dots or bubbles. But they remain political and partial. Behind efficient, dazzling abstractions lie journeys that require far more time and space to grasp.

Charles Minard, "Carte figurative des pertes successives en hommes de L'Armée Française dans la campagne de Russie 1812–1813" (1869).

Charles Minard, "Les émigrants du globe" (1862).

4

The Pulse of Global Passage

Listening to Logistics

CONCERNED WITH THE MOVEMENT of people and money and things, logistics constitutes a system of material mediation, or intercession, writ large.[1] That system has long relied on myriad media forms for its efficient operation: calendars, clocks, towers, maps, addresses, stamps, compasses, astrolabes, searchlights, GPS, and so forth.[2] These logistical media, Judd Case explains, "are detectors, orderers, and arrangers. They establish points of view [and] become collection points for information."[3] While logistics enlists various media technologies in its operation, it doesn't readily lend itself to macro-scale mediation. Many have tried: consultants, engineers, and artists have sought to render global capitalism visible by mapping it, flow-charting it, tracking it via satellites and sensors, photographing its indexical landscapes, and capturing its flows on film.[4] Yet ultimately, logistics, as a "deeply incoherent, contradictory, conflicted, and competitive domain," Alberto Toscano explains, possesses a "fundamental opacity."[5]

That opacity presents an opportunity for another mode of representation and investigation: listening. Logistical systems are assemblages of maps and surveillance footage and customs forms, but they're also symphonies of beeps and shouts and fog horns. Listening has long been central to logical operations, and sounding media—from booming canons to voices to RFID tags—have long regimented its operations. I've written elsewhere about the value of engaging infrastructure through sound; I argued that listening to infrastructures can help us understand their mechanisms and rhythms of operation, as well as how their broader spatial contexts function as sites of sonic communication.[6] Logistics *is* a rhythm; it's an orchestration of infrastructures to facilitate movement, a means of synchronizing disparate temporalities. And sound is well qualified to mark those rhythms, register logistics' political and cultural dynamics, sound out its environments of operation, and capture its affective dimensions. This chapter demonstrates how sound, in rendering logistics differently *sense*-able, offers us a new way of listening through its contradictory, conflicted opacity.

We'll discover that logistics both compels and conditions various modes of listening. Diagnostic, orientational, and defensive listening enable dockworkers, deckhands, soldiers, and factory and maintenance workers to appraise the proper functioning of the system; to coordinate actions (both compliant and disruptive); to assess their own safety; and, if necessary, to get out of harm's way. Ethical and critical listening can help us to tune into the system's power dynamics and to recognize, even empathize with, other logistical subjects, including those on the other end of the supply chain. While it might seem that critical listening would benefit from an outsider's perspective, we'll come to see that it, like all other modes of listening, can take place from anywhere: on the dock, in the fields, or at the supermarket. Listening-as-method is particularly well suited for thinking across logistics' scales of operation, attuned to the resonances between the micro and macro.[7] We can lend an ear to local operations and attend to individual logistical agents, while also listening from a remove—across space and time, through abstraction or speculation—to sound out big patterns and macroscale rhythms. We can extrapolate from the sonic qualities of particular logistical nodes—from the cacophony of the battlefield to a quiet respite at the bow of a container ship—to index the flows of goods and capital, bodies and affect, throughout the system. Logistics also offers up countless sonic stimuli for our consideration: languages, both natural and artificial; environmental sounds; objects' resonances; electronic signals; and machinic rhythms. Such a crowded acoustic field has made it increasingly necessary for us to supplement our own ears with machinic sensors and algorithmic processors, creating cyborgian listening subjects.

All this is to say: listening to logistics attunes us to new dimensions and dynamics of logistical systems past and present, *and* it enables us to think anew about what it means to listen in an age of global capitalism and automation. In what follows, we'll acknowledge logistics' sonic histories and reverberations—from slave ship to cotton field, battlefield to factory floor, seaport to distribution center. Then we'll examine how new sound technologies and modes of machinic, algorithmic listening might allow us to better understand the logistical operations that undergird our everyday existence—and, perhaps, to imagine new systems that embody different values.

Echoes from Slave Ship to Battlefield: Laboring Bodies

Stefano Harney and Fred Moten remind us that even the earliest logistical systems resounded: "Modern logistics is founded with the first great movement of commodities, the ones that could speak. It was founded in the Atlantic slave trade."[8] These voices expressed suffering, labor, empathy toward one another, deference toward their captors, and, in moments of protest—itself a form of counterlogistics—authority. The bodies containing those voices may have even used "the material conditions of their imprisonment—instruments of labor, chains, and the [resonant wooden] ship itself"—to register affect, or to communicate furtively with one another, without words.[9] Here, sounding and listening were means of coordinating action, compliant or rebellious; expressing fear and pain; and soliciting or extending empathy and care.

Once those enslaved people made it to the Americas, their voices often united in song in the cotton fields and, later, on chain gangs. "Work songs" have long regimented the productive movements of hunters and herders, seamen and lumberjacks—but on the plantation, they served to coordinate and discipline captive bodies compelled into labor and noisemaking.[10] As Frederick Douglass explained: "Slaves are expected to sing as well as to work. A silent slave was not liked either by masters, or by overseers. . . . There was generally more or less singing among the teamsters at all times. It was a means of telling the overseer, in the distance, where they were, and what they were about."[11] Yet the work songs also occasionally served as an outlet for laborers to mock their masters and imagine escape, as a sort of speculative logistical soundtrack. Here, in the fields, sounding and listening served as means to coordinate local action, disclose orientation from afar, and imagine the disruption of logistical operations.

While African Americans' spirituals have echoed across generations, most enslaved and oppressed voices are lost to history. Saidiya Hartman asks how, in the archive of African slavery—an archive that erases and suppresses African voices and cultures—one might "listen for the groans and cries, the undecipherable songs, the crackle of fire in the cane fields, the laments for the dead, and the shouts of victory, and then assign words to all of it? Is it possible to construct a story from 'the locus of impossible speech' or resurrect lives from the ruins"?[12] Hartman gives voice to these silences through "critical fabulation"—by offering a counterhistory, extrapolated from the archive, about what *might have* resounded or been said.[13] Such speculative listening represents an epistemology and historical method that could allow us to re-sound all those suppressed voices and silenced noises that chart out the rhythms and geographies of logistics' pasts. And perhaps we needn't feel compelled to translate those shouts, songs, and crackles into words, as Hartman proposes; perhaps rather than becoming a story, they can blend into a centuries-long lament whose refrains remind us that the dark patterns of the past are still with us today.[14] Listening, here, is a speculative method for resuscitation, for historical analysis and political critique.

Music then extended into sites of industrial labor. Modern psychologists, informed by new theories of scientific management, found that music broadcast onto the factory floor served to increase workers' productivity.[15] And now, in the postindustrial workplace, where service workers and "creatives" toil away in clamorous open-plan offices, music often serves as a means of defense, a way of isolating oneself from ubiquitous ambient distractions.[16] In the factory and the office, listening—whether public or private—still serves as a means of logistical alignment; it allows one to either engage or disengage with one's acoustic environment in order to sync up with the assembly line or the office Slack channel.

Sonic logistics have long been of critical importance in another workplace: the battlefield. Some historians and etymologists regard logistics as a fundamentally military affair. Antoine-Henri Jomini famously described logistics as "the practical art of moving armies": "strategy decides where to act; logistics brings the troops to this point; grand tactics decides the manner of execution and the employment of troops."[17] Military officers were *practicing* logistics long before the term emerged in the nineteenth century. In the days before real-time electronic communications, the sounds of battle were among their primary cues for the deployment of troops and resources. Charles D. Ross has documented how the vast, topographically variable battlefields of the US Civil War necessitated that officers practice a form of distant listening in order to discern the location of nearby military activity and advancing threats.[18] Many officers failed to account for "acoustic shadows," which occur when topography, air temperature, wind speed and direction, fog, snow, and terrestrial obstructions like trees and buildings either make nearby sounds inaudible or amplify the sound of distant activity, making it seem closer than it actually is.[19] Such acoustic anomalies shaped command decisions and, Ross claims, determined the outcome of the war. Here, listening is a means of detection and (dis)orientation.

The increasing use of trench combat, machine guns, airplanes, and submarines in World War I necessitated yet more "diagnostic" modes of terrestrial, submarine, aerial, and mechanical listening, both close and distant. Troops had to be able to discern the location of friends and enemies and to distinguish the acoustic signatures of their aircraft and artillery.[20] The early twentieth century brought many new sonic logistical media. Judd Case explains how war horns, acoustic locators, orthophones, sound mirrors, static dishes or walls, telephones, radar, sonar, and, eventually, radio offered (often imperfect) means of acoustic detection and location, surveillance, and sonic command. These new sonic logistics and logistical media also cultivated new listening cultures *off* the battlefield, specifically around radio and the telephone, in the postwar years.[21]

Sonic weapons—from indigenous instruments to long-range acoustic devices to buzzing drones—have also been used as a means to repel enemy troops or "neutralize" insurgents.[22] Radar and sonar are used to make maps, particularly of subterranean, subglacial, and seafloor regions that escape a visual survey.[23] And the electromagnetic spectrum has become a battlefield itself, with communication jammers a widely deployed weapon. "Communications, navigation, battlefield logistics, precision munitions—all of these depend on complete and unfettered access to the spectrum, territory that must be vigilantly defended from enemy combatants," Brendan Koerner reports in *Wired*.[24] On today's battlefield, our reliance on machine-aided listening both enhances troops' abilities to orient and target, and serves as a potential source of disorientation. In other words, the sonic infrastructure itself can be a liability—much like the acoustic environment of the Civil War battlefield.

Sounding Out Supply Chains

After World War II, many industrial and commercial leaders sought to deploy the lessons of the battlefield—that "practical art of moving armies"—in their own sectors. "For business management," Deborah Cowen writes, "a 'revolution in logistics' took shape in the 1960s that entirely transformed the ways that corporations imagine, calculate, plan, and build spaces of production and of distribution and gradually remade the global economy."[25] Logistics' acoustic applications echoed in this new terrain. But even well before the rise of a "business science" of logistics, sounds played a crucial role in the movement of goods and people. Elevated voices were once the means by which dockworkers secured work. In 1857, Henry Mayhew described the "scuffling and scrambling, and stretching forth of countless hands high in the air, to catch the eye of him whose nod can give them work. . . . All are shouting; some cry aloud his surname, and some his Christian name; and some call out their own names, to remind him that they are there."[26] Those same voices were then deployed during long shifts to ensure the efficient movement of goods, equipment, and bodies. Managers shouted orders, and longshoremen called out verbal cues to one another. In more recent years, those voices have extended their reach via VHF maritime mobile band radio. Radio connects agents on dock, on deck, in cranes perched high above the action, and in vessel traffic control, all speaking a machinic patois that maximizes efficiency and intelligibility. Today, as yesterday, bells, whistles, horns, and alarms are part of the mix, too, warning of the comings and goings of ships and equipment, both close and distant. Listening on the docks has long been a means of recognition, logistical coordination, and self-defense.

The equipment itself makes quite a racket. Yet that racket contains useful information and thus requires close listening. According to a recent report from a team of occupational health researchers, a fifty-five-year-old dockworker

> reported exposure to frequent impact noise from metal striking metal. He noted that, when operating the crane, he had to shout to be able to communicate to a co-worker nearby. He did not wear hearing protection, saying that he needed to hear sounds (such as that of the overhead crane when he was loading), and to shout communication when he we operating the crane. For 1 or 2 hours a day, he operated a forklift in a refrigerated warehouse, where noise from the refrigeration units was so loud that he had to shout to communicate with a co-worker at arm's length. He did not wear hearing protection when he drove the forklift because of the need to hear warning signals and communication from co-workers.[27]

Not surprisingly, all that close listening causes hearing loss. And according to Jake Alimahomed-Wilson, it's been embedded in the masculine culture of longshoring. When Elbert Kelly Jr. started working on the docks, "the industry was extremely dangerous." Yet nowadays, he told Alimahomed-Wilson, "we see people that are so fearful . . . It annoys me when a . . . driver pulls up and says: can I have earplugs? And we used to work all kinds of dangerous jobs. Nobody asked for no damn earplugs."[28] Here, cultivated listening techniques serve as means of orientation and coordination among humans and machines—and, just as importantly, as means of self-definition and medical diagnosis.

Cacophony is a sonic index of a busy port, of readily circulating goods and laboring bodies, of a strong global economy.[29] In other words, what's bad for dockworkers' eardrums is ultimately good for business. As ethnographer Charmaine Chua explains, "A quiet port is logistics' nightmare."[30] And there are countless forces that have the power to silence particular nodes within the supply chain: from labor disputes to truck shortages to ports' failure to "scale-up" in order to accommodate ever-bigger ships. Chua explains that local snafus can easily become global: "Built on precisely-timed coordination between shippers and suppliers, the system is so vulnerable that what might have been a minor shock in the past today produces a domino effect that has worldwide echoes." Her sonic metaphor hints at an acoustic methodology: we can use the quiet port as a diagnostic for disruption within the broader logistical system. Local silence can signal global discord. Yet listening closely to that local calm should also compel us to ask, as Hartman advocates: Who is silenced? What is erased? What local economies or marginalized communities are affected by this stasis?

The ship in transit inhabits another acoustic environment. The sea, John Durham Peters suggests, is "a natural laboratory for altered sense rations," and Chua has written eloquently about her own sensory experience of riding the supply chain aboard a container ship from Los Angeles to Taipei.[31] I quote Chua at length:

> The bow of the ship is the only place . . . that affords a modicum of silence. To get there, you walk down the length of the narrow grey deck, flanked on one side by containers crowded into towering stacks that scrape and creak against each other as the ship cuts through the waves, and on the other by the powerful sweep of a wind so strong that you have to fight not to be blown backwards. At the foremost tip of the ship, you climb a few steps onto a large open deck . . . and suddenly, the mechanical roar of the ship falls away. . . . [From there,] you can look outward onto an endless, unbroken horizon of ocean in near quiet, and almost think that the ship is barely moving.[32]

This romantic image of escape—which is kind of the open-sea version of wearing noise-canceling headphones in an open-plan office—reminds us again that there are pockets of restorative silence within this cacophonous system; that the human laborer, in an act of self-preservation, must occasionally unplug from the logistical system, turn down the volume. Chua also writes of the inaudible voices of the ships' crew, many of whom are Filipinos separated from their families for weeks or months at a time. "In non-places," like a ship adrift in international waters, on a monotonous sea, "no one can hear you cry," she writes, implying that many workers have reason to despair.[33] (Yet marine life can hear everything, amplified. The incessant submarine sounds of shipping and mining and military operations prove not only destructive to their *own* logistical sensibilities but lethal.[34]) Logistical listening, as we see here, is a means of both self-preservation and self-destruction.

Most consumers onshore are oblivious to that movement and its attendant roars and whimpers. Logistics' "entire network of infrastructures, technologies, spaces, [and] workers," Cowen says, "remains tucked out of sight" for most of us.[35] It remains mostly inaudible too: we rarely hear the whirr of conveyor belts, the roar of the refrigeration units, or the stifled sobs of the cooks and engine crew. And we can't discern, from amidst the distant roar of overhead jets, which might emanate from the FedEx 777 delivering our Amazon Prime order (though there has been much romanticization of certain logistical sounds—particularly the distant train whistle and foghorn). "In the past," Allan Sekula writes, "harbor residents were deluded by their senses into thinking that a global economy could be seen and heard and smelled. The wealth of nations would slide by in the channel."[36] Today's logistics traps the sounds and smells of those global commodities in steel containers. Yet if we listen closely, as well as from a distance—extrapolating across time and space, as Hartman proposes—we can still hear the tones and rhythms of the supply chain that brings those goods to us.

Before they're deposited at our doorstep—by truck, by pushcart, or, perhaps soon, by drone—those packages are cycled through a distribution center. Unlike a traditional warehouse, where things are stored, the distribution center sorts and redirects; it "keeps stuff in motion."[37] Again, sounding technologies help to orchestrate that movement. While the trucks, trains, robots, products, and people circulating through and around these centers are tracked via radio frequency identification tags, the distribution center's workers, or "pickers," are guided by voice-picking software.[38] As Jesse LeCavalier explains, "A synthesized [female] voice directs the worker to different locations in the distribution center, prompting him or her to pick certain quantities of particular items. The worker then vocally confirms the completion of each task."[39] Listening is a means of orientation and synchronization.

Because our workers are focused on close listening to the super-fast-talking automated voice, they're unable to use their *own* voices to communicate with others—anyone other than the computer, that is. With no time wasted on socialization, pickers can maximize their performance. A worker can ask the machine, "How am I doing?" and the software will deliver a progress report. And because the system can be programmed to speak in workers' native languages, LeCavalier says, "It demonstrates a greater capacity for communication with workers than many human managers."[40] As a company spokesperson told LeCavalier, it's "like having a supervisor stand over your shoulder."[41] It's a means of disciplining the ears and, by extension, the body, in order to "integrate workers into the system and calibrate the rhythms of their movements with the needs of an automated system of stuff," Cowen proposes.[42] And then, at the consumer end of the supply chain, at the grocery store checkout, a coda: the barcode beep, that human-intelligible sound of global trade reduced to a micro-scale, machine-readable graphic. Listening offers confirmation that we're doing our jobs, as pickers and consumers, properly.

Listening to Signal and Spectrum

While all these sounding technologies were being designed or adapted to serve military and commercial logistical purposes, engineers were also employing logistical principles in building out infrastructures for these media. Poles and wires, antennae and repeaters, microwave relay towers and base stations were—and still are—deployed logistically, to facilitate the efficient movement of signals and use of the electromagnetic spectrum. The history of signal traffic logistics is a bit too complex for us to address here, but there are many other resources—from studies in historical archaeology to government records—that document sound's logistical past.[43] In one particular study, Kimberley Peters describes how pirate radio broadcasters sometimes situated themselves on converted ships in the logistically and legally fluid space of the sea—a "space of vast proportions and depth," which facilitates signal transmission, and, simultaneously, a space in-between national and international regulations, floating amid the laws of land and sea and air.[44] These broadcasters took advantage of their scalar in-between-ness. (The Defense Advanced Research Projects Agency [DARPA] is now exploiting the unique properties of the submarine seascape to develop a sonic underwater GPS system, Posydon, to aid with the navigation of unmanned underwater vehicles.[45])

The fluidity of the electromagnetic spectrum has presented its own jurisdictional challenges. Governments have tended to chop it up, like parcels of real estate, and regulate its use. Yet "as billions of phones, appliances, drones, traffic lights, security systems, environmental sensors, and other radio-connected devices sum into a rapidly growing Internet of Things (IoT)," government agencies and technology companies are using artificial intelligence to listen to the electromagnetic spectrum as a whole, algorithmically, to propose means for re-orchestrating and auditing its use so as to accommodate more signaling media and ensure space for the right ones.[46] NEC says that its radio sensing system can be used for "the monitoring of radio signals in crowded areas (stadiums, rail stations, airports, etc.), the planning of optimum deployment and operation of wireless infrastructure, and the management of radio spectrum and the detection of illegal radio."[47] The Mitre Corporation, a government-sponsored research organization, has advocated for radio frequency spectrum management to ensure that spectrum is allocated appropriately to serve critical services, like air traffic control, national defense, and homeland security.[48] DARPA has even proposed using such machine-learning-aided distant listening to shift from the "current practice of exclusive allocations governed by license agreements for specific frequencies," to a new "paradigm of shared spectrum."[49] These modes of macro-scale listening, if translated into policy and infrastructure-building, could potentially reorient the logistical maneuvering of signals themselves.

What else might we learn about logistics by listening from a distance, algorithmically? Some cities deploy networked sound sensors at distributed locations to assess noise pollution, much of which is caused by logistical systems. City officials correlate those noise readings with data about road surfaces, vehicle counts, traffic speed, topology, and other variables, then create daytime and nighttime sound maps that help managers make decisions about noise reduction policies. Here, Claudio Coletta and Rob Kitchin proclaim, "We have a set of algorhythms at work, algorithmically measuring, processing, and analyzing urban sound and its rhythms."[50] John Mannes reports that several companies are developing systems to automate the sonic monitoring of mechanical systems—railways, oil drills, power plants, and so forth. Some players in this field are building training sets with sound samples of well-behaved machines, while others listen across a vast array of systems, identify anomalies, and invite engineers and other experts in to help them analyze and classify those aberrant sounds.[51]

In both of these examples, the machine listens algorithmically, then enlists a human to listen closely in order to diagnose individual anomalies or explain meaningful patterns. Artist-researchers Wesley Goatley and Georgina Voss use machinic and algorithmic forms of listening in order to make those macro-scale patterns perceptible and affectively "graspable" (if not transparently intelligible) to human listeners. *Familiars* is "an immersive installation that materializes the presence, function, and fragility of the unseen logistical infrastructure that underpins the modern world."[52] The duo used new software-defined radio receivers (which essentially "virtualize" traditional radio hardware components, like mixers and amplifiers, as software) to intercept radio signals broadcast by nearby planes, ships, and trains to register their location and identity. Goatley and Voss then "transmuted" the data into ambient sound and a big, live map on the floor.

Each mode of transit requires its own mode of "listening" for systemwide data. Harvesting data from planes, they found, was relatively easy; "they openly broadcast their position, altitude, speed, and heading on the 1090 MHz radio frequency for other aircraft and ground control."[53] Container ships, via their onboard automatic identification system, also openly transmit data at 161.975 MHz and 162.025 MHz about their position, speed, and destination port—yet Goatley and Voss found that their terrestrial reception of these marine vessels was subject to acoustic shadow. In order to intercept the ships' signals, they'd have to be in direct line of sight; the artists' own logistical positioning determined their ability to access the ships' logistical data. In the United Kingdom, trains communicate via the Global Systems for Mobile Communications–Railway, a closed network. Voss and Goatley couldn't legally decode the correspondence, but they could detect, at 876–880 MHz, when encoded messages were sent. By whom or where, and what that message said, they couldn't know. But when they detected a signal, they illuminated the rail network on their map. Silence registered as light.

The artists captured sounds recorded in cargo ships, plane cockpits, and air control towers, and mixed those into sonic tags that were then assigned to each vessel on the map. Those tags were meant to signal the location of individual craft and, simultaneously, reveal "the hidden human activity within them."[54] Despite these myriad correlated logistical data sets and the artists' attempts to integrate visual and sonic modes of representation, the map still ultimately highlighted the difficulty of modeling logistics in its totality. Rather than evidencing a "fundamental opacity," as Toscano proposes, Goatley and Voss's work instead offered an intentional epistemological messiness. These transportation data, and the logistical systems they represent, are shaped, deformed, rerouted, and thwarted by all kinds of obstacles—weather, electromagnetic interference, topographic impediments, borders, regulations, and pirates of the marine and virtual varieties. *Familiars*, rather than promising a precise God's-eye view, instead offered only a partial multisensory understanding of the logistical systems that make our world move—as well as the data moving behind it.

Sound, Goatley told me, is well suited to disabuse us of our delusions of omniscience and aspirations to see the world through a "conquering gaze from nowhere."[55] As Donna Haraway proposes, "We must be hostile to easy . . . holisms built out of summing and subsuming parts," much like those totalizing logistical maps and black-boxed logistical software systems. Instead, we should aspire to a "self-critical partiality" that allows us to imagine "worlds less organized by axes of domination"—worlds in which, perhaps, we can hear the Filipino seamen's laments, or the deafened blue whale swimming aimlessly below the ship, or the unemployed dockworker in a quiet port city.[56] Sound, Goatley says, "offers both a form of sensing larger rhythms, repetitions, and patterns in space in an embodied fashion distinct from the visual," and it also allows for an intimate engagement with these systems.[57]

Familiars prompts us to ask what we can know through listening—and what kinds and scope of knowledge it represents. Listening across logistics' scales helps us to orient ourselves within its interlocking systems: to feel the rhythms of its local nodes, to recognize and give voice to its local agents, to re-sound its ambient environments and, at the same time, to extrapolate from the micro-scale in order to imagine the orchestration of goods and capital and bodies throughout the system, to hear the pulses of global passage. This "telephoning" out, expanding the scale of attunement (more often, now, with the aid of algorithmic ears), allows us to sound out bigger patterns—cacophonies and silences, harmonies and discord—in global capitalism. By rendering logistics *sense*-able, listening-as-method proposes new epistemological frameworks for what we can know about logistics' silenced pasts and encrypted data, and how we sonically register its operations through logistical media. Listening can supplement our other means of logistical mediation—like maps and flowcharts and photographs of shipping containers—to offer new tools of ethical investment and political critique.

NOTES

Thanks to the editorial team, Rick and Megan Prelinger, Kenneth Tay, Nick Anderman, Jesse LeCavalier, Wes Goatley, Georgina Voss, Benjamin Tausig, Nikolaus Wegmann, Bernhard Siegert, Ute Holl, and the Princeton-Weimar Media Theory Summer School attendees.

1. For relevant images and videos, please see the author's website: "The Pulse of Global Passage: Listening to Logistics (2018)," *Words in Space*, accessed January 13, 2021, http://wordsinspace.net/shannon/the-pulse-of-global-passage-listening-to-logistics-2018/.

2. Judd A. Case, "Logistical Media: Fragments from Radar's Prehistory," *Canadian Journal of Communication* 38, no. 3 (2013): 379–95; John Durham Peters, "Calendar, Clock, Tower," in *Deus in Machina: Religion and Technology in Historical Perspective*, ed. Jeremy Stolow (New York: Fordham University Press, 2013), 25–42.

3. Case, "Logistical Media," 381.

4. See Alberto Toscano and Jeff Kinkle, *Cartographies of the Absolute* (Washington, DC: Zero Books, 2015): 190–217.

5. Alberto Toscano, "Lineaments of the Logistical State," *Viewpoint Magazine*, September 28, 2014, https://www.viewpointmag.com/2014/09/28/lineaments-of -the-logistical-state/.

6. See, e.g., Shannon Mattern, *Clay and Code, Data and Dirt: Five Thousand Years of Urban Media* (Minneapolis: University of Minnesota Press, 2017); and Shannon Mattern, "Ear to the Wire: Listening to Historic Urban Infrastructures," *Amodern 2: Network Archaeology*, October 2013, http://amodern.net/article/ear-to-the-wire/.

7. Recent work on "distant listening," which takes inspiration from the literary-critical methods of close and distant reading, has been applied across literary criticism, history, music, radio, and sound studies. Readers can find a partial bibliography at Shannon Mattern (@shannonmattern), "Thank you! There's are a few approaches to this method," Twitter, June 11, 2018, 9:31 p.m., https://twitter.com/shannonmattern/status/1006348170618646528.

8. Stefano Harney and Fred Moten, *The Undercommons: Fugitive Planning and Black Study* (Wivenhoe, UK: Minor Compositions, 2013), 92.

9. Danielle Sheehan, "Deadly Notes: Atlantic Soundscapes and the Writing of the Middle Passage," *Appendix* 1, no. 3 (2013), http://theappendix.net/issues/2013 /7/deadly-notes-atlantic-soundscapes-and-the-writing-of-the-middle-passage.

10. Ted Gioia, *Work Songs* (Durham, NC: Duke University Press, 2006).

11. Frederick Douglass, *Life and Times of Frederick Douglass: From 1817 to 1882*, ed. John Lobb (London: Christian Age Office, 1882), 28

12. Saidiya Hartman, "Venus in Two Acts," *Small Axe*, no. 26 (2008): 1–14, 3; "impossible speech" is drawn from Stephen Best, "The African Queen," unpublished essay.

13. Hartman, "Venus in Two Acts," 11.

14. See also Jennifer Lynn Stoever, *The Sonic Color Line: Race and the Cultural Politics of Listening* (New York: NYU Press, 2016).

15. Readers can find a partial bibliography at Shannon Mattern (@shannon-mattern), "Offloading some citations to cut my word count!," Twitter, March 28, 2019, 11:01 p.m., https://twitter.com/shannonmattern/status/1111463285138882560.

16. Nicola Dibben and Anneli B. Haake, "Music and the Construction of Space in Office-Based Work Settings," in *Music, Sound and Space: Transformations of Public and Private Experience*, ed. Georgina Born (New York: Cambridge University Press, 2013), 151–68, 152.

17. Baron Jomini, *The Art of War*, trans. Capt. G. H. Mendell (Philadelphia: J. B. Lippincott, 1862), available at https://archive.org/stream/bub_gb_fMpCIcomOFIC/bub_gb_fMpCIcomOFIC_djvu.txt.

18. Charles. D. Ross, *Civil War Acoustic Shadows* (Shippensburg, PA: White Main Books, 2001).

19. Gordon Berg, "The Sounds of Silence," HistoryNet, December 14, 2016, https://www.historynet.com/the-sounds-of-silence.htm.

20. Axel Volmar, "In Storms of Steel: The Soundscape of World War I and Its Impact on Auditory Media Culture during the Weimar Period," in *Sounds of Modern History: Auditory Cultures in 19th- and 20th-Century Europe*, ed. Daniel Morat (New York: Berghahn, 2014), 227–55, 246.

21. For more resources on "listening in combat" and how military listening transformed postwar everyday listening practices, see Shannon Mattern (@shannonmattern), "Some resources re: 'listening in combat' and how military listening transformed everyday post-war listening practices," Twitter, March 28, 2019, 11:05 p.m., https://twitter.com/shannonmattern/status/1111464413691871232.

22. For sample resources, see Shannon Mattern (@shannonmattern), "On sonic weapons (just two here - but there are LOTS more)," Twitter, March 28, 2019, 11:35 p.m., https://twitter.com/shannonmattern/status/1111471915473035264.

23. For sample resources, see Shannon Mattern (@shannonmattern), "On how radar and sonar are used to make maps, particularly of subterranean, subglacial, and seafloor regions that escape a visual survey," Twitter, March 28, 2019, 11:09 p.m., https://twitter.com/shannonmattern/status/1111465277114535936.

24. Brendan Koerner, "Inside the New Arms Race to Control Bandwidth on the Battlefield," *Wired*, February 18, 2014, https://www.wired.com/2014/02/spectrum-warfare/.

25. Deborah Cowen, *The Deadly Life of Logistics: Mapping Violence in Global Trade* (Minneapolis: University of Minnesota Press, 2014), 6.

26. Henry Mayhew, *The Great World of London* (London: David Bogue, 1857), 35.

27. Thais C. Morata, David C. Byrne, and Peter M. Rabinowitz, "Noise Exposure and Hearing Disorders," in *Occupational and Environmental Health: Recognizing and Preventing Disease and Injury*, ed. Barry S. Levy, David H. Wegman, Sherry L. Baron, and Rosemary K. Sokas (New York: Oxford University Press, 2011), 461–74, 468.

28. Quoted in Jake Alimahomed-Wilson, *Solidarity Forever? Race, Gender, and Unionism in the Ports of Southern California* (London: Lexington Books, 2016), 137.

29. For more on market noise, see Shannon Mattern (@shannonmattern), "On the continuing role of noise in an economy based on algorithmic transactions and high-frequency trades," Twitter, March 28, 2019, 11:46 p.m., https://twitter.com/shannonmattern/status/1111474659160195073.

30. Charmaine Chua, "The Quiet Port Is Logistics' Nightmare," *Empire Logistics*, September 21, 2015, http://www.empirelogistics.org/dispatches/the-quiet-port.

31. John Durham Peters, *The Marvelous Clouds: Toward a Philosophy of Elemental Media* (Chicago: University of Chicago Press, 2015), 62.

32. Charmaine Chua, "Landlessness and the Life of Seamen," *Empire Logistics*, September 28, 2015, http://www.empirelogistics.org/dispatches/landlessness-and -the-life-of-seamen. Nick Anderman, who's also traveled aboard a container ship, describes the sound of "maritime metal . . . twisting and flexing against oceanic forces." He wonders what these sounds "might tell us about the global flows of capital that underpin the movement of the ship in the first place?" Nick Anderman, "Sounding Maritime Metal: Listening to Global Trade at Sea," presented at Society for Social Studies of Science, Boston, August 31, 2017.

33. Charmaine Chua, "In Non-Places, No One Can Hear You Cry," *Empire Logistics*, October 6, 2015, http://www.empirelogistics.org/dispatches/in-non -places-no-one-can-hear-you-cry.

34. Max Ritts, "Amplifying Environmental Politics: Ocean Noise," *Antipode* 49, no. 5 (2017): 1406–26.

35. Cowen, *Deadly Life of Logistics*, 1.

36. Allan Sekula, *Fish Story* (Düsseldorf: Richter Verlag 2002), 12.

37. Cowen, *Deadly Life of Logistics*, 111.

38. See, for instance, Anja Kanngieser, "Tracking and Tracing: Geographies of Logistical Governance and Labouring Bodies," *Environment and Planning D: Society and Space* 31 (2013): 594–610.

39. Jesse LeCavalier, *The Rule of Logistics: Walmart and the Architecture of Fulfillment* (Minneapolis: University of Minnesota Press, 2016), 164.

40. LeCavalier, *Rule of Logistics*, 167.

41. LeCavalier, *Rule of Logistics*, 166.

42. Cowen, *Deadly Life of Logistics*, 126.

43. For relevant resources, see Shannon Mattern (@shannonmattern), "On the logistics of signal traffic," Twitter, March 28, 2019, 11:13 p.m., https://twitter .com/shannonmattern/status/1111466298159087616.

44. Kimberley Peters, "Tracking (Im)mobilities at Sea: Ships, Boats and Surveillance Strategies," *Mobilities* 9, no. 3 (2014), 414–31, 426.

45. Jack Stewart, "DARPA Wants an Underwater GPS System for Seafaring Robots," *Wired*, May 16, 2016, https://www.wired.com/2016/05/darpa-wants -underwater-gps-system-seafaring-robots/. Thanks to Nick Anderman for the reference.

46. DARPA, "The Radio Frequency Spectrum + Machine Learning = A New Wave in Radio Technology," August 11, 2017, https://www.darpa.mil/news-events /2017-08-11a.

47. NEC, "NEC Develops Radio Sensing System to Visualize Use of Radio Spectrum in Real Time," October 3, 2016, https://www.nec.com/en/press/201610 /global_20161003_02.html.

48. Mitre, "Radio Frequency Spectrum Management," accessed June 16, 2018, https://www.mitre.org/publications/systems-engineering-guide/enterprise -engineering/enterprise-technology-information-and-infrastructure/radio -frequency-spectrum-management.

49. DARPA, "The Radio Frequency Spectrum."

50. Claudio Coletta and Rob Kitchin, "Algorhythmic Governance: Regulating the 'Heartbeat' of a City Using the Internet of Things," *Big Data and Society* (July–December 2017): 1–16, 11. Algorhythmics is a reference to the media-archaeological "machine listening" work of Shintaro Miyazaki.

51. John Mannes, "The Sound of Impending Failure," *Tech Crunch*, January 29, 2017, https://techcrunch.com/2017/01/29/the-sound-of-impending-failure/.

52. Wesley Goatley, "Familiars," http://www.wesleygoatley.com/familiars/.

53. Georgina Voss and Wesley Goatley, "The Secret Signals That Rule Our Transport Networks," *BBC Future*, April 27, 2016, http://www.bbc.com/future/story/20160426-the-invisible-language-of-trains-boats-and-planes.

54. Goatley, "Familiars."

55. Donna Haraway, "Situated Knowledges: The Science Question in Feminism and the Privilege of Partial Perspective," *Feminist Studies* 14, no. 3 (1988): 575–99, 581.

56. Haraway, "Situated Knowledges," 585.

57. Wesley Goatley, personal communication, June 5, 2018.

LOGISTICAL INSTRUMENTS

Efficiency, Automation,
Interoperability

PART II

BENEATH THE GREAT WHITE WAY

Logistics is a second-order operation, the optimization of networks well understood. The colonial encounter in the Americas was itself such an operation. Europeans found open space already cleared by burning forests and hunting animals. They occupied sites whose inhabitants had been decimated by disease. They benefited from their proximity to local sources of knowledge. And as they moved into the interior of North and South America, they found and appropriated the extensive networks of trails that covered the land.

One of the most famous of these networks was the Incan road system (Qhapaq Ñan). When they landed, the Spanish found thousands of kilometers of paved or compacted roads, dotted with storehouses separated by a day or two of travel. While the Incans did not originate the system, they had greatly extended it to smooth over the fractured geography of the Tawantinsuyu. From one end to the other, relays of runners carried messages as armies transported supplies. Ill-suited to the horses and wagons of the conquistadors, the roads were nevertheless instrumental for the administration of the Incan Empire.

While the Spanish destroyed many of these roads in their conquest, throughout the rest of the new world native trails organized the shape of neo-European settlement, becoming critical points of connection that persist even to this day. The island of Manhattan, of course, was originally home to the Lenape and Wappinger peoples, and New York City's iconic Broadway was once recognizable to native travelers as the Wickquasgeck trail.

5

Colonization's Logistical Media

The Ship and the Document

I.

Since media theory loves its primal scenes, let us begin with a fragment regarding John Cabot's 1497 encounter with what is today called Newfoundland. That year, the Duke of Milan received word of Cabot's report about a sea "swarming with fish, which can be taken not only with the net but in baskets let down with a stone" and from which Cabot and his companions "could bring so many fish that this kingdom would have no further need of Iceland, from which place there comes a very great quantity of the fish called stockfish."[1] These reports signal the formation of an international economy based on codfish that would have wide-ranging historical implications. They mark an important flashpoint in a long historical trajectory in which lands, waters, and peoples around the globe were reconfigured by a European orientation toward logistics. The North Atlantic cod fisheries established a continuing back-and-forth of ships, men, and matériel between the so-called Old World and the New, the extraction of staple resources for European markets—first fish, later fur, lumber, gold, and oil—and the depositing of European infrastructure and populations across the continent. These campaigns of conquest and, eventually, colonization were at core about logistics: the design and systematization of circulation, the movement people, things, and data across time and space.

Logistics, which in the twentieth century became a science of "supply chain management," seeks optimization. It employs a suite of media and techniques that calculate and choreograph so as to maximize efficiency in the circulation of people, things, and data. Logistics desires the minimization of spatial or temporal impediments and the eradication of barriers. As Paul Virilio famously argued, logistics attempts to remake the world as a frictionless field of pure circulation.[2] It is an increasingly dominant concept in contemporary understandings of economy, ecology, and even sociality. Examples spring easily to mind: Amazon's vast network of distribution centers, UPS trucks that dot urban landscapes, and, most notably, container ports around the globe like Shanghai, Singapore, Rotterdam, Dubai, and Los Angeles. Innovative uses of automation, robotics, and machine learning are designed for and beta tested in these enclaves prior to being adopted in other settings. In such spaces, computational and mechanical engineering converge in the modus operandi of interoperability: the seamless integration and porting of physical objects, people, and computational systems. The content of an individual shipping container is of secondary importance to the smooth operation of the system that has been designed to move it through space and time.[3] This logistical medium is the message because with it comes interoperability, standardization, and synchronization. The aesthetics of these land-seascapes is otherworldly, but the fantasies they materialize are entirely human: the world bent to our will, operationalized for continuous circulation. Logistics is a condition of what Marxist media theorist Atle Mikkola Kjøsen describes as *Bestand*-in-motion.[4]

Though their scale, scope, and intensity are unprecedented, these logistical operations are nothing new. As long as there have been military campaigns and large-scale patterns of settlement and migration, humans have devoted time and labor power to optimizing the movement of people, things, and data. What thinkers like Martin Heidegger, Hannah Arendt, Karl Marx, Paul Virilio, and, more recently, Anna Tsing diagnose as particular to modernity is the codification of these actions into sciences and the privileging of this vision of the world. Earthly terrain is reframed as an impediment to be overcome or neutralized; people and things are abstracted into units to be calculated, circulated, and "scaled"; time becomes a series of discrete units to be saved, optimized, compressed, or even transcended.[5] This logistical orientation takes material form today in global infrastructures that are inscribed into the world and its inhabitants: the internet, of course (and earlier telecommunication networks upon which it was built), but also projects like China's Belt and Road initiative that terraform in the name of circulation and exchange.[6] Such projects, Benjamin Bratton argues, are different articulations of a vast "Stack" in which a dizzying array of human and nonhuman operators are ported together in planetary-scale assemblages.[7]

These diagnoses require additional historical depth. In this essay, I emphasize the centrality of logistics and logistical media to early modern projects of European conquest and colonization. Because these projects sought to overwrite competing Indigenous knowledges, values, economies, and relations, I synthesize concepts and methods from media theory and settler colonial studies. The latter field shows colonization as still ongoing processes of extracting wealth and resources that simultaneously displace or attempt to erase indigeneity.[8] But colonization, I argue, goes beyond extraction and encompasses, in media-theoretical terms, processes of *inscription* over land, peoples, creatures, things, and their interrelations. Colonization has always been, in other words, an infrastructural project. Beyond noting how "logistics," as a science of circulation, continues to be a primary vehicle of these multifaceted and multiscalar processes, I more specifically recast histories of colonization through the lens of what John Durham Peters calls "logistical" media.[9] These are media forms and techniques that function differently than transmission- or storage-based media. Logistical media are processual; they orient, locate, and organize words, things, people, and data. They are gatekeepers of basic categories of time, space, and experience—ancient, such as calendars, clocks, towers, and lists, or modern, such as radar, algorithms, platforms, or even tents and tear gas.[10] Logistical media of proto-colonial economies, such as Cabot's cod fisheries, include tall ships, nets, barrels, inventories, schedules, maps, shipping manifests, crown charters, compasses, and canoes.

Such logistical media are derived from "cultural techniques" of ordering, calculating, observing, and measuring that become scalable or standardized through a mix of use, technical implementation, or edict.[11] Though not often considered as "media," they are essential nodes in the operative chains by which European colonial order becomes inscribed over life, land, labor, and imagination. As a concept, then, "logistical media" addresses Eve Tuck and K. Wayne Yang's point that the question "'what is colonization?' must be answered specifically, with attention paid to the colonial apparatus that is assembled to order the relationships between particular peoples, lands, the 'natural world,' and 'civilization.' Colonialism is marked by its specializations."[12] Because logistical media take a variety of forms and operate at varying scales, I adopt a multiscalar approach to analysis, moving from Eurocentric visions of global conquest to the smaller-scale media by which such visions were inscribed over land, people, and things. I take two paradigmatic examples: the ship and the document. Both facilitate movement and circulation, most obviously, but they are also *interfaces* (between land and sea, between imperial centers of Europe and the colonial "margins," between individuals and the state); they render things *interoperable* (gathering and "porting" what otherwise would remain disaggregated, whether people, things, or data); and they *inscribe* (creating parameters within which relations and circulation unfold on land and at sea). In each of these functions, ships and documents materialize a European logistical orientation that opens with the onset of modernity.

II.

Cabot's and di Soncino's letters about stockfish point to a signal moment by which to trace the emergence of this orientation, but there are others. Stefano Harney and Fred Moten suggest, "Modern logistics is founded with the first great movement of commodities, the ones that could speak. It was founded in the Atlantic slave trade. Founded against the Atlantic slave."[13] The large-scale abstraction of human life into the commodity form and its movement as matériel mark for Harney and Moten the moment at which the core tenets of logistics—optimization, efficiency, speed, expansion—took hold. Much has been written on the violence of European logistics in the context of the slave trade.[14] Until recently, relatively little research has considered its implication in the structure and operations of North American colonization and settlement. The lives and lands that Europeans sought to render according to this logistical orientation had been to that point under the stewardship of the continent's thousands of Indigenous communities. Europeans first arrived to fish but later learned to navigate coastal waters and rivers, to move inland, trap, and, eventually, to settle. In making each transition they skimmed knowledge from First Nations about land, animal, navigation, technique, and climate before attempting to displace and dismantle systematically the traditions and practices from which such knowledge was derived.[15] That the European project was not entirely successful is a testament to the care with which these communities have protected their languages, traditions, and kin, and the labor with which they repair damages inflicted on them.[16]

This struggle is ongoing; colonization was neither entirely successful nor has it been eradicated, as we are reminded by recent Indigenous resistances to settler infrastructure projects including the Dakota Access Pipeline, British

Columbia's Northern Gateway Pipeline, or Muskrat Falls in Newfoundland. Shiri Pasternak and Tia Dafnos demonstrate how state power and "resiliency" are exerted through the expansion of these infrastructure projects. They argue this development has been precisely coordinated to deter and defer Indigenous claims of sovereignty and jurisdiction.[17] Pasternak and Deborah Cowen build on this work, as well as on Cowen's seminal research into logistics' "deadly" lives, to reframe settler colonialism in Canada as a project of ongoing infrastructural violence.[18] Such work complements that on logistics and the Atlantic slave trade by showing contemporaneous processes of contact, extraction, and European settlement that sought to render, displace, or otherwise "contain" Indigenous bodies, epistemologies, and relations.

To this research we should add analyses of, on the one hand, the critical role of logistical media to the operations of European imperialism and setter colonialism and, on the other, lessons from competing Indigenous media of transport, exchange, and congress. Concepts from media theory—*inscription, technique, port, interface,* and *cancellation,* among others—can describe both the varying scales at which processes of colonization unfold and the important role of logistical media in enacting or resisting such processes. To demonstrate, I turn now to two examples: the ship and the document.

III.

Ships are media that activate logistical operations through interoperability. The term *interoperability,* first used in military settings before being adopted in discourses of computation, describes bringing into conjunction two or more separate and seemingly incompatible entities. To humans, land and sea are separate spheres of activity with fundamentally different orders and protocols for survivability. Water-faring vessels like ships (but also canoes, rafts, and submarines) make land and sea interoperable. They bring land onto sea. They are a unit that accepts both human foot and waterline. From the human point of view, they render the sea navigable. A previously confounding zone becomes one of conquest, measure, management, and extraction. From the perspective of cargo and logistics, ships make land and sea commensurate for the movement and transport of people, things, and data.

The effects of this logistical medium are cascading. European ships of the early modern period were not the first ocean-faring vessels, nor even the first to cross the Atlantic. But innovations during this period in design and shipbuilding led to rapid expansion in the size and volume of ships, as well as the frequency and predictability of transatlantic seafaring.[19] As Bernhard Siegert shows, shipbuilding progressed steadily throughout the sixteenth century from a craft in which "design and construction were not yet separated" (the *mezzaluna* or "whole-mould" method bent wood for each frame of the ship using elastics and rope according to the guide of the master frame) into a disaggregated process that began with lines on paper and Euclidean geometry. Siegert writes, "Once he relocates from the shipyard to his office to conduct his work at the drawing board, the master shipwright transforms into an architect. In other words, this occurs when shipbuilding becomes paperwork."[20] Such shipbuilding activity could accelerate and scale as it became more readily transferable from person to person, and place to place, in memory supports like equations and drawings, and in storage media like books.

As techniques of shipbuilding and navigation became more mathematically precise and replicable, possibilities for seafaring expanded to offer ever more humans a medium by which to unbind themselves from land, to venture into the ancient mysteries of the sea and toward what European eyes saw as "white space" at the edge of the map.[21] The possibility of human presence in such spaces was not considered or even conceived; they were "empty with a telos of filling," to borrow Peter van Wyck's formulation of more recent settler visions of the north.[22] As Siegert writes, "The ship is a colonial and scientific technology, a medium of overseas trade or ceremonial exchanges, a war machine, a technology for harvesting fish and other ocean riches," and yet it is more than all of that, he notes, quoting Michel Foucault, who wrote it is "for our [European] civilization . . . the greatest reserve of imagination."[23] Ships were designed to allow humans to tap into the previously unnavigable vectors of ocean and wind currents. The tall ship of European voyages of exploration was therefore not simply a vessel that facilitated the movement of matériel and men but a logistical medium that established an entirely new horizon of space and time. In the words of Siegert, "The ship makes space. By setting out and carrying man, 'that terrible wonder,' into open waters, it transforms the sea, hitherto devoid of any sense of place or history, into something inscribed by both."[24] The ship is the medium by which the sea becomes conceptually transformed into a zone of transportation, extraction, and exchange to be exploited and leveraged, bent to human will. A similar understanding leads Virilio to locate the birth of modern logistics in seafaring since the open horizon of the sea taps into an imaginary of frictionless and omnidirectional movement over and through not only water but also land and, eventually, air—in other words, the world as pure logistical field.[25] Water-faring vessels, particularly European tall ships, are a crucial step in the genealogy of such imaginaries, in which land is understood as not more than an impediment, a temporary zone to be portaged so that cargo can return to the oceanic vectors that are, for Virilio, the true home of logistics.[26]

Harold Adams Innis's account of the early cod fisheries understands the European tall ship in such a way, as an interface between land and water that turns the sea into a zone of extraction and a channel of transfer between landed ports. Because the ship aggregates divergent people, things, and data, Innis characterizes it as the basic unit of this sixteenth-century economy (instead of, for instance, the company, contract, or formal partnership, units that were constitutive of the North American fur trade economy).[27] Captains and *bourgeois* (outfitters) of individual ships in France, Portugal, Spain, and England recruited sailors and fishermen; secured capital; and brokered agreements for provisions such as salt, sugar, and flour—and in so doing bore the brunt of risk. Thus Innis writes: "The wide distribution of small loans, the high rate of interest, and the financial structure by which dependence was placed primarily on those directly concerned with the industry were possibly a result of heavy losses but more probably of the overwhelming importance of the vessel as a unit . . . it demanded the initiative of large numbers carrying on the industry from small vessels. The demands were reflected in aggressive commercialism in contrast with large-scale company organizations."[28] The vessel is here understood as the basal unit of a larger totality, and through its operations we can glean much about that larger structure. It helps Innis, for instance, understand the importance of what he calls "unused capacity" to nascent operations of European extraction, colonization, and empire. Put simply, filling empty cargo space for voyages between continents required a huge amount of attention, planning, and resources. How and with what each vessel was filled had far-reaching implications for patterns of European arrival, contact with First Nations, and eventual settlement. Vessels from salt-rich Spain, Portugal, and France, for instance, carried salt and equipment from Europe for "greening" (salting) the catch on board. These voyages therefore had little need, in the earliest decades of the fishery, to land in New England or Newfoundland, deferring contact with Indigenous communities. England, on the other hand, was salt-poor and thus reliant on trade. To reduce this dependency, English crews developed an on-land technique of "dry curing" that required less salt and took advantage of sunny coastal areas, such as at Newfoundland's Avalon Peninsula. But because the number of men required to dry cure exceeded the number required to sail, more men made the voyage than could return once the catch was brought aboard. This surplus of manpower results in British crews spending long periods on and near land earlier than their continental rivals, with some even staying behind to winter in Newfoundland and New England.[29] British control of these cod-rich waters pushed the French fishery north to the Gaspé Peninsula and St. Lawrence Seaway, the gateway to the interior of the continent. The French moved farther up the St. Lawrence, expanding the scope of contact and trade with Indigenous communities and building infrastructure for an ongoing trade of valuable beaver pelts. Permanent settlements of New France, the earliest on the North American continent, soon followed.[30]

Logistical media of the cod fisheries like the tall ship delineate not just spatial zones within which people, things, and information intermingle but also rhythms of time. The steps of each voyage, from planning, outfitting, sailing, fishing, and salting, to returning, offloading, exchanging, and reinvesting, followed the seasons. This was not just for obvious reasons related to navigation but also due to temporal demands of the market related to, for instance, religious ritual (Catholic markets demanded fish for certain days of the week and for certain festivals; Protestant markets did not).[31] The North American continent and its waters thus became inscribed by European logics of space, time, and power derived from cultural techniques of eating, exchanging, shipbuilding, navigating, and even worshiping that took place thousands of kilometers away. Understanding the tall ship as the basic unit of this international economy, as a logistical medium through which categories of experience and patterns of culture emerged, brings this layer of European conquest and colonization into view.

Though beyond the scope of this essay, we might consider other waterfaring vessels integral during the period of early contact between European and Indigenous communities, such as the birchbark canoe, in similar terms. For more than 350 years, circa 1500–1850, the canoe rendered land and water interoperable, providing a medium by which the valuable commodity of fur could be moved more efficiently and with less friction over vast distances. Once appropriated by Europeans, it became an interface between the North American continent's interior river systems and its deepwater ports at Montreal and Boston. The canoe, like the tall ship, was not simply a passive container but an active agent that shaped the character and rhythm of contact between Indigenous communities and European traders. This idea is central to Innis's analysis of the fur trade, leading him to suggest, "we have given to the maple [tree] a prominence which was due to the birch" and no doubt inspiring his colleague A. R. M. Lower's infamous (and probably apocryphal) quip that "Canada is a canoe route."[32]

IV.

My second example is the document, a logistical medium that seeks to inscribe and entrench colonial systems of governance and control over North American land and its inhabitants. Exemplary in this regard is the monopoly charter issued by King Charles II of Britain in 1670 to the "Governor and Company of Adventurers of England, trading into Hudson's Bay," granting an exclusive trading monopoly as well as mineral and exploratory rights to the Hudson's Bay Company (HBC). Charles named his cousin, Prince Rupert, the first governor of HBC and christened the territory in question Rupert's Land (a name it carried for two hundred years). The swipe of this pen had cascading effects. It legitimized the further incursion of fur traders into the continent's interior and thus brought dozens of First Nations and hundreds of communities living in Rupert's Land under the sway of European logistics. It was also a document with a high degree of what Bernd Frohmann calls "documentality," the ability to "produce, afford, allow, encourage, permit, influence, render possible, block, or forbid the generation of marks, traces or inscriptions in its arrangements with other things."[33] The charter stood at the center of a proliferation of legal and governance documents. Through these, the sovereignty of the Crown and its agents would be asserted over, or inscribed into, land, people, waterways, and animal inhabitants. *Inscription* is a useful concept here. It describes the material techniques of crafting and circulating documents that produced Charles II's monopoly charter, the maps through which that European vision of North American territory would be standardized, and the legal apparatus that would seek to enforce colonial rule. As a metaphor, it describes a wider set of assumptions and general orientation toward land, people, and data that Europeans brought with them—the world as *Bestand* ("standing reserve")—and how this orientation would be inscribed as colonial infrastructure to crowd out and undermine extant Indigenous systems of transport and assembly.

With charter in hand, such alternate epistemologies, social and commercial relationships, or systems of governments—between Europeans and First Nations, but also between and among First Nations—were, in the mind of HBC company men and the Crown, *cancelled*. Cornelia Vismann's media theory of files reminds us that cancellation has been an essential technique of European law, order, and documentation since antiquity. The word *cancel* derives from the Latin *cancelli*, the "latticed and hence transparent bars" that originally delineated the Roman chancellery as a space of law, order, and power.[34] She shows the importance of door stewards (*cancellarius*) who granted or barred access to this space of the judge and the law. This mediating function migrated into the world of paper, eventually describing the activities of scribes who acted as gatekeepers of the symbolic order of the law in producing final drafts of documents. They used the lattice pattern to cross out earlier drafts and annotations, rendering them null and void, and thus wielded immense power. This power arises not from generative acts of creation but through negation of what came before. In Vismann's words: "Crossing out, it seems, is more elementary than the more productive act of writing down. Deleting rather than writing establishes the symbolic order of the law."[35]

A similar logic of cancellation describes how colonial interests used paperwork to exert dominance over land, people, and things. In a brief commentary from 1927, Innis offers a close reading of a newly discovered constitution of the North West Company (NWC). Dated 1790, it was, at the time of Innis's writing, the earliest known of any such document. Though "constitution" implies creation or origin, Innis cautions against such an interpretation. His commentary instead shows how this document arose as much or more from a negation of what came before, a cancellation. In order to be absorbed into the nascent colonial state, existing ad hoc relationships between individual traders or with First Nations that did not pass through the legal apparatus of the European colonial state had to be written over by this new document. In its very existence, the constitution seeks to render null and void all previous arrangements or competing claims to authority over trapping territory, equipment, or relationships with individual trappers (Indigenous or non). Innis carefully retraces these earlier relations through canoe licenses, schedules, agreements pertaining to the transport of furs and payment of Indigenous trappers, the building of forts and storehouses, and so on.[36] The 1790 constitution voided these earlier agreements under British law, which rested on the sovereignty of the Crown and its apparatus of documentation. It was a list of legal clauses. Like any list, it drew certain things together to the exclusion of all others.[37] It made interoperable this particular series of European actors, interests, capital, and supply chains. Like all contracts under European law, it pre*scribed* certain actions. It programmed all parties to act in certain ways (but not others), thus enhancing confidence that the relationships defined therein would endure. Any and all relationships with parties external to the agreement became secondary.

In so doing, it inscribed a series of relations in terms that were legible to Crown and colonial power. It was thus not a beginning, the "origin" of the North West Company, but an endpoint of a more heterogeneous set of relations and hierarchies. It established settler power not through creation but through cancellation of what came before.

The inscription of a European juridical-legal order over land and people is even more obvious in view of the westward march of settlement. Previously, throughout the seventeenth and eighteenth centuries, a variety of techniques had been used in eastern and central Canada to mark agreements arising from early contact between Indigenous and European communities. As Europeans moved west, these were replaced by a rationalized and numbered treaty system, applied across the prairies, that refused to incorporate competing epistemologies or interpretations such as had been present in earlier arrangements. The numbered treaties offered as little interpretive flexibility as possible. They were designed to be fixed in place according to settler law and order, and inoperable for competing epistemologies or claims to sovereignty. Viewing such treaties as more than legal documents, as logistical media, offers localized views on the transition from early colonization, in which agreements were less standardized according to European legal traditions, to settler colonialism, a longer-lasting structure.[38] The Indian Act (1876) and the Dominion Lands Act (1872) similarly testify to the Crown's attempts to use techniques of documentation to exert power and authority over land and people.[39] Rereading the histories, and presents, of settler colonialism through this lens shows that it is not a structure enacted strictly through brute force and abject racism (though there always has been plenty of both), but often more subtly and insidiously through techniques of documentation.

But "cancellation," importantly, is not the same as erasure. It always leaves a trace. As Vissmann writes about cancellation in the world of writing, "The more thorough the cancellation, the less visible the traces left behind by the deletions. But sometimes 'slips'—irregularities, displacements, mistakes—remain."[40] Going beyond colonial archives, scholars from Indigenous studies have recentered such traces, that is, relations and modes of documentation that did not pass through the bottleneck of European law and that were founded on principles other than extraction, circulation, and exchange. Wampum belts, for instance, documented agreements, events, and relationships using images, patterns, and colors crafted from wampum shells rather than ink, paper, or alphanumeric scripts. Wampum has a long history that extends well prior to contact. Tehanetorens writes that the practice began among Atlantic Coastal First Nations before spreading inland. It was eventually used to document encounters and arrangements with Europeans, particularly in the sixteenth and seventeenth centuries (during which shells were valued so highly that settlers briefly adopted them as currency).[41] The Two Row Wampum Treaty (1613) between the Dutch and Iroquois, for instance, signaled the recognition of both parties to coexistence. Two parallel rows of purple wampum were set against a background of white, which, in Audra Simpson's words, "represents the sea of life that each row metaphorically shares. One purple row represents an Iroquois vessel and the other a European vessel. Although they share the same sea, they are separate and parallel; they should not touch or disturb each other or try to steer the other's vessel even though they share the same space. Between the vessels are chains that connect them to each other; these are to be shined and maintained by one or the other vessel."[42] Tehanetorens explicitly suggests the Iroquois vessel is a canoe, the Dutch one a ship, emphasizing the importance again of these vessels in mediating not just the logistics of the fur trade but also the social relationships of contact between First Nations and Europeans.[43]

Similarly, John Borrows points to wampum as an important marker of Indigenous agency in treaty negotiations such as in the Treaty of Fort Niagara in 1764. Too often, Borrows argues, First Nations are understood only to have been acted on during such processes, rather than as "active and powerful partners in making provisions for the future relationship between the parties."[44] At Niagara, these relations took shape in an agreement that incorporated European and Indigenous epistemologies alike: paper documents, signatures, wampum belts, oral speeches, and gift exchanges were all crucial elements of the covenant. In reminding us of the importance of Indigenous modes of documenting this agreement, Borrows argues that its grounding principles—the affirmation of Indigenous sovereignty and territorial rights in the spirit of mutual recognition and respect—were a legally binding context brought by all parties to subsequent treaties. This context, he argues, must therefore inform any interpretation of these agreements, legal or otherwise. The power of wampum belts to offer such historical and legal testimony is likely why they have been, at best, routinely refused by Eurocentric juridical processes or, at worst, greeted with outright violence.[45]

Such traces, marginalized by colonial histories, continue to be recentered by Indigenous and Indigenist scholars and activists working across such decolonizing projects as land repatriation, community building, educational reform, legal claims, and more. An understanding of colonization in logistical terms—as ongoing processes of inscription and attempted cancellation, but also, importantly, of resistance and refusal—similarly preserves space for that which exceeds, precedes, and survives. It may therefore help deflate histories of North America that presume from nothing came something 150 years ago, or 400, or whatever colonial "origin" may be posited.

V.

In this essay, I have recast fragments from the variegated histories of colonization in terms of its "logistical media," the forms and techniques that orient, order, and establish basic categories of time, space, and power. Such analysis brings specificity to our understanding of how European conquest and exploration became inscribed as a longer-lasting structure of settler colonialism. Recasting water-faring vessels as logistical media shows how they render land and sea, center and periphery, ocean and river interoperable, porting these otherwise disaggregated spaces and times together. Recasting documents as logistical media helps us to see them as more than traces of past activities or events but rather as intermediaries that activate certain possibilities and seek to cancel others. Through the ship the European colonial project of North America became writable. Through the document it became written.

The concepts and methods of "logistical" media theory provide a vocabulary for understanding the operations of colonial power at an ontological level, across seemingly diverse realms of paperwork, navigation, extraction, communication, and exchange. The focus of this essay has been North America, but we should develop similar analyses of colonial encounters elsewhere. What were the logistical media that facilitated Europe's "scramble for Africa"? By what techniques did the Dutch and English East India Companies inscribe the European logistical orientation over South Asia? What were the logistical media of resistance and refusal? Such questions invite debates and concepts from settler colonial studies into media theory, bringing a political valence that is often absent from such research. From the other direction, media theory brings fresh concepts, such as interoperability, cancellation, and inscription, to bear on modernity's colonial structures and legacies. Given the degree to which these legacies imprint contemporary systems of circulation, communication, and exchange, such interdisciplinary frameworks seem urgently required.

1. Raimondo di Soncino, quoted in Mary Quayle Innis, *An Economic History of Canada* (Toronto: Ryerson Press, 1935), 2; and Harold Innis, *The Cod Fisheries* (Toronto: University of Toronto Press, [1940] 1978), 11.

2. Paul Virilio, *The Original Accident* (Cambridge: Polity, 2007).

3. A sampling of literature on shipping containers includes Deborah Cowen, *The Deadly Life of Logistics* (Minneapolis: University of Minnesota Press, 2014); Marc Levinson, *The Box: How the Shipping Container Made the World Smaller and the World Economy Bigger* (Princeton, NJ: Princeton University Press, 2006); Craig Martin, *Shipping Container* (London: Bloomsbury, 2016); and Allan Sekula, *Fish Story* (Düsseldorf: Richter Verlag, 1995), among many others.

4. *Bestand* is Heidegger's term, usually translated as "standing reserve," to describe a condition in which the world and its inhabitants are understood as dead or subservient matériel to be marshalled for human ends. The most extensive treatment of the concept is in "The Question concerning Technology," in Martin Heidegger, *Basic Writings*, ed. David F. Krell, trans. William Lovitt (New York: HarperCollins, 1993), 307–41. Kjøsen's formulation of logistics as "*Bestand*-in-motion" is so far unpublished.

5. For a powerful analysis of modernity and scale, see Anna Tsing, "Supply Chains and the Human Condition," *Rethinking Marxism* 21, no. 2 (2009): 148–76; and Anna Tsing, "On Non-Scalability," *Common Knowledge* 18, no. 3 (2012): 505–24.

6. A sampling of the recent literature to engage such questions includes Dwayne Winseck and Robert Pike, *Communication and Empire: Media, Markets, and Globalization, 1860-1930* (Durham, NC: Duke University Press, 2007); Nicole Starosielski, *The Undersea Network* (Durham, NC: Duke University Press, 2015); Miriyam Aouragh and Paula Chakravartty, "Infrastructures of Empire: Towards a Critical Geopolitics of Media and Information Studies," *Media, Culture and Society* 38, no. 4 (2016): 559–75; Jesse LeCavalier, *The Rule of Logistics: Walmart and the Architecture of Fulfillment* (Minneapolis: University of Minnesota Press, 2016); and Martin Danyluk, "Capital's Logistical Fix: Accumulation, Globalization, and the Survival of Capitalism," *Environment and Planning D: Society and Space* 36, no. 4 (2018): 630–47.

7. Benjamin Bratton, *The Stack: On Software and Sovereignty* (Cambridge, MA: MIT Press, 2015). See also Benjamin Bratton, *The Terraforming* (Moscow: Strelka Press, 2019).

8. I use the term *colonization* rather than *colonialism* to signal these processual and temporal aspects. I am attentive to arguments made by Aimee Carrillo Rowe and Eve Tuck, among others, that not all colonialisms are the same. *Colonization* is a processual term that can, I hope, bring further precision to understanding the transition from, for instance, the "colonialism" of the early fur trade (that was primarily "external" colonialism, about wealth extraction) to the "settler colonialism" that came after (in which Europeans came to stay and in so

doing displaced and sought to erase Indigenous life and land). Recent texts by Aimee Carrillo Rowe and Eve Tuck ("Settler Colonialism and Cultural Studies," *Cultural Studies ↔ Critical Methodologies* 17, no. 1 [2017]: 3–13) and Eve Tuck and K. Wayne Yang ("Decolonization Is Not a Metaphor," *Decolonization: Indigeneity, Education and Society* 1, no. 1 [2012]: 1–40) inform this point. See also seminal texts by Patrick Wolfe (*Settler Colonialism and the Transformation of Anthropology* [London: Cassell, 1999]) and Lorenzo Veracini ("Introducing Settler Colonial Studies," *Settler Colonial Studies* 1, no. 1 [2012]: 1–12).

9. See John Durham Peters, "Calendar, Clock, Tower," in *Deus in Machina*, ed. Jeremy Stolow (New York: Fordham University Press, 2013), 25–42; and John Durham Peters, *The Marvelous Clouds* (Chicago: University of Chicago Press, 2015).

10. See Judd Case, "Logistical Media: Fragments from Radar's Prehistory," *Canadian Journal of Communication* 38 (2013): 379–95; Liam Cole Young, *List Cultures: Knowledge and Poetics from Mesopotamia to BuzzFeed* (Amsterdam: Amsterdam University Press, 2017); Ned Rossiter, "Logistical Worlds," *Cultural Studies Review* 20, no. 1 (2014): 53–76; and Anna Feigenbaum, "Resistant Matters: Tents, Tear Gas and the 'Other Media' of Occupy," *Communication and Critical/Cultural Studies* 11, no. 1 (2014): 15–24.

11. "Cultural techniques" is the English translation of the German concept of *Kulturtechniken*. For overviews of this concept, see Bernhard Siegert, *Cultural Techniques: Grids, Filters, Doors, and Other Articulations of the Real*, trans. Geoffrey Winthrop-Young (New York: Fordham University Press, 2015), 1–17; Geoffrey Winthrop-Young, "Cultural Techniques: Preliminary Remarks," *Theory, Culture and Society* 30, no. 6 (2013): 3–19; Bernard Dionysius Geoghegan, "After Kittler: On the Cultural Techniques of Recent German Media Theory," *Theory, Culture and Society* 30, no. 6 (2013): 66–82; and Young, *List Cultures*, 39–43.

12. Tuck and Yang, "Decolonization Is Not a Metaphor," 21.

13. Stefano Harney and Fred Moten, *The Undercommons: Fugitive Planning and Black Study* (Wivenhoe, UK: Minor Compositions, 2013), 92.

14. In addition to Harney and Moten, *The Undercommons*, see Robin Blackburn, *The Making of New World Slavery: From the Baroque to the Modern, 1492–1800* (New York: Verso, 1997); and Simone Browne, *Dark Matters: On the Surveillance of Blackness* (Durham, NC: Duke University Press, 2015).

15. Harold Innis, *The Fur Trade in Canada* (Toronto: University of Toronto Press, [1930] 1970), 386–89. See also Arthur Ray, *Indians in the Fur Trade* (Toronto: University of Toronto Press [1974] 1998).

16. I am mindful of Eve Tuck's call to move beyond "damage-centered" research that frames Indigenous experiences and voices only in terms of brokenness or failure ("Suspending Damage: A Letter to Communities," *Harvard Educational Review* 79, no. 3 [2009]: 409–28). I hope to make a small contribution to efforts in Indigenous and settler colonial studies toward unsettling narratives of nation that presume Indigenous erasure or absorption, and which overem-

phasize individuals like John A. MacDonald (Canada's first prime minister), ideas like "manifest destiny," sublime technologies like the railroad, or policy directives such as Canada's Indian Act.

17. Shiri Pasternak and Tia Dafnos, "How Does a Settler State Secure the Circuitry of Capital?," *Environment and Planning D: Society and Space* 36, no. 4 (2018): 739–57.

18. Shiri Pasternak and Deborah Cowen, "Trans Mountain Pipeline Another Colonial Project Asserting Jurisdiction over Indigenous Lands," *Star* (Toronto), April 24, 2018; Cowen, *Deadly Life of Logistics*; and Deborah Cowen, "Following the Infrastructures of Empire: Notes on Cities, Settler Colonialism, and Method," *Urban Geography* 41, no. 4 (2020): 469–86.

19. Paul Butel offers an expansive maritime history of the Atlantic in *The Atlantic* (London: Routledge, 1999). Stephen Berry's *A Path in the Mighty Waters* (New Haven, CT: Yale University Press, 2015) focuses on life aboard transatlantic ships during the great European migrations of the eighteenth century. Other classic studies of seafaring, ships, and the maritime imaginary include, among many others, Bronislaw Malinowski's *Argonauts of the Western Pacific* (London: Routledge, [1922] 2014); Hans Blumenberg's *Shipwreck and Spectator* (Cambridge, MA: MIT Press, 1985); Fernand Braudel's three-volume study of *The Mediterranean* (Berkeley: University of California Press, [1949] 1995); and Peregrine Horden and Nicholas Purcell's *The Corrupting Sea* (Hoboken, NJ: Wiley-Blackwell, 2000).

20. Siegert, *Cultural Techniques*, 152.

21. Siegert, *Cultural Techniques*, 130–46.

22. Peter van Wyck, *The Highway of the Atom* (Montreal: McGill-Queen's University Press, 2010), 202.

23. Siegert, *Cultural Techniques*, 68.

24. Siegert, *Cultural Techniques*, 70.

25. Virilio, *Original Accident*, 83–101; see Benjamin Bratton, "Introduction: Logistics of Habitable Circulation," in Paul Virilio, *Speed and Politics*, trans. Mark Polizzotti (Los Angeles: Semiotext(e), [1977] 2006), 7–25, 8.

26. A similar argument is developed through a Marxian framework by Danyluk in "Capital's Logistical Fix," building on Edna Bonacich and Jake Wilson, *Getting the Goods: Ports, Labor, and the Logistics Revolution* (Ithaca, NY: Cornell University Press, 2008), and Keller Easterling, *Extrastatecraft: The Power of Infrastructure Space* (New York: Verso, 2014).

27. Innis, *Cod Fisheries*, 41–42.

28. Innis, *Cod Fisheries*, 42.

29. Harold Innis, "Unused Capacity as a Factor in Canadian Economic History," *Canadian Journal of Economics and Political Science* 2, no. 1 (1936): 1–2. See also Liam Cole Young, "Salt: Fragments from the History of a Medium," *Theory, Culture and Society* 37, no. 6 (2020): 135–58.

30. Innis, *Cod Fisheries*, 30–51.

31. Innis, "Unused Capacity," 2.

32. Innis, *Fur Trade in Canada*, 15–20, 388–90, 497.

33. See Bernd Frohmann, "The Documentality of Mme Briet's Antelope," in *Communication Matters: Materialist Approaches to Media, Mobility, and Networks*, ed. Jeremey Packer and Stephen B. Crofts Wiley (London: Routledge, 2012), 173–82, 175.

34. Alois Walde and Johann Baptist Hofmann, quoted in Cornelia Vismann, *Files: Law and Media Technology*, trans. Geoffrey Winthrop-Young (Stanford, CA: Stanford University Press, 2008), 17.

35. Vismann, *Files*, 26.

36. See Harold Innis, "The North West Company," *Canadian Historical Review* 8, no. 4 (1927): 308–21, 309–13. See also Innis, *Fur Trade in Canada*, 311.

37. Jack Goody, *The Domestication of the Savage Mind* (Cambridge: Cambridge University Press, 1977), 76–81; and Young, *List Cultures*, 16–17, 23–35.

38. Patrick Wolfe's seminal work urges a conception of settler colonial invasion as a "structure" rather than an event. See Wolfe, *Settler Colonialism*, 163.

39. Simpson recalls Deskaheh's (Levi General) efforts to assert Iroquois sovereignty and treaty rights in the 1920s by trying to get Six Nations recognized as a nation by the League of Nations. When this failed and Canada began to enforce the Indian Act, Deskaheh urgently called for an understanding of "citizenship as a colonizing technique." See Audra Simpson, *Mohawk Interruptus: Political Life across the Borders of Settler States* (Durham, NC: Duke University Press, 2014), 136 and 222. For more on the Indian Act and the documentary techniques of the state, see Danielle Taschereau Mamers, "Settler Colonial Ways of Seeing: Documentary Governance of Indigenous Life in Canada and Its Disruption," PhD diss., University of Western Ontario, 2017.

40. Vismann, *Files*, 27.

41. Simpson, *Mohawk Interruptus*, 222.

42. Simpson, *Mohawk Interruptus*, 221.

43. Tehanetorens [Ray Fadden], *Wampum Belts of the Iroquois* (Ohsweken, ON: Iroqrafts, 1983), 10–11.

44. See John Borrows, "Wampum at Niagara: The Royal Proclamation, Canadian Legal History, and Self-Government," in *Aboriginal and Treaty Rights in Canada: Essays on Law, Equality, and Respect for Difference*, ed. Michael Asch (Vancouver: University of British Columbia Press, 1997), 155–72, 169.

45. Belts of the Six Nations, for instance, were seized by the Royal Canadian Mounted Police as it forcibly disbanded the Nations' traditional governments in the 1920s; see Simpson, *Mohawk Interruptus*, 222.

ALWAYS ALREADY
ASSEMBLED

When investigative journalism began to unravel the reach of production for mobile technology companies such as Apple, Nokia, and Samsung in the late 2000s, consumers were surprised at the sheer scale of these supply chains. The release of Apple's first comprehensive supplier list in 2011—and the institution of its yearly progress report audits—offered a partial picture of the truly world-spanning requirements for assembling contemporary media technologies. The complex materiality presented in these reports struck many as something altogether new—another hallmark of the digital era. But there are similarities between the rare and precious resources demanded by high-tech objects and the sort supplied for century-old components in telephones, typewriters, and sewing machines. What audits don't reveal is that media have long been global productions, and the pathways that have furnished their production will persist long into the future.

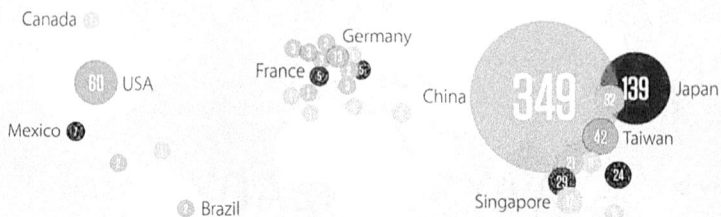

Supplier map included in Apple's "Supplier Responsibility Report" for 2013 operations (2014).

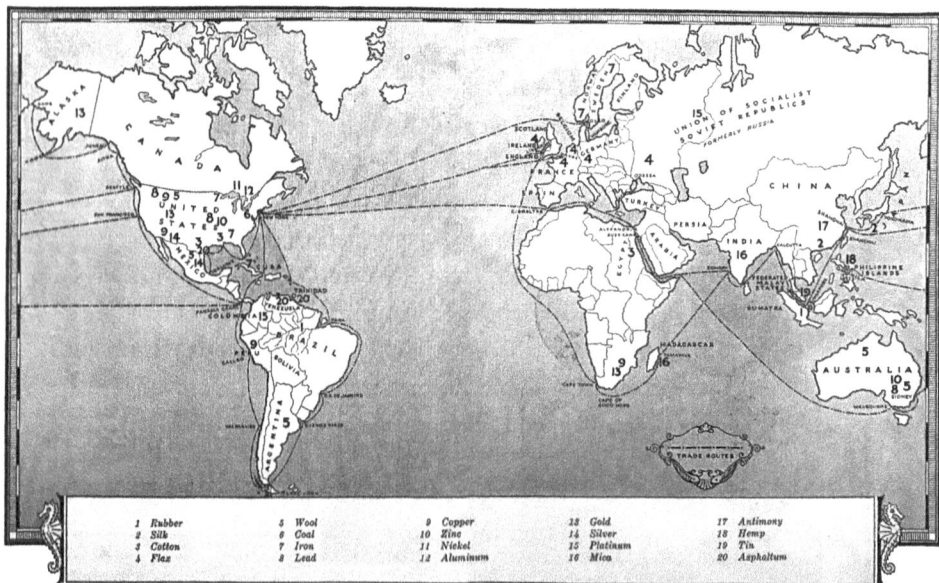

Western Electric materials map as pictured in Western Electric, *From the Far Corners of the Earth* (1927).

6

"Every Man within Earshot"

Auditory Efficiency in the Time of the Telephone

"SIRI, CANCEL MY UBER." "Alexa, order toner from Prime Now." "Hey, Google, turn up the lights." In speaking these commands to the rapidly proliferating army of voice-activated assistants that have come to occupy my daily life, I am not simply preparing to write this chapter. I am connecting myself to a vast network of people and machines. My voice travels through electrical lines and radio waves, populating database tables that feed the operations of logistical software systems. As it increments their inventories, it may connect me to the logistical laborers who circulate invisibly throughout the city. Or perhaps it reaches farther, to the remote factories spread along the world's perceptual periphery, activating the endless assembly lines of robots—human and nonhuman alike—that churn out the designs my voice has called into being. When my order has been stamped with the barcode digitizing its distribution, when it has been picked up, packed, and placed on pallets bound for cargo containers and transport trucks, only then is it ready to be shipped back to join others of its kind in an apartment full of smart things. And the marvelous thing is that there is no longer the need to click or call. My voice resonates with a networked power. Directed to devices of logistical listening, this ready ensemble provides a mode of address where one's wish really is one's command.

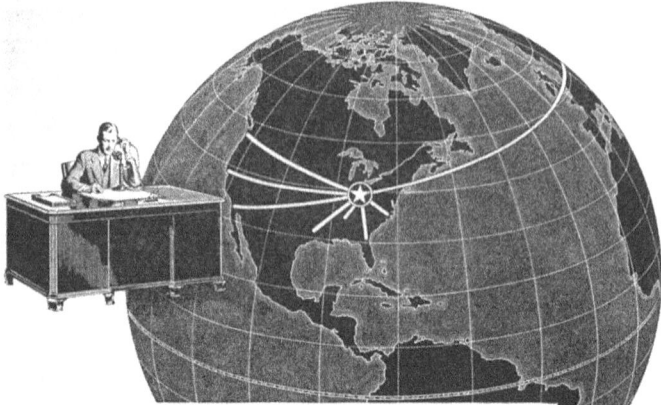

The vice-president in charge of purchases says: "The way business is conducted today, I couldn't function without Long Distance."

PROMPT AND EFFICIENT
BUYING BY TELEPHONE
brings important savings to this large company

6.1 Bell Telephone advertisement (1932).

There is something strange about the recent ascendance of speech as a means for the remote operation of these large-scale systems of global supply. The electric age has been rife with new sorts of interfaces, from buttons on keyboards to the movement of mice and gestures drawn on glass. But *speech* has rarely proven to be the most reliable. And yet, here it is, with its old-fashioned and purportedly more *human* qualities of interaction presented to privileged consumers as a more accessible and, consequently, more approachable kind of communion than those prior forms of computer-coordinated connection. But in this suggestion the voice is not really a vehicle for communication. It is a signal of demand. The devices that answer to its call are again sites for a demonstration of the supposedly diminished vocal power that once established the domination of master over servant. As perceptions of the network of human sociality flatten, their loathsome hierarchies are reinscribed in the speech between humans and nonhumans. This form again becomes an index of the rules of a system, one that reaffirms its structures of control to all connected constituents. It builds on a logistics of operation that has long figured speech not only as a more convenient interface, but as a more *efficient* one.

The contemporary sense of efficiency was introduced to Western discourse with the transformation of the small shop into the modern enterprise at the end of the nineteenth century. As production moved out of the confines of the craft hall, the effort to install a more orderly mode of operation enrolled everything from paperwork and procedure to the architecture of the shop itself. Efficiency, the stewards of this *system* argued, was what would set their new pattern of production apart. To suggest a process as "efficient" was to connect it to a more modern means of scientific, economic evaluation. As a model for placing one prescription for production against another, the only problem was that almost no one seemed able to say what it was that they were measuring.

That the *idea* of this evaluation came about before any particular means to conduct the comparison may seem surprising. After all, efficiency has become as much a part of daily life as it has the workings of the global supply chain. As a universal evaluation of operation, few could contest its fundamental place in structuring what Anna Tsing has called "supply chain capitalism."[1] Over fifty years ago, Lewis Mumford had already remarked on the strands of supply that circled great metropoles in the "aimless giantism of the whole." So long as capital held sway over these distant sources of supply, he suggested, this growth could proceed indefinitely.[2] And indeed, efficiency is *the* measure by which capital manages the movement of men, women, and machines necessary for this indefinite suspension. It is the force that links the local and global, transforming and deterritorializing the fragmented bounds of borders. Always and everywhere its effect is to prolong capital's unending growth, to ease the friction of logistical flows, and to "build up and create a smooth and straight up space" of possibility. If the world is a vast ocean, then efficiency means to render it everywhere a "sea without winds or waves."[3]

Despite this ubiquity, definitions of efficiency have proven elusive and unstable. What does it mean, after all, for something to be *efficient*? Does it suggest an operation that requires the fewest steps, needs the smallest assembly of actors, or costs the least amount of money? Perhaps the most common understanding is of a certain speed of operation. But logistics has an unusual relationship with this final definition, one that means efficiency cannot be easily divorced from other conceptions like flexibility and order. For the logistician, speed is not so much an objective reality as it is a subjective one. As Paul Virilio has noted, the relativity of this perception is fundamental to the dromological design of modernity. Speed, like efficiency, is a multifarious measure.[4]

Governance by speed, Virilio's work suggests, is logistics.[5] It is the rate of movement over time. But logistical time is neither fast nor slow. It is simply more regular, more ordered and orderly. The cargo container is not concerned with the raw speed of shipment but with an organizational consistency that can produce instantaneous access for consumers. The distribution of the modern warehouse was based less on new technologies of movement than it was approaches to organizing the mechanics of those moves. It is in the seamlessness and regularity afforded by practices of planning that we approach the logistical sublime. Here is the sea without wind or waves, for its passage is the product of manpower alone. Efficiency is found in the delivery of a more regular and reliable speed of connection, of communication, and, it may be most plainly said, of anticipation.

There is a particularly heightened affordance for this anticipatory action in the design of contemporary communication. Speech-enabled assistants like Siri and Alexa are, after all, not designed as "search engines." They are "do engines," devices for connecting the promises of action-by-app to the great age of agents, where servants—indentured rather than digitized—set off in response to their master's voice.[6] Speaking to these artificial analogues is to open an interface to the vast reaches of the global supply chain, one enabled through the connective capabilities of a newly networked internet of things. But it is not faster because it is triggering something new. It is faster because it is activating something that has already been carefully assembled.

That the phone is the most frequent container for this kind of connection, though, is suggestive. It not only speaks to the ways in which media devices have long served to abstract and obfuscate the networks that bring them into being, it foregrounds the ways in which logistical media are intertwined with the kinds of logistical operations they both anticipate and encode. This is a container, after all, that carries a long-standing association with a certain kind of speech—and, I will argue, a certain idea of efficiency. We might very well say that efficiency finds functional form as an auditory mode of analysis, one tied to an imagination of a logistics of network operation premised on the abstraction and operationalization of conventional geography. Over the course of this chapter I will not only demonstrate this auditory efficiency in the time of the telephone, but I will argue for its fundamental importance to the understanding of logistical operation itself.

Soul of Prosperity

At the beginning of the twentieth century, Harrington Emerson, a man who would come to be called the "high priest of efficiency," began his exploration of the term on an entirely conventional sort of sea. "The Guamanese," Emerson wrote of the newly American island, "have few wants and these, lavishly supplied by prodigal Nature." And while it may have been Captain Leary who, as the island's first governor, determined that they "ought to work," it was Emerson who clarified that this obligation should be to work "efficiently." That this was a concern for the work of *system* was because, while "primitive" peoples and medieval peasants had labored alike, they had not done so in any sort of orderly way. As a means of measuring productive potential, the idea of efficiency was, Emerson suggested, not "an ethical or financial or social problem." It remained, as yet, "an engineering problem."[7]

This was certainly the view held by practitioners of scientific management, including its infamous inventor, Frederick Taylor. Efficiency, Taylor suggested, was an object born of system, one that could, through clear engineering and careful examination, be restructured and reworked. The journalist Herbert Casson suggested that Taylor's and Emerson's programs were one and the same, the only difference being in the elegance of their argument. The result of the inquiry would be, Taylor evocatively offered, akin to the production of precious good—the "soul of prosperity" for the individual as well as the nation.[8] The irony was that rather than feeding the soul of human workers it would instead produce their equivalence with the machinic sort that lacked one. And, of course, that efficiency would prove to be a similarly slippery substance.

Indeed, the most peculiar thing about the fundamental object of analysis for this new method of management was how little could be said about it. Herbert Casson suggested that its differing definitions arose from the same basic assumption.[9] Efficiency, he noted, was imagined as a material good. It was something first to be constructed, then to be conserved. But while there was no doubt that the object of "both the workmen and the management" should be the "maximum of efficiency," most disagreed on how to measure it. Taylor's solution would be realized in his time and motion studies, but general understanding relied less on clear ideals of future practice than it did the more accessible *inefficiencies* of the present ones.[10] As Alfred Marshall explained, while "the efficiency of the workers" may have had an ambiguity in its recognition, its absence did not.[11] Inefficiency was something that was evident, but it was so only in *lack*, a lack of order and, more important, a lack of *system*. It was convenient, then, that the installation of system and the elimination of inefficiency went hand in hand. It was from "want of system" that one could find the signs of inefficiency—the "cause of waste" of both "time and material." It was in shops "where promiscuous work is done," where one "may often find the floor covered with litter, heaps of cuttings under every lathe, machine, or bench."[12] Emerson argued that efficiency followed from "the elimination of all needless wastes, in material, in labor, and in equipment." In many respects, systematizers adopted the sort of progressive posturing found in the work of the hygienists. "Dust is the microbe of laziness," as the chain-store specialist Herbert Collins remarked.[13]

But while it was true that one "can see and feel the waste of material things," the "awkward, inefficient, or ill-directed movements of men," Taylor reflected, "leave nothing visible or tangible behind them." And it was in this "general disorder," he believed, that the true spirits of inefficiency dwelled—a kind of *miasma* seeping out of the woodwork to workmen "naturally influenced by their surroundings."[14] An 1891 letter by J. A. Gilkerson spoke to this deeper philosophy. "Like causes," he wrote, "produce like effects."[15] His invocation of David Hume was an expression of what appeared to his contemporaries to be an elemental order, extending from the desk of the firm's owner down to the scraps on the shop floor—indeed, even deeper, to those very *qualities* of the men who swept them. While Casson believed that efficiency should not just be taken as synonymous with system, because "the most useless and wasteful actions can be done in the most systematic way," troublingly often the argument was made solely through this sort of moral imperative.[16] Whatever could be outlined, iterated, and explained in the confines of "system" could be classified within the associated rubric of "efficiency"—by "standardization," "rationalization," and "routine."[17] While Hume's intuition had been to explain the workings of the natural world, this application had arrived in the pages of shop journals by a circuitous route. Not only would the ordering of men and materials be alike in this new science of system, they would each be subject to the same mode of analysis. It was, as Emerson had intimated, hardly natural.

In defining efficiency as an operation of engineering, the stewards of system built a means of evaluation applicable to humans as well as to nonhumans. The efficiency of one was now able to be measured against that of the other. The result was that man and machine increasingly *became* alike—for neither were, for the efficiency theorist, purely a product of nature. As *System* magazine put it, "human and mechanical equipment" must both be kept to "a certain standard." They had been made interchangeable, and so each was reduced to the bounds that these new standards set out. But although many of the systematizers imagined efficiency in purely mechanical terms, the coming of electric life offered an alternative interpretation for measuring the spirit of the "human machine."[18] It was one that could be made accessible to the demands of efficient, electric speech.

Standards of Efficiency

Western Electric was the manufacturer of the telephone for the Bell System. It was also an electrical supplier, and in the early decades of the twentieth century the zeitgeist of electrical modernity haunted shareholder meetings and advertising copy alike. As it extolled the promise of electric futurity to an increasingly orderly US industry, Western Electric came to embrace a particular rhetoric of flexibility, system, and, above all, efficiency. With a vision of the "electric home" and the "electric business," Western Electric marketed products wired for control and command.[19] Electricity was the "twentieth century servant," Western explained. As such, it offered a truly universal means through which to organize human activity. "Why have two standards of efficiency," it asked, when all managerial operations now required the instantaneity of electric life?[20]

This call to electrical efficiency and communicative modernity as the preferred pattern of daily life came to eclipse, at least within Western Electric, Bell's old refrain of "universal service." This ideal, influenced by Western Union's company line, had been the framing vision of telecommunication for decades.[21] But by the 1910s, Western Electric had begun to look for a new message, one that could unite its electrical and telephone interests. The answer, the company believed, lay in system. Western had already adapted these standards of management into the operation of the firm. The company's Hawthorne Works, after all, was famously the site of Elton Mayo's experiments with worker productivity in the 1920s.[22] Just as it had pursued prior paradigms of business practice in its marketing, the company now came to sell the emerging efficiency of electric life.[23]

"The executive who believes in the theory of scientific management," Western explained, "equips his office with Western Electric Inter-phones."[24] In the telephone, Western may have already had an electric object that collapsed the operative fabric of time and space, but it was in ancillary products that the company first marketed this logistical spatiotemporality to firms invested in the promises of systemic management. "If efficiency is the science of saving useless motion," Western wrote, products like the "inter-phone" were to be synonymous with it. "Why go yourself," the company asked, "when you can telephone?" "Modern business," it proclaimed, "must be keyed up"—each department and division electrically connected for "instant communication."[25] If a belief in the spirit of electrical efficiency ran rampant during this period, it came to its most sublime sensibility within the tools of communication.[26]

The interphone was functionally analogous to an intercom, a telephone without the telephone network. Its advantage was that Western could market it outside the internal constraints of the Bell System. As a result, spatial geographies at the small scale—from office desks to factory floors—became a case study for telephonic efficiency. "Wasted steps," Western wrote in one advertisement, "are wasted dollars . . . little thieves that carry off the profits, yet often go unchecked." The very objects of office life were made to testify to this inefficiency: "if your floors could show the steps you waste."[27] These experiments in marketing auditory efficiency positioned telephony as a more precise means of production. "Is your organization running you?" read one notice in 1916. "Are your department heads and foremen continually at your elbow?" "Are you besieged by your subordinates with a thousand interruptions?" Through the interphone a firm could make sure it answered only to demand. Fibrous tendrils of capillary control stretched out, allowing managers to "keep [their] fingers on the whole plant," their staff "within arm's reach."[28]

One of the consequences of invoking this call to a telephonically inflected electrical efficiency was to exchange images of human mediators like messenger boys and central operators for electrical intermediaries like interphones and loudspeakers. Bell's "spirit of service" was replaced with a haunting message of direct auditory efficiency. The result was a radical dehumanization of communicative practice. While figures like the operator would still remain present long into the twentieth century, nonhuman actors increasingly came to supplant their more animated analogues. It was not just the promise of an auditory mode of access, but of a direct, unmediated one. The efficiency of the interphone was, after all, that there was "no operator needed."[29] In a Western Electric office one could reach "every man within earshot" not with "number please" but by "button-touch."[30]

It may not be surprising that the maker of the telephone preached the potential for telephonic efficiency. But the firm had come slowly to this realization. As a nineteenth-century bureaucracy, Western's sense of system had been patterned on paperwork. The company did not telephone its suppliers, nor did it ask its customers to call.[31] Indeed, Western seemed hesitant to employ the telephone as an interface to any of its networks. Toward the latter half of the 1910s, Western's annual "Supply Year Book" became notable for being one of the earliest of its publications to make any sort of reference to

6.2 Western Electric Company advertisements (1916).

taking orders by telephone. But while some editions did (reluctantly) direct readers to "telephone our nearest house," even these instructions still made clear an assumption for business to be conducted by mail order.[32]

Eventually this started to change. It was with the expiration of the original telephone patents in the closing decade of the nineteenth century that Western Electric first began to advertise its telephone offerings alongside its electrical ones. But it wasn't until the 1920s that it fully integrated the device into its marketing strategy. When it did, an auditory idea of efficiency meant that, for the maker of the telephone, there was finally something to say about *speech*. In Western's writing, the telephone's disembodied voice became a spectral projection of intention, an unmediated messenger for the logistical designs of demand. Advertising copy carried the same message the telephone did. "Your voice carries your commands," it declared, "direct to the party at the other end of the wire." This kind of disembodied directness, instantaneity, and, indeed, *efficiency* soon became a familiar refrain. "Your own voice is your best messenger," Western entreated, why bother to "explain your wishes to a messenger boy," when you can "send your voice" instead.[33] So, too, the company learned, could these calls carry the protocols of production from one distant point on the network to another.

6.3 Western Electric advertisement (1914).

While it is noteworthy how few of Western's publications initially afforded the telephone any particular kind of communicative import for the process of assembly, this was not the case outside the company. It had been obvious to purchasing agents and salesmen that, in concert with the catalog, the telephone was a powerful part of an emerging logistical apparatus for the control of consumption. In the 1905 *Book on Selling,* Frank Lomas of the Lomas Hardware Company wrote that, with the "growing use of the telephone in country districts," not only could a regular customer "notify his merchant if goods he has purchased are not what he wished," but "he can send in his order, and have it booked almost as well as though he were there," and subseqently have it sent out by the deliveryman for efficient delivery to his door.[34]

As Western Electric embraced this logistical sensibility, it came to position itself as a kind of universal supplier. Just as Western's warehouses made it a singular source of supply for its customers, the telephone now represented the only efficient connection to them. Unintentionally or not, this precipitated the collapse of the prevailing system of assembly, the logistical efficiencies of telecommunication coming to envelop the whole of distribution. Once lauded as bringing nations together, the telephone would now serve to make manufacturers more distant from them. Indeed, by the 1920s Western no longer saw itself as just an electrical outfit or a telephone manufacturer. Through the connective constitution of the telephone it had become the supplier of suppliers. It was a position the company assumed with remarkable authority.

"If your dealer cannot supply you," Western's publications increasingly emphasized, "we will." Through the auditory efficiencies of the telephone, Western came to imagine itself primarily as a logistics company, one with a reputation as the foremost distributor of electrical technologies and telephonic materials. It was the culmination of a practice that reached back to the turn of the century. As early as 1909, Western had begun to offer twenty-four-hour shipments of "poles, pins, cross-arms, insulators, wires," and other items, "when you want it."[35] While the 1915 "The Making of the Voice Highways" conceded that some of the company's cables would ship "three to four weeks" after receipt, "certain types" could be sent immediately—and more each year.[36] The company had then claimed "thirty distribution houses"; the *Telephone Register* recorded forty-two by 1924, and at the end of the decade, fifty-two. These networked nodes of supply, backed by the company's Hawthorne and Kearny Works, made Western a universal emblem of availability. It could now market itself that way. Notices asked businesses to "make your order book your store house" with "an electrical supply room within easy call." This was the Western Electric Distribution House, a "source of supply" that, through the efficient reach of the telephone, was ready to serve as "your own reserve."[37]

For Western, merging the auditory efficiency of the telephone with the work of managing the supply chain became a way of encapsulating the network of production into a singular point of call—enrolling scores of businesses and agents within a subscription of supply. The potential for industry was profound. Advertisements in the 1925 *Manufacturer's Record* suggested that this held the cure for the "purchasing agent's nightmare." While the agent of an industrial plant may already be a "champion bookworm," even he, Western wrote, "must be appalled by the mass of catalogues and sales literature which confronts him every time he wants to buy something." By offering to search markets "the country over" with "exacting specifications," Western became the center of an electric exchange that could relieve the "burden of buying." For storekeepers, purchasing became as efficient as picking up the phone—supplies "ready at your call."[38] The telephone transformed into an unrivaled technology of design and demand, with the distant sites of directories reconfigured as telephonic storehouses. Activated by auditory impulse, they were limited only by the reach of the wires.

In his 1920 *Economic Consequences of Peace*, John Maynard Keynes considered this new power a contemporary equivalent to Adam Smith's "long sea and long land carriage." For a "man of capacity or character at all exceeding the average," Keynes wrote, life now offered "at a low cost and with the least trouble, conveniences, comforts, and amenities beyond the compass of the richest and most powerful monarchs of other ages." Such a person, he suggested, "could order by telephone, sipping his morning tea in bed, the various products of the whole earth, in such quantity as he might see fit, and reasonably expect their early delivery upon his doorstep."[39] The telephone, after all, could now place its subscribers within earshot of thirty million others, in "more than a score of widely separated lands." It enabled "merchant or manufacturer" alike to send their words "one-third of the way around the world," bringing them "within arm's reach the trade of markets thousands of miles away." How could this not be the very soul of prosperity? The telephone stood at the center of a vast logistical network with ever-widening horizons. It was, Western proclaimed, "the empire of the voice."[40]

From Western's first marketing experiments with the interphone to its proclamation of an all-encompassing auditory empire, the particular idea of efficiency that the firm carried forward had been structured and shaped by the peculiar confines of telephonic speech. Unlike telegraphy, telephony had always tended toward a particular kind of synchronicity in communication. It was awkward to distribute. Had the first telephone call not been a demand? "Mr. Watson—come here—I want to see you." The result, Graham Bell recorded—to his "delight"—had been the ready answer to his request.[41] Telephonic speech demanded an immediacy of listening, of response, that Western now came to align to a particular perception of system and efficiency. In the promise of immediate and seemingly *unmediated* interaction, the auditory efficiencies of the telephone could collapse old measures of distribution and manufacture into the spreading activation of the network. When regional Bells or external clients needed to address some matter of supply, they needed only to speak to Western Electric. "The Western Electric gets it," as the Chicago supply agent H. H. Henry wrote.[42]

Infused with calls to electrical "efficiency" carried forward by the legacy of Western's interpretation of Taylorism, the promise of instantaneity introduced the telephone to patterns of communication previously unmediated by technological means. But this was premised on an even more peculiar proposition: the strange acceptance of listeners that the movement of the telephone, that is to say the movement of the vocal cords and speech entering the receiver, was somehow a kind of nonmovement, the pure efficiency of communication. And in some ways whether this was true hardly mattered. With its promises of geographic and temporal contraction, the telephone's placement as an efficient means for mediative collapse was as real as the marketing could make it.

The imagination of telephonic speech, here, as a different kind of motion—nonmotion from the point of view of practitioners of system—had the effect of off-loading movement throughout the network, distributing it to assembled nodes of supply the world over. Given the scale of modern manufacture, it is banal to suggest that this technique found a receptive audience in the new enterprises of the Global North. In many ways, these signals weren't speech in the conventional sense at all. Even as they absented a certain kind of caller from the human concerns of communication, they could still be heard by individuals removed not only in space but in time—pulses cascading down to the farthest reaches of the supply chain. Through the auditory efficiencies of the telephone came a kind of logistical assembly only possible through the expansion of the productive apparatus to a point where it was no longer visible. The telephone was not only the product of an increasingly unseeable supply chain but the one with the power to produce them. And all that was lost in this new imagination was the image of the network itself. This is, after all, the era of the audit. The supply chain can no longer be seen, so it has to be heard.[43] While the telephone, for Western, may not yet have been explicitly offered as a constituent of this new network of creation, it already figured as both an auditory agent of supply and a communicative technology of demand—divorced from the implications of what either might entail.

Logistical operation requires the elimination of the fractures and friction that come along with geographic space—to render them immaterial, invisible, and inconsequential. Rescaled along global lines, they become "rewoven into increasingly complex spatial configurations."[44] Contemporary logistical software manages these formations through abstract interfaces that govern communication along the supply chain, the factory cities, the distribution channels, all reduced to icons and tables. But the real abstraction is the network itself. Through telephonic connection, the device *became* the network. The floor beneath the manager's office had been made as proximal as any distant supplier, each a number to be operated by voice command. Logistical space is networked space, equivalent and interchangeable. It is founded, as Deborah Cowen has explained, on a "dramatic recasting of the relationship between making and moving."[45] But it is really an auditory assembly. As such, it is making *without* moving.

The digital devices of logistical listening promise precisely such an assembly. One where packages appear on doorsteps, cars arrive in an instant, and apartments clean themselves. As the world looks expectantly to the handmaidens of what may prove a new age of auditory efficiency, one must be cautious of the designs of their demands. Just as the calls of an emerging industry of electrical operation brought a new, and largely unknowable, network into being, one must wonder of the inevitable and unpredictable productions that might now be birthed. The logistical distribution of a new class of workers, not littered to the geographically distant peripheries of global capital, but living in its midst—stand ready for the call. Siri, build me a supply chain.

NOTES

1. Anna Tsing, "Supply Chains and the Human Condition," *Rethinking Marxism* 21, no. 2 (2009): 148–76.

2. Lewis Mumford, *The City in History* (New York: Harcourt, 1961), 539.

3. Niccolò Cuppini, Mattia Frapporti, Floriano Milesi, Luca Padova, and Maurilio Pirone, "Logistics and Crisis: The Supply Chain System in the Po Valley Region," Teaching the Crisis: Geographies, Methodologies, Perspectives, 2013, accessed January 13, 2021, http://teachingthecrisis.net/logistics-and-crisis-the-supply-chain-system-in-the-po-valley-region-2/index.html.

4. Paul Virilio, *War and Cinema: The Logistics of Perception*, translated by Patrick Camiller (London: Verso, 1989), 74–75.

5. Benjamin Bratton, "Introduction: Logistics of Habitable Circulation," in Paul Virilio, *Speed and Politics*, trans. Mark Polizzotti (Los Angeles: Semiotext(e), 2006 [1977]), 7–25, 12.

6. Jenna Wortham, "A Personal Assistant on Your iPhone," *New York Times*, February 5, 2010; and Dylan Tweney, "Siri Launches Voice-Powered iPhone 'Assistant,'" *Wired*, February 5, 2010.

7. Harrington Emerson, *Efficiency as a Basis for Operation and Wages* (New York: Engineering Magazine, 1909), 5–6, 15.

8. Frederick Taylor, *The Principles of Scientific Management* (New York: Harper and Row, 1911), 5, 140; Frederick Taylor, *Scientific Management* (Westport, CT: Greenwood, 1972 [1947]); and Frederick Taylor, *Shop Management* (New York: Harper and Row, 1911).

9. Herbert Casson, "The Story of Emerson, High Priest of the New Science of Efficiency," *American Review of Reviews* 48, no. 3 (1913): 305–15.

10. Taylor, *Principles of Scientific Management*, 12.

11. Alfred Marshall, *Elements of Economics* (London: Macmillan, 1899), 260.

12. "How to Do It, and How Not to Do It," *Scientific American Supplement* 4, no. 88 (1877): 1400; and W. H. Booth, "Transactions of the Inefficient Club," *American Machinist*, October 12, 1911, 679–82.

13. Herbert Collins, "Radium Rays from the Sales Manager," *System* 8, no. 1 (1905): 10–11.

14. Taylor, *Principles of Scientific Management*, 5, 140.

15. J. A. Gilkerson, "Letter on the Foreman," *American Machinist*, July 9, 1891, 6.

16. Casson, "The Story of Emerson," 305–6.

17. Gilkerson, "Letter on the Foreman."

18. "Increasing Efficiency of Men and Machines," *System* 7, no. 4 (March 1905): 329.

19. Western Electric, "My Electric Home," 1915, and "Are You Giving Your Wife a Square Deal?," 1917, N. W. Ayer Collection, National Museum of American History (NMAH); F. X. Cleary, "Selling to the Rural Districts," *Printer's Ink* 70, no. 8 (February 23, 1910): 11.

20. Western Electric, "Electricity: The Twentieth Century Servant," 1915, and "Why Have Two Standards of Efficiency?," 1916, N. W. Ayer Collection, NMAH.

21. George David Smith, *The Anatomy of a Business Strategy: Bell, Western Electric, and the Origins of the American Telephone Industry* (Baltimore: Johns Hopkins University Press, 1985).

22. See F. J. Roethlisberger and William J. Dickson, *Management and the Worker* (Cambridge, MA: Harvard University Press, 1939); and Richard Gillespie, *Manufacturing Knowledge: A History of the Hawthorne Experiments* (Cambridge: Cambridge University Press, 1993).

23. An advertisement in 1909, for example, addressed piece-work payment schemes. Western Electric, "Put Your Power on 'Piece-Work,'" 1909, N. W. Ayer Collection, NMAH.

24. Western Electric, Inter-phones Series, 1911, N. W. Ayer Collection, NMAH.

25. Western Electric, "Quick Inter-communication," Inter-phones Series, 1915, and "Why Go Yourself When You Can Telephone," Rural Telephone Series, 1910, N. W. Ayer Collection, NMAH.

26. Henry Thayer, who had been president of Western Electric since 1909, reflected on this development in "The Western Electric Company and Its Relation to the Bell System," *Bell Telephone News* 6, no. 3 (1916): 5–8.

27. Western Electric, "Wasted Steps Are Wasted Dollars" and "If Your Floors Could Show the Steps You Waste," Inter-phones Series, 1916, N. W. Ayer Collection, NMAH. Perhaps the earliest example is AT&T's "Save Time and Steps," 1910, N. W. Ayer Collection, NMAH.

28. Western Electric, "Is Your Organization Running You?," Inter-phones Series, 1916, N. W. Ayer Collection, NMAH. This was later recalled in "Your Whole Staff at Arms' Length," 1924, and "Keep Your Fingers on the Whole Plant," 1925, N. W. Ayer Collection, NMAH.

29. Western Electric, "Factory Supervision from Private Office," Inter-phones Series, 1911, N. W. Ayer Collection, NMAH.

30. Western Electric, "Every Man within Earshot," Inter-phones Series, 1914, N. W. Ayer Collection, NMAH.

31. Perhaps Western Electric's reticence owes something to Bell's longstanding anxiety that subscribers remained uncomfortable with the device. See Elinor Carmi, "Taming Noisy Women," *Media History* 21, no. 3 (2015): 313–27.

32. Western Electric, *Supply Year Book* (New York: Western Electric Company, 1916).

33. Western Electric, "Quick Inter-communication," Inter-phones Series, 1915; "Call Your Foreman with Western Electric Inter-phones," Inter-phones Series, 1912; and "Why Go Yourself When You Can Telephone," Rural Telephone Series, 1910—all N. W. Ayer Collection, NMAH.

34. Frank Lomas, "How the Country Merchant Meets the Competition of the Catalogue House," in *The Book on Selling: The Business Man's Library*, vol. 4 (New York: System Company, 1905).

35. Western Electric, "Western Electric Service," "Line Construction Material," and "24-Hour Shipments," 1909, N. W. Ayer Collection, NMAH.

36. Western Electric, "The Making of the Voice Highways," 1915, Trade Literature Collection, NMAH.

37. Western Electric, "Locked!" and "Make Your Order Book Your Store House," 1924, Trade Literature Collection, NMAH. And later, "Some Lamp Storerooms You Didn't Know You Had," 1929, Trade Literature Collection, NMAH.

38. Western Electric, "Purchasing Agent's Nightmare—And How to Cure It," 1925, Trade Literature Collection, NMAH.

39. John Maynard Keynes, "Europe before the War," in *Economic Consequences of Peace* (New York: Harcourt, Brace and Howe, 1920), 9–26, 11–12.

40. AT&T, "Telephone Almanac," 1930, AT&T Archives.

41. Alexander Graham Bell, Laboratory Notebook, 1875–76 (March 10, 1876).

42. H. H. Henry, "The Work of the Supply Department," *Bell Telephone News* 2, no. 7 (1913): 6–7.

43. See Shannon Mattern, "The Pulse of Global Passage: Listening to Logistics," this volume.

44. Charmaine Chua, Martin Danyluk, Deborah Cowen, and Laleh Khalili, "Introduction: Turbulent Circulation: Building a Critical Engagement with Logistics," *Environment and Planning D: Society and Space* 36, no. 4 (2018): 617–29, 621.

45. Deborah Cowen, *The Deadly Life of Logistics: Mapping Violence in Global Trade* (Minneapolis: University of Minnesota Press, 2014), 103.

LOGISTICAL SOFTWARE

Software began in supply chain management, when paper parts and paper products became bound up in punched cards and magnetic tape after World War II. Richard Lilly, who was responsible for IBM's production and inventory control system (PICS), recalls that, at first, it was just *system*—"there was no software at all." When computational control of production arrived in 1961, it did so in an already familiar logistical form: the bill of material processor (BOMP), developed by IBM programmer Gene Thomas. This was the foundation of the more comprehensive package IBM released five years later. When five former IBM employees left in 1971 to start SAP (Systeme, Anwendungen, und Produkte, or Systems, Applications, and Products), they took this legacy to the design of their R-series enterprise resource planning system.

SAP is the software system used for the design and coordination of most of the world's supply chains. Replacing warehouses and workers with screens of icons and tables, checkboxes and pop-up windows, its view of the supply chain is almost entirely abstract. As it spreads production across a vast array of software components, it allows users to manage ordering, manufacturing, packing, and shipping as they schedule work shifts and product movements in intervals as small as a second. Compiling past performance against future projections, blurring production and distribution, these opaque and dense acronyms—BOMP, PICS, ERP, SAP—name the genealogy of the hidden algorithms that orchestrate workers' lives the world over.

Screenshot of SAP Transportation Management 9.4 ("Transportation Cockpit") (2016).

7

Logistical Media Theory, the Politics of Time, and the Geopolitics of Automation

Provincial Media Theory

Like all theory, media theory is troubled by its provincialism, even if it struggles to take note of this common condition. As many readers may recall, Martin Heidegger famously refused a professorial chair in Berlin, instead preferring to stay in the provinces.[1] While the negative attributes of repressive culture, neurotic personas, and social intolerance are readily piled on the experience of provincial life, there nonetheless remains something positive to be said about provincialism: it can provide conditions for the crafting of unique concepts that, when combined with deep historical knowledge, generate a legacy that spans generations. But what happens when ontological conditions change from the security of the earth to the technical contours of media systems? How might such a transition from governance of the self and community to technical architectures of biopolitical control also register an epochal shift of geopolitical proportions as automation increasingly takes command?

Such questions speak to contemporary technological conditions, prompting an exploration of concepts immanent to or coextensive with media situations of patterns and prediction, complexity and control, contingency and failure.

Wherever social life manifests in the world, the specter of provincialism appears as a potential organizing condition and institutional horizon with epistemological implications for disciplinary formation, including media theory. Provincial thought all too often functions as an impasse to engaging contemporary media-infrastructural forces and modes of practice that shape the lives of many.

To foreground the provincial as a limit horizon for media-theoretical analyses of power is not to make a distinction between the provincial and some variant of neoliberal globality. We are always-already provincial. This is our situation. Provincialization is a historical process that afflicts both centers and margins of empire.[2] Indeed, the effects of provincialization on modes of thought may be more profound in spaces that assume the status of center—a structural position or worldview almost always at variance with the cosmopolitanism of strangers. For media theory, the provincializing effect is at once disciplinary and institutional, just as it is geocultural. We could also add that the provincialization of media-theoretical idioms is technical and historical. Software updates build on and inherit the faulty design of legacy architectures. So does media theory, tinkering at times in different institutional, social, and cultural settings that may register, with a degree of delay, as a school of thought. The Kittler School, The Annenberg School, The New School. 4chan becomes 8chan. And then relaunches as 8kun.

Critically attending to the materialities that define the media situation quickly makes apparent the complication of importing conceptual imaginaries and theoretical tropes that may have accumulated kudos and gained admirers in part due to the economies of publishing and social desire for celebrity scholars who spawn individual and collective neuronal stimulation. The provincializing effect of the knowledge industries concocts asymmetrical forms of reception and circuits of distribution. Dominant knowledge is decoupled from the materialities of the media situation. The trick is to collectively design transversal relations and technical architectures that stitch provinces together in ways that unsettle social-technical regimes of perception and knowledge production. Cohesion is but a gesture, albeit one that is ratified by the political economy of scale and institutional cultures of consent. Concepts have a limited reach. Philosophy, for instance, rarely generates new concepts these days and more often than not functions to police thought and restrict invention, preferring instead to trawl over the fortified remains of received ideas.

Alert to the intersection between geopolitics and geoculture, and cognizant of computational infrastructures such as data centers and smart grids that generate new sovereign forms, this essay assumes neither the nation-state nor planetary-scale digital platforms ("stacks") as the primary configurations of governance specific to the automation of economy and society.[3] In approaching the problematic of contemporary geopolitics, I set out the case in this essay for practices of method and analytical techniques that start with the media question, which so often nowadays is also an infrastructural question. First and foremost, the media question is alert to the material tendencies and properties of technological forms and their cybernetic systems. As such, the media question is attuned to the environment of technological operations.[4] Devising a media-theoretical approach to address historical and contemporary conditions is therefore antithetical to template theory if one wishes to engage and encounter the world, which is a world fractured by multiple lines of crises that cross ecology and society, economy and politics. Template theory is something like the compulsion to take canonical views and reapply them across conditions and situations regardless of the nuances of phenomena and field of forces. While our historical condition is not entirely new in all aspects, there is a sense of singularity at the current conjuncture that, if nothing else, invites us to revisit ideas of what theory is, what it can do, and what its response to the world might be. In devising a critical theory of our times, we need media-theoretical approaches alive to the dynamics of the world made technical—approaches that are alert to epistemology and history, but not reducible to them.

Within systems of algorithmic governance, epistemology has become subsumed into techniques of policing society. But the calculus of power is never total. Submission is not the only option. The production of concepts derived from the operational logic of platform architectures can provide explanatory models of the empirical world. Forms of counter-knowledge to algorithmic power can, for example, be produced by reverse engineering or modelling computational operations that exert pressure on performance regimes endured by labor.[5] Media theory need not be obliged or beholden to the ethnographic methods of science and technology studies and cognate fields since it is through the question and instantiation of power that logistical media theory can make intelligible the variational conditions of automated worlds. To the extent that standards enable the technical and organizational interoperability of communication protocols, the capacity for technologies of automation to extend their geopolitical command of territory is challenged by the advent of competing hegemons, as evident in the competition between Chinese and US firms to develop artificial intelligence and machine learning services, which are central to major shifts in automation driven by data extraction, accumulation, and analysis. How these technological developments then play out within specific settings, such as Amazon or Alibaba fulfillment centers in Kuala Lumpur, Brieselang, Grolsheim, or Sydney, adds to the uneven and unforeseen ways in which power is forged from and against the contingencies of labor dispute, technical inoperability, infrastructural failure, supply chain mishaps, environmental intrusion, and the like.

To advance critical inquiry into computational conditions that organize economy and society, politics and subjectivity, requires a study of how power is generated within and by digital infrastructures, systems, operations, and practices. The objective here is to establish empirical coordinates that provide an analytical basis for populating disciplines in the humanities and social sciences, and possibly elsewhere, with a conceptual vocabulary coextensive with contemporary technological conditions. The operational logic of digital communication technology can furnish concepts of power able to describe and explain emergent geopolitical forces. Logistics is geopolitical because it requires new frontiers of extraction. Time is one of the primary frontiers operative within logistical media of communication, control, and coordination. The phantasm of real time is pervasive across the logistical industries, and indeed, the extraction of value from supply chain systems and labor regimes is time-critical. Yet the actual synchronization of real time necessarily evades digital networks of communication since the relationship between time and value is made possible by temporal differences specific to the technics of logistical media.[6] A temporal interval inherent to the operational logic of the digital unsettles the politics of decision. Distributed across networks of supply and demand, the seriality of the interval as technically differentiated time conditions the space of politics. As Bernhard Siegert notes, "Once we read the synchronic segments diachronically, time appears as a function of space."[7] Advancing a critical geopolitical account of automation, this essay explores the political potential of the interval as a concept immanent to the operation of logistical media.

The Geopolitics and Chronopolitics of Media

Data sets define our situation. Such a post-Kittlerian dictum speaks to the massive accumulation of data required to train software to respond to variables within controlled environments. Data on legislation related to driving law within any particular province or state, for instance, fulfill just one category in the parameters of operation necessary for the production of autonomous vehicles. The programming of contingency as it relates to unforeseen objects launching unexpectedly in front of a moving car is again specific to cultural situations. Children, elderly people, a jogger, dogs, balls, or any other object or thing moving in ways that could produce an accident are going to vary according to cultural and social habits. The rule-bound tendencies of urban populations in western and northern Europe are dramatically different from the behavior of pedestrians on the busy streets of Rome, let alone somewhere like Kolkata or Jakarta. The situation, in other words, has become the test bed for a world not easily translatable.

Optimization, control, metrics, dashboards, prediction, preemption, tasks, lists, ranking, transaction, raw data, autonomy, adaptivity, statistical induction, replication. These are some of the many typologies, categories, actions, routines, and processes from which to compile a logistical media theory immanent to the technics of artificial intelligence and machine learning. The coordinates and contours of a media theory attentive to technologies of automation, for example, need to discern how a geocultural encoding within software engineering indexes an optic onto the geopolitics of the tech industry. Whether it is Salesforce, a customer relationship management platform, or Elon Musk's investment in autonomous cars, the parameters of operation coded into these systems are informed by the cultures from which they emerge.[8] But the traffic here is by no means one-way. Parameters and protocols also generate cultural forms, practices, problems, and modes of expression. Witness, for instance, the currency of terms like *algorithmic cultures*, *software cultures*, and *network cultures* to identify and describe the ways in which culture is always-already technical and, nowadays, computational. The cybernetic process of feedback and contingency makes situations distinct. Variabilities that compose communication systems will exert capacities that produce conflicts and struggles within specific media-cultural arrangements.

Automated customer service technologies and process management systems from companies such as Tencent and Alibaba hold default cultural settings that are not equivalent to the platform capitalism stemming from Silicon Valley. To take just one example, the business models of tech firms such as Amazon and Alibaba manifest in substantively different ways with regard to the structure and management of warehousing facilities, which are effectively test beds for machine learning systems. Amazon invests substantially in infrastructure, including construction of its own warehouses, while Alibaba's development of third-party digital platforms mirrors its preference to establish partnerships with existing companies in the logistics and warehousing industry. Such differences can be understood, in part, as cultural variations of similar material forms, namely, the warehouse.[9] The ways in which material, infrastructural forms that share a similar typology then populate the world has territorial implications. When territory is understood in technological terms, the warehousing software operations of Amazon and Alibaba index a geopolitical dimension to their business practices.

In short, the geopolitics of data economies signals an emergent contest of territoriality that unsettles post–World War II geopolitical world orders defined by the legacies of colonialism, intergovernmental treaties and trade agreements, legal regimes, and supranational organizations such as the World Trade Organization, the World Bank, the Association of Southeast Asian Nations, and the like. The rise of China over the past decade as a world hegemon, manifest in transcontinental infrastructural projects such as the Belt and Road Initiative, provides one key to an emergent geopolitical remaking of territory. The development of software systems as logistical media designed to manage activity and govern the movement of people, finance, and commodities in tandem with supply chain infrastructures offers another point of entry into a study of the relation between technical systems, territorial arrangements, and geopolitical configurations. Such an investigation would include an analysis of the role of standards and protocols, which are central to the efforts of firms especially, in maximizing the potential for interoperability across operations whose spatial relations are orchestrated by economic interests channeled through the nexus of software and infrastructure.

Here one might take note of two Chinese government policy initiatives, "Made in China 2025" and the "New Generation Artificial Intelligence Development Plan."[10] These strategic plans on artificial intelligence and machine learning lend an optic onto the contours of geopolitics through infrastructure. Oscillating between exuberant business and tech media reports on a thriving start-up sector and the ominous rise of state-endorsed surveillance programs, China is engaged in a political economic tussle with the United States to expand its geopolitical power, modulated through algorithmic architectures and digital infrastructures. With a massive digitally connected population at hand to generate the volume of data required to fuel the training of machine learning systems, China's State Council is poised to become "the premier global AI innovation center" by 2030.[11] The transfer of intelligence from the human mind to the logistical state registers the geopolitical status of media as a technology of governance in the management of economy and society.

Within an Innisian framework, the "territorial state" of ancient civilizations and their empires was predisposed toward a spatial or temporal bias as a result of the material properties of prevailing transport systems and communication technologies.[12] And this made civilizations and empires vulnerable to external forces able to exploit such infrastructural oversight or limits to capacity. The logistical state, by contrast, encompasses both dimensions simultaneously. The global networks of supply chains expand the territorial reach of producers and suppliers required for the operation of the logistical state. Enterprise resource planning (ERP) software systems calibrate labor productivity and coordinate the movement of goods and finance in an approximation of real time, and data centers store, process, and transmit the data integral to logistical operations governed by computational systems. These are the infrastructural components that generate the possibility of imperial rule for the logistical state. Importantly, the spatial and temporal dimensions described here are not synchronic or spatial equivalents. Time and space are peculiar to each, forming layers or, more likely, a complex undulation of planes that overlap and intersect on some occasions while colliding and disconnecting on others.[13]

Media are geopolitical because they extend over space. And they are also chronopolitical because they produce the rhythms and pulses of economy, labor, and life. The allusion to the writings of urban theorist Paul Virilio on "dromology" (the "science" of speed) is no accident here, although I invoke the term quite differently.[14] Virilio's chronopolitics of speed and acceleration of history exceeding the human capacity to govern space may be offset against another theorist of time and technology, namely, German media archaeologist Wolfgang Ernst and his organizing concept of chronopoetics.[15] Where Ernst offers a micro-description of the temporal properties of media forms that impact on perception and epistemology, Virilio diagnoses how the acceleration of time wrought by technological intensification in effect decimates the assertion of human life to self-govern.

In *Polar Inertia*, Virilio registers the triumph of "real time" over "real space."[16] With such terms of reference, we may consider Virilio as the first theorist of logistical media, even if nineteenth-century colonial technologies such as telegraphy inaugurated the social-technical experience and perception of time eclipsing space. Whether it is the exertion of labor, the outputs of manufacturing processes, the packing of inventory, the distribution and delivery of goods, the management of workplaces, the monitoring of air particles, the anticipation of accidents, or the preemption of crime—all are instantiations of contemporary logistical media where the *chronos* of calculation is calibrated by digital media of real time. Virilio was perhaps too hasty in prioritizing the temporal dimension of media and communication technologies when, indeed, the political-poetic beauty and horror of logistical media lie in their capacity to command space and time simultaneously.

Logistical media depart from Harold Innis's concern that all communication media are prone to either a spatial or a temporal bias.[17] Logistical media approximate real time and may be regarded, historically, as the first media of quasi equilibrium. Both spatial and temporal dimensions of logistical media jostle for primacy in the shadow of interoperability. However, like economic theory that supposes an optimum balance in supply and demand will result in a general equilibrium of market forces and "perfect competition," projecting a condition of equilibrium or balance onto logistical media only holds to the extent that the phantasm of an interoperable model of real time excludes dissonance and the far-from-equilibrium forces or disequilibrium operating within any system. As Niklas Luhmann notes, the metaphor of a "balance of trade" took root in the seventeenth century, and "by the end of that century it also motivated the idea of an international, specifically European, balance of power between nations (or political factors)."[18] Inherently provincial in cosmopolitical outlook, the equilibrium assumed by classical economics as a possible stabilizing mechanism or condition of behavior in markets and geopolitical relations between nation-states is underscored by disturbance. Luhmann points out that "imbalance or disequilibrium might function as a condition of stability."[19] Jeremy Walker and Melinda Cooper reverse this assessment in their account of the influence of ecologist Crawford S. Holling on neoliberal approaches to financial, environmental, and security crises: "the long-term expectation of stability may be inherently destabilizing."[20] Given the partiality of knowledge and uncertainty of forecasting technologies, which include automated techniques of preemption and prediction, a necessary condition of disequilibrium is the force of the constitutive outside. A world exists external to techno-economic operations. The organization of space and time is not reducible to relations of cause and effect, inputs and outputs.[21] As I discuss below, the temporality of the interval internal to the operation of the digital is pregnant with that which evades capture in the binary switch between zeros and ones.[22] Within this slither of time subsists a universe of possibility from which a politics of time may emanate as "a competition or struggle between . . . different forms of temporalization."[23]

The idea of logistical media as a system of relative equilibrium does not result in a balanced society, as Innis supposed, with power and control kept in check. Rather, across any number of reports and academic studies we find an increasing disparity in the distribution of economic wealth and a widening gulf across the class spectrum between the wealthy and the rest.[24] The political economy of automation technologies and the monopoly effects of platform economies produce further divides in the form of highly uneven access to and distribution of data that drive machine learning systems, despite the often prevalent ideologies of openness. These forms of division in economy, society, and data are obtained through seemingly conflictual modes of organization: the centralization of planned economies as distinct from data scattered across network architectures and digital infrastructures. Common to the multiplication of organization and distribution is the consolidation and entrenchment of division.

Paradoxically, the quasi equilibrium of logistical media generates an intensification of disequilibrium in Virilio's sense of human disorientation and the surrender of decision. Pure chronopolitics is the complete annihilation of time, a temporality with no past, present, or future—time as the pulsation of sensation amplified to serve capital's appetite of synchronic extraction. This is the end point of logistical ambition: the instantaneity of capital accumulation unshackled from the externality of the interval.[25] The temporality of the interval restores to logistical media the property of bias. With the interruption of time offered by the logic of the interval, media again become a scene of contestation and power made manifest.

Spatial Scales and Technical Regimes

Set against the predicament of provinciality, the transcontinental perspective I adopt across a number of collective research projects foregrounds the variational ways in which digital technologies of control and *inter*operability are troubled and disrupted by social-technical instantiations of *in*operability.[26] Systems, in other words, are always prone to breaking down. Networking, as Geert Lovink reminds us, is also about notworking.[27] Such forms of unsettling regimes of power manifest in many ways. Take, for example, peasant communities in the new IT town and smart city of Rajarhat on the outskirts of Kolkata who engage in willful acts of infrastructural sabotage in response to the violence of dispossession wrought by the West Bengal government's invocation of a colonial administrative remnant, the Land Acquisition Act of 1894. In tandem with changes to this Act in 2013 and the Special Economic Zone Act of 2005, the government was able legally to conjure a zoning technology for Rajarhat designed to attract foreign capital to finance the transformation of fertile agricultural land and fisheries into non-agricultural use.[28] Peasant populations numbering in the tens of thousands experienced economic and social displacement as a result of this process of "primitive accumulation," or what David Harvey prefers instead to term "accumulation by dispossession."[29] In the case of Rajarhat, the expropriation of land and the partial remobilization of peasant labor forced into "service villages" are the conditions of possibility for the logistical city and its data economy. Infrastructural sabotage of roads and fiber-optic cables is one way of thinking the constitutive outside that attends the media-infrastructural transformation currently underway across many sites in the world.

In the case of electronic waste industries in China we see a quite different form in which "supply chain capitalism," to invoke a term by anthropologist Anna Tsing, is confronted with the limits of protocological totality.[30] The logistical software architectures that feature in shipping industries, warehousing, and distribution centers are also operative within supply chains that shift toxic infrastructural and technological waste around the planet. However, there is a strong informal sector at work in the collection and dismantling of discarded, decommissioned electronic devices. This informal sector does not use the hugely expensive, technically complicated, and frequently bug-prone enterprise resource planning software such as that produced by SAP and Oracle. Rather, the often-illegal e-waste industry maintains its networks using everyday software preinstalled in computers or easy to download—MSN, Skype, Weibo, and so forth. Or at least that's how the informal sectors in the e-waste industries were working in Zhejiang around ten years ago.[31]

My point is that the universe of software in the informal sector presents a protocological incompatibility or border with high-end ERP software. This means that the logistical world driven by an impulse to make everything accountable, calculable, and transparent is confronted with a constitutive outside not figuring within the technical operation of the interval—secondary economies of waste that, due to protocological disjunctures and platform silos, are not registering within meta-level technologies of control despite their inclusion within a larger ecology and economy of waste. Wherever it subsides, waste carries a potential value, as evidenced in the mass accumulation of data made valuable again by analytics, machine learning, and so forth. The constitutive outside also generates a special form of subjectivity: the production of what I call nongovernable subjects, which is an interesting proposition in a country like China where, as we repeatedly hear, there is a massive rise in investment and research and development in artificial intelligence and facial recognition technologies.

Recent governmental technologies like Alibaba's Sesame Credit system and the platform variations that make everything and everyone visible and financialized within a control paradigm of preemption and prediction are hardly exclusive to China. Such technologies are being rolled out across the world. It's important to note that while Anglophone news media report on China's facial recognition technologies and social credit systems of Tencent and Alibaba as if they were totalizing technical regimes, there is considerable variation in platform architectures and their techniques of capture across and beyond the provincial spaces of the nation.

The extent to which these data extraction and aggregation platforms step into the world with such power is indicative of the erosion of trust and amplification of despair and depression following decades of social upheaval wrought by structural and economic transformation. Computational systems and technical architectures may address the problem of trust in transactional ways that scale. However, despair and depression tend not to respond well to "solutions." If the production of subjectivity is key to processes of capital accumulation, is there a temporal regime that is also specific to processes of subjectivation? Since the production of subjectivity intersects with the technics of production, this is also a question of time and technology. In short, what is the time of digital media? And can the temporality of digital media hold implications for geopolitical formations? Operations of digital media have both temporalized attributes and temporalizing capacities. They interact cybernetically with environments, but they also create new temporal orders, producing a politics of time.

Decisionism and the Interval

In some ways the media question has become more uncertain than ever. If media were once supposed to have an organizing, transformative power to produce effects, giving rise to the academic discipline of "media studies," nowadays the nexus between media power and disciplinary borders is less certain. Yet the battle persists over who owns the infrastructure and data of communication, who designs and controls the standards and protocols, and who determines the right to be heard. These are among the core features that continue to define the media question. Media theory seems eclipsed by the ubiquity of its objects. As technologies of mediation increasingly find their way into societies of sensation and economies of calibration, the monopoly of knowledge hitherto enjoyed by the discipline of media and communications is now harangued in a world where everyone is an expert. Within the academy, many disciplines claim the authority to speak about digital technologies—mathematicians, urban planners, engineers, biologists, health scientists, sociologists, and architects, to name just a few.

Across society at large we are all invited to comment and find it increasingly difficult to extricate ourselves from the pressure to connect. Yet a crystallization of thought often enough emerges from moments of crisis—if that is indeed the current situation of media theory. While many of us identify with transdisciplinary methods or embrace forms of disciplinary promiscuity, there remains a distinction of media theory within environments governed by digital objects. As media approach a universal condition of integration with labor and life, the organic and inorganic, the question of power becomes amplified. Media theory asserts its ontological and epistemological dimensions when a curiosity in the material properties and tendencies of communications media is coupled with a critical interrogation of the operation of power.

If calculation machines have displaced representational regimes, then the ontological properties of media become secondary to the procedural routines of sorting, classifying, correlation, pattern recognition, prediction, and preemptive action. If power is understood as immanent to processes of subjectivation and technics of governance, then the production, distribution, and force of power are similarly internal to these more epistemological procedures as distinct from the ontological properties of media. But it is a mode of power whose limit is defined by the interval.

As much as systems of classification aspire to totality, their logic is haunted by the intervention of the fissure that distinguishes one category from the next. Within ecological conservation professions this problem is referred to as the taxonomic impediment in which insufficient information and knowledge of planetary biodiversity can be overcome by additional training of taxonomists and museum curators. Certainly this is one way to formulate a discourse to make claims on funding for the future of particular professions. But it does not address the epistemological void and political potential that subsists in the interval between zeros and ones, which is also the mathematical foundation of the digital and the basic architecture on which computational procedures are built.

The concept of the interval can thus be understood as a space of pure contingency and unintelligibility or incommensurability: the interval comprises that which evades the power of decisionism but is nonetheless subject to it. In contrast to the "discrete points" of the digital—the *decisionism* of the digital, if you will—the world of the analog is defined by "continuous variation."[32] In defining the relation between the digital and the logic of division, Alexander Galloway writes: "As the one dividing in two, the digital describes processes of distinction or decision. Both distinction and decision involve the separation of a formerly indistinguishable mass into separate lumps. To decide means to choose, but it also means that the choice has been rendered into discrete paths that may be chosen."[33] This illusion of freedom instantiates the engineering constraints that define the situation of media.

When such a notion of decision "motivated" by the digital is extended to a consideration of Carl Schmitt's notion of decisionism, the power to decide inflects the operation of the digital as an assertion of sovereign media.[34] While for François Laruelle, in Galloway's account, the event of the decision is "a kind of *static preemption*,"[35] which we might understand in Schmittian terms as a potency of suspension not yet cleaved to material transformation (politics of action), the decisionism of the digital nonetheless is also setting futurity in motion insofar as the parameters of the decision always-already assume and, importantly, reveal a contour of possibility. In other words, a prehistory attends the event of static preemption. Concretely, one might point to the ways in which engineers program into the functionality of software systems algorithmic routines that have already defined the set of permutations possible in the course of finite combinations and computational processes. The technical a priori or preemptive logic of computational decision is internally coherent to the extent that it precludes the disruptive force of the outside.[36] The outside to decision is contingency: the crash, the virus, protocological inoperability across platforms, and any number of material perturbations (labor strikes, climatic interference, infrastructural sabotage, failure, etc.).

In digital facilities such as data centers, low latency is the optimal economy of time. To be sure, low latency is not equivalent to real time. In the case of high-frequency trading, low latency is key to the time required to switch packets of data containing information on financial derivatives or to algorithmically analyze stock options and market performance. Indeed, as Florian Sprenger argues in his long-form essay on the politics of micro-decisions and communication networks, real-time information is "technically impossible to attain."[37] Through an extended reading of Paul Baran's technical paper "On Distributed Communication Networks" (1964),[38] Sprenger retrieves the political and epistemological significance of interrupted time that arises from "bursts of information" that define the transmission of data divided into packets and switched from node to node across network architectures. The micro-decisions made by computational systems in the process of switching packets of data are never instantaneous but rather "in time," creating a human perception and experience of simultaneity or "real time" in the traffic of information.[39]

Of the many riveting insights developed across Sprenger's essay, perhaps none is more significant for network politics than his identification of technical interruptions that accompany decision-making processes specific to the operation of digital networks.[40] Interruption can also be understood as a form of temporal interlude or interval manifest in the switching of packets. When interruption conditions the possibility of decision by machines, a form of vulnerability is inherent to sovereign power migrated from the subject to data-processing systems and digital infrastructures. In network architectures, control proceeds on the basis of interruption that defines the instantiation of decision, as packets of data switch at nodes in the system. Such is the internal limit, as noted, to the decisionism of the digital. Unlike Schmitt's conception of sovereignty as the power of the state to assert a legitimate right to decide the exception, within network architectures, decision exceeds the sovereign state: the act of control is a technical operation predicated on interruption, or what I have defined in this essay as the digital logic of the interval. Paradoxically, the sovereign act of technical decision is necessarily interrupted. At this moment the interval conditions the passage of decision.

Politics of the Nondigital

It is tempting to attribute to the analog the verdancy of materiality in all its splendor. Yet we know all too well the materiality of the digital: from the monocrystalline silicon substrate of printed circuit boards to the architectural form of data centers stuffed with server racks, from the copper alloy of coaxial cable to the bodies in pain that mine elemental metals such as copper from the Chilean mountains.[41] As a technological object and electronic system, the digital is both produced and conditioned by multiple variants of the material world. Needless to say, at an operational level the digital is constitutive of habits and routines across a panoply of institutional settings, urban systems, and industrial sectors to the extent that what at first glance might appear as nondigital—the work of teaching and administration in universities, preparing meals in a commercial kitchen, or driving long-haul trucks across the Nullarbor Plain that stretches from the east to west coasts of Australia—is in fact intimately tied to and can be read back against the digital.

The material world, in other words, is losing sight of itself. Which is not to say that it vanishes so much as persists in ways beyond registration and external to the calibration machines of the digital. Outside the calculated emptiness of the interval blossoms the triumph of material worlds not yet surrendered to the command of the digital. The earth's tectonic plates continue to punctuate the surface of the planet with fault lines, volcanoes, and earthquakes. The celestial motion of stars, comets, and planets negotiate gravitational forces. The moon tugs away on oceans and rivers. The worm makes its way through crevices in the sand. These are forms of materiality not touched in substantive ways by the digital, if at all. As ubiquitous as digital media and computational operations are in daily life and economy, their reach is not total. Needless to say, the extension of the digital is sufficient enough to attract critical attention. That is obvious.

In the society of metrics, neopositivism assumes authority within the disciplinary context of both the university and organizations such as government departments, think tanks, nongovernmental organizations, lobby groups, and service companies tasked with the production of knowledge. Paradoxically, one task for a media theory of the digital is to pursue thought and practice that is nondigital.[42] This amounts to a politics as well, a politics that contests the digital decisionism of calculation and code, synthesis and connection, procedure and preemption. When decision is dependent on the numeric, the technics of interruption assures the orientation of data by the activation of the TCP/IP protocol in the instance of packet switching. At a functional level this form of interruption is not an act of revenge immanent to the logic of the digital. But subsisting in the interruption is an interval that enunciates the nondigital component of digital operations. The micro-temporality of the interval signals the externality of the digital.

A media theory of the digital explores the properties of media to devise an aesthetics of disappearance in the society of tracking. The generation of social-technical systems of nonstandardization and indeterminacy amounts to a politics of secrecy and nontransparency alive to contingency and the incomputable.[43] The political question of how to stage and make operational an "aesthetics of disappearance" would turn back, precisely, to the digital logic of the interval. An aesthetics of disappearance consists of media, because they are ubiquitous; the digital, because its binary decisions don't register the materiality of the interval; and the material, because the interval evades total accountancy by the digital. Within an aesthetics of disappearance, or what we might now call the materialities of digital media, time accumulates, no matter the micro-temporality of the interval within computational systems whose operationality requires machine decision. Time outside extraction technologies is time that pulsates to rhythms, time that has not been captured by chronopolitics in Virilio's understanding of that term. The heartbeat of an insurgent geopolitics is the multiplication of the interval.

NOTES

1. Martin Heidegger, "Why Do I Stay in the Provinces?," in *Heidegger: The Man and the Thinker*, ed. Thomas Sheehan (Abingdon, UK: Routledge, 2017), 27–30.

2. I am thinking here of Dipesh Chakrabarty, *Provincializing Europe: Postcolonial Thought and Historical Difference* (Princeton, NJ: Princeton University Press, 2000).

3. See, respectively, Immanuel Wallerstein, *Geopolitics and Geoculture: Essays on the Changing World System* (Cambridge: Cambridge University Press, 1991); and Benjamin Bratton, *The Stack: On Software and Sovereignty* (Cambridge, MA: MIT Press, 2015).

4. See Erich Hörl, "Introduction to General Ecology," in *General Ecology: A New Ecological Paradigm*, ed. Erich Hörl with James Burton (London: Bloomsbury Academic, 2017), 1–73.

5. See, for example, Robert W. Gehl, "(Critical) Reverse Engineering and Genealogy," *Le foucaldien* 3, no. 1 (2017), DOI: 10.16995/lefou.26.

6. Thanks to Florian Sprenger for bringing these points to my attention.

7. Bernhard Siegert, *Cultural Techniques: Grids, Filters, Doors, and Other Articulations of the Real*, trans. Geoffrey Winthrop-Young (New York: Fordham University Press, 2015), 102.

8. For an analysis of Salesforce and the relationship between epistemology and algorithmic governance, see Eva-Maria Nyckel, "Investigating Organizational Powers of Process Management Systems through the Origins of Process Management: Taylorist Techniques in Contrast to Salesforce Technology," unpublished paper, 2017.

9. See Dara Orenstein, *Out of Stock: The Warehouse in the History of Capitalism* (Chicago: University of Chicago Press, 2019).

10. See State Council of the People's Republic of China, "Made in China 2025," May 19, 2015, http://english.www.gov.cn/policies/latest_releases/2015/05/19/content_281475110703534.htm; and State Council Notice, "New Generation Artificial Intelligence Development Plan," July 2017. An English translation of the latter is available at Graham Webster, Paul Triolo, Elsa Kania, and Rogier Creemers, "A Next Generation Artificial Intelligence Plan," *China Copyright and Media* (blog), July 20, 2017, https://chinacopyrightandmedia.wordpress.com/2017/07/20/a-next-generation-artificial-intelligence-development-plan/.

11. Elsa Kania, "China's Artificial Intelligence Revolution," *The Diplomat*, July 27, 2017, https://thediplomat.com/2017/07/chinas-artificial-intelligence -revolution/.

12. See Harold A. Innis, *The Bias of Communication* (Toronto: University of Toronto Press, 1951).

13. Here, I am drawing on Ned Rossiter, "Imperial Infrastructures and Asia beyond Asia: Data Centres, State Formation and the Territoriality of Logistical Media," *Fibreculture Journal* 29 (2017), http://twentynine.fibreculturejournal .org/fcj-220-imperial-infrastructures-and-asia-beyond-asia-data-centres-state -formation-and-the-territoriality-of-logistical-media/.

14. See Paul Virilio, *Speed and Politics*, trans. Mark Polizzotti (Los Angeles: Semiotext(e), 1986 [1977]). See also John Armitage, "Beyond Postmodernism? Paul Virilio's Hypermodern Cultural Theory," *CTheory* (2000), https://journals .uvic.ca/index.php/ctheory/article/view/14598.

15. On Virilio's concept of *chronopolitics*, see Paul Virilio and Sylvère Lotringer, *Pure War*, trans. Mark Polizzotti (New York: Semiotext(e), 1983); and Eric Wilson, "Chronopolitics," in *The Virilio Dictionary*, ed. John Armitage (Edinburgh: Edinburgh University Press, 2013), 45–47. See also Wolfgang Ernst, *Chronopoetics: The Temporal Being and Operativity of Technological Media*, trans. Anthony Enns (London: Rowman and Littlefield, 2016).

16. Paul Virilio, *Polar Inertia*, trans. Patrick Camiller (London: Sage, 2000).

17. Innis, *The Bias of Communication*.

18. Niklas Luhmann, *Introduction to Systems Theory*, trans. Peter Gilgen (Cambridge: Polity, 2013), 26.

19. Luhmann, *Introduction to Systems Theory*, 27.

20. Jeremy Walker and Melinda Cooper, "Genealogies of Resilience: From Systems Ecology to the Political Economy of Crisis Adaptation," *Security Dialogue* 42, no. 2 (2011): 143–60.

21. See Sandro Mezzadra and Brett Neilson, *The Politics of Operations: Excavating Contemporary Capitalism* (Durham, NC: Duke University Press, 2019), 5.

22. Suffice to say, one would be hard-pressed to identify a messianic dimension within global logistical industries, yet there is some structural affinity here with Peter Osborne's reading of Walter Benjamin's critique of historicism and the temporality of modernity: "New-time (*Neuzeit*) becomes the now-time (*Jetztzeit*) of a materialist messianism for which the exteriority of the messianic is found to be paradoxically immanent to the structure of temporality itself." Peter Osborne, *The Politics of Time: Modernity and Avant-Garde* (London: Verso, 1995), 116.

23. Osborne, *The Politics of Time*, 116.

24. Among such studies perhaps none has gained more attention and fewer readers in recent years than Thomas Piketty, *Capital in the Twenty-First Century*, trans. Arthur Goldhammer (Cambridge, MA: Harvard University Press, 2014).

25. It is important to note that empirically, and therefore analytically and conceptually, capital accumulation does not function exclusively through some incremental logic of increasing speed. Rather, there are multiple and often conflicting temporalities that underpin capital accumulation. The phenomenon of "slow steaming" in the shipping industry, for example, is pushed by pressures of capital accumulation that includes energy costs, labor strikes in ports, smaller cargoes, reduced traffic in global commodity flows, etc. A multitude of time, in other words, defines the economies of the logistical industries. My point, however, concerns the temporality of logistical media. See Brett Neilson and Ned Rossiter, "Still Waiting, Still Moving: On Migration, Logistics and Maritime Industries," in *Stillness in a Mobile World*, ed. David Bissell and Gillian Fuller (London: Routledge, 2011), 51–68.

26. These projects include Transit Labour: Circuits, Regions, Borders (2009–12), http://transitlabour.asia; Logistical Worlds: Infrastructure, Software, Labour (2013–17), http://logisticalworlds.org; and Data Farms: Circuits, Labour, Territory (2016–20), http://www.datafarms.org/.

27. Geert Lovink, "The Principle of Notworking: Concepts in Critical Internet Culture," public lecture, Hogeschool van Amsterdam, February 24, 2005, http://www.hva.nl/lectoraten/documenten/0109-050224-lovink.pdf.

28. See Ishita Dey, Ranabir Samaddar, and Suhit K. Sen, *Beyond Kolkata: Rajarhat and the Dsytopia of Urban Imagination* (New Delhi: Routledge, 2013).

29. David Harvey, *The New Imperialism* (Oxford: Oxford University Press, 2003).

30. Anna Tsing, "Supply Chains and the Human Condition," *Rethinking Marxism: A Journal of Economics, Culture and Society* 21, no. 2 (2009): 148–76.

31. During this time I was conducting collective field research on e-waste industries with my students at the University of Nottingham, Ningbo. Material from their research can be found at http://orgnets.cn. See also Ned Rossiter, "Translating the Indifference of Communication: Electronic Waste, Migrant Labour and the Informational Sovereignty of Logistics in China," *International Review of Information Ethics* 11 (2009), http://www.i-r-i-e.net/issue11.htm.

32. See Alexander R. Galloway, *Laruelle: Against the Digital* (Minneapolis: University of Minnesota Press, 2014), xxix.

33. Galloway, *Laruelle*, xxix.

34. For an overview of Schmitt's thinking on sovereign power, see Carl Schmitt, *Political Theology: Four Chapters on the Concept of Sovereignty*, trans. George Schwab (Chicago: University of Chicago Press, 2005).

35. Galloway, *Laruelle*, 20.

36. For a fascinating account and critique of the technical a priori, see Stefan Heidenreich, "The Situation after Media," in *Media after Kittler*, ed. Eleni Ikoniadou and Scott Wilson (London: Rowman and Littlefield, 2015), 135–53.

37. Florian Sprenger, *Micro-Decisions: Snowden, Net Neutrality, Internet Architectures*, trans. Valentine A. Pakis (Lüneburg, Germany: Meson Press, 2015), 97.

38. Paul Baran, "On Distributed Communications Networks," *IEEE Transactions* CS–12, no. 1 (1964): 1–9.

39. See Sprenger, *Micro-Decisions*, 98.

40. See Sprenger, *Micro-Decisions*, 111–13.

41. See Ned Rossiter, "Copper," in *The Oxford Handbook of Media, Technology, and Organization Studies*, ed. Timon Beyes, Robin Holt, and Claus Pias (Oxford: Oxford University Press, 2020), 160–71.

42. See Galloway, *Laruelle*, xxix.

43. See Timon Beyes and Claus Pias, "Secrecy, Transparency, and Non-Knowledge," in *Non-Knowledge and Digital Cultures*, ed. Andreas Bernard, Matthias Koch, and Martina Leeker (Lüneburg, Germany: Meson Press, 2018), 39–51, https://meson.press/books/non-knowledge-and-digital-cultures/. See also M. Beatrice Fazi, *Contingent Computation: Abstraction, Experience, and Indeterminacy in Computational Aesthetics* (London: Rowman and Littlefield, 2018).

SUPPLY CHAIN MEDIA

Digitization, Globalization, Exploitation

PART III

"IT'S LOUD AND IT'S TASTELESS AND I'VE HEARD IT BEFORE"

Logistics made fashion fast. Streamlining supply chains, Zara, H&M, Uniqlo, and Forever 21 accelerated production and distribution to get their clothes onto racks in mere weeks. This speed multiplied the traditional fall and spring seasons to fifty-two "micro-seasons." Supercharged by YouTube shopping "haul" videos and Instagram celebrity feeds, stocks are replenished weekly; the cheap clothes hardly last longer than their social media cycles. While fashion has been an analog social medium for class communication since the nineteenth century, fast fashion is a digital information medium—a series of classless, post-brand advertisements for entrepreneurial selves. Through endless feedback loops, social media parasitically extracts information about consumer taste from the very users who use it to assemble their online identities.

But fast fashion is so yesterday. Now Zara struggles to catch up to online-only upstarts such as Misguided, ASOS, and other "ultrafast" clothiers that go from design to point of sale in a week—with hundreds of new products added to their sites daily. As women of color in the Global South absorb the impact of consumer desire, rivers around the globe fill with industrial dyes, and landfills overflow with synthetic fabrics. With the workers who make them fast becoming new consumers, the piles of polyester and slowly rotting sequins will only grow. "It's loud and it's tasteless and I've heard it before," sang David Bowie. This quaint complaint makes us long for the days when lack of originality seemed to be the only problem with fashion.

8

Carry That Weight

The Costs of Delivery and the Ecology of Vinyl Records' Revival

IN OCTOBER 2018 I traveled to Detroit for Making Vinyl, the second annual gathering of nearly three hundred "great minds all along the vinyl value chain—from the pressing plants to the mastering facilities and PVC manufacturers [polyvinyl chloride, records' raw material] to the plater/stamper makers and lathe cutters to the labels and indie retailers."[1] New vinyl sales had been climbing for thirteen consecutive years, from under $1 million annually to more than $14 million, and records now made up their largest market share of music sales since Nielsen began distinguishing between physical and digital formats.[2] The number of record pressing plants in the United States had doubled in the past decade, with a dozen opening from Oregon to south Florida.[3] Spirits were high at the conference, and camaraderie infused the proceedings. The veterans coached the neophytes, while innovators and experts exchanged ideas, and everyone welcomed an academic interloper.

Over the course of Making Vinyl's two days, it became clear that shipping was a stressor widely shared among the attendees. A panel of new plant proprietors (seven white men in their thirties and forties, three with beards) all agreed that their biggest surprise in starting up had been the ratio of "costs to goods," and when one speaker assured the audience that "no one is getting rich from this," another quipped, to knowing laughter, "Except FedEx and UPS." The fabrication of records unfolds across several intricate operations, and few facilities are equipped to handle more than one, so delicate intermediate materials are transported from station to station (to station). Profit margins are razor-thin for every phase of vinyl manufacturing, which only raises the stakes of delivering parts and materials between them, and any production delays can be especially costly for goods with release dates scheduled months in advance. During a session devoted to quality and standards, a call for standardized packaging protocols struck a chord. Discussion zeroed in on transport between shops, and horror stories were shared about heavy boxes stacked too high and missed deliveries left to cook in the summer sun. Someone relayed the lore of a bicycle company having reduced damage 80 percent by mislabeling their products' lean rectangular boxes as flat-screen TVs, and everyone acknowledged the inadequacy of "FRAGILE: RECORDS" as a label to alert the uninitiated. Near the end of the session, a suggestion to invite representatives from the US Postal Service and leading shipping companies to the next Making Vinyl met with nods, murmurs of affirmation, and applause.

Once a vinyl record has been made, the audio information etched in its grooves cannot be streamed or downloaded, so any distribution and sales entail further physical relocation. Today the majority of vinyl is purchased online, virtually all of which is then mailed from sellers to buyers. (A substantial portion of records bought online is shipped internationally.) Listening to vinyl requires far less energy than streaming, but internet sales have delocalized traffic and dramatically increased the resources devoted to shipping records. In a sea of content readily accessible online, vinyl offers a sort of divergence culture in an era of media convergence. Like so many "alternative practices in the age of the Anthropocene," however, vinyl's supply chains retain "a dependency on mainstream architectures from global logistics to data centers and the perpetuation of an international division of labor."[4] Making and moving records today are both reliant on shipping, and it turns out that the revived vinyl economy is every bit as conditioned by logistical infrastructures as those digital formats to which records purportedly offer an alternative.

In this chapter I address the environmental and economic costs of shipping along vinyl's contemporary supply chains. There are essentially two ways to reduce the ecological impact of vinyl records: curtailing the consumption of energy and other resources in their trafficking, and reducing the toxicity of their fabrication. Accordingly, I devote a section each to vinyl traffic and fabrication, and along the way I consider how the same digital technology facilitating vinyl's booming sales can be utilized logistically for the sake of both ecology and efficiency. Vinyl is, after all, a nonbiodegradable plastic, and so in the third section I suggest how logistical media might help govern the amount of new material entering the supply chain in the first place. I conclude by noting how the analysis of the vinyl revival offered in this chapter might provide a model for logistical media studies that counts environmental costs among its animating concerns.

No shortage of ink has been spilled over the culture and commerce of vinyl records' revived popularity, but scholarship exploring vinyl's ecology is scant.[5] My aim here is not to determine whether vinyl is greener than other music formats but rather to provide an overdue accounting of vinyl's "ecological context." The "intersecting histories of chemical, mechanical, and electrical processes [comprise] the ecological context" of a particular medium or format, and here I add a consideration of the logistical media that sustain the contemporary production, distribution, and consumption of vinyl records.[6] After being accepted rather than actively embraced by nearly all listeners during the middle decades of the twentieth century, vinyl's revival gives the lie to Walter Benjamin's famous critique of art and its mechanical reproduction: records are mass produced and industrially manufactured, yet they are now prized for their authenticity, for what Benjamin would call their aura. This rearticulated appeal of vinyl records, as an analog exception in a digital world, makes them an ideal case study for demonstrating the centrality of logistical media to popular culture in any format today, both off- and online. With its "obstinate material form," vinyl also provides a model for foregrounding ecological contexts as both the subject and stakes of analyses within the burgeoning interdisciplinary field of critical logistics studies.[7]

Vinyl Goes Digital

When I attended Making Vinyl in 2018, vinyl sales had been growing for more than a decade. Total sales of physical musical media were down to 10 percent of total industry revenue, yet vinyl sales were continuing to climb, while CDs were plummeting alongside downloads.[8] Vinyl's compatibility with streaming exemplifies what some media scholars have taken to calling our "postdigital" condition.[9] Vinyl is the leading case study in David Sax's popular book, *The Revenge of Analog*, and Sax's formulation that "digital [technology] helped save the very analog record it nearly killed" signals the centrality of the internet for contemporary vinyl commerce as well as for the format's rearticulated appeal.[10] Ironically, vinyl's new value is enhanced by its perceived distance from the same technology appreciated by buyers and sellers alike as fueling the contemporary vinyl marketplace. While vinyl's commercial infrastructure has migrated online, the format's materiality tethers it logistically to nondigital media. Chief among vinyl's postdigital logistical media are mail services. Every record made entails the transport of intermediate materials, and every online sale of a record occasions its packing and delivery.[11] Secondhand sales aren't tracked by the industry, and despite the decade of booming sales of new vinyl, "the bulk of records traded, sold, and played today" are on at least their second owner.[12] This fact makes vinyl uniquely green among popular media, rivaled only by books, and the thriving online markets in used records underscore the centrality of shipping in the revitalized vinyl economy.

Amazon, of course, sells more new records than any other single retailer, as well as a healthy share of used records, but all told, more than two-thirds of new records are sold by independent merchants, as are most used records. Small shops (and individuals who flip records online) utilize the same, or at least the same sorts of, logistical media—digital and nondigital—to facilitate their sales and organize their inventory as a behemoth like Amazon does at an exponentially vaster scale. Independent shops and individuals selling used records populate sites like eBay and Craigslist, not to mention Discogs, the world's "biggest and most comprehensive music database and marketplace."[13] Started as a "hobby project" in 2000, the site is now "like Wikipedia for music," with nearly half a million users contributing to entries for more than six million artists and more than ten million recordings. Unlike Wikipedia it also lists nearly fifty million items for sale, more than thirty-three million of which are vinyl records. Not only has Discogs matured into an authoritative database as well as sales platform, but its roles as each are inextricable: purchases on Discogs are monitored by buyers and sellers, in turn helping to set the going rate for records in shops and on other websites. Discogs embodies the centralizing, if not outright monopolizing force of "platform capitalism," albeit on a smaller scale than an all-encompassing retailer like Amazon.[14]

No company has been more central to the logistical remediation of the vinyl marketplace than Discogs. Not only are millions of used as well as new records bought and sold via Discogs annually, but many of its more than seven million site visits per month are price checks from sellers and buyers. The time-honored tradition of "crate digging" has long been a source of profit as well as pleasure for record collectors, but now Discogs has upended the practice by providing ready access to prices and availability for novices alongside connoisseurs.[15] Discogs also affects the production of new records, both directly and indirectly, as no label worth its salt can afford to ignore the site's trove of data. Recently labels have begun to float potential reissued releases with a Discogs entry, gauging interest before deciding whether to start the presses.

Most record stores list at least some inventory on Discogs, usually their more rarefied fare, but their presence is dwarfed on the site by free agents selling records to help earn a living, to fund their own vinyl habit, or both. Shoppers can sort copies of a record for sale by price, condition, age, and location; users who keep a "want list" are alerted as soon as any copies are posted for sale; and buyers and sellers are expected to leave reviews for one another. Many individual sellers will follow up repeatedly with buyers, imploring them (cheerfully) to leave a positive review, often offering (or withholding) their own in exchange. (Discogs members are also assessed with a "buyer's rating," based on sellers' feedback.) In order to ensure that reviews remain positive, individual sellers often decide they must absorb the added expenses of refunds and return shipments. In the contemporary vinyl marketplace, risks and costs have been redistributed in patterns resembling those in other sectors of the retail economy that have been logistically remediated by "platformization."[16]

Dusty Groove emerged during the late 1990s as one of the first online retailers of records (or of anything else), and now it also has one of the largest and most-established record stores among scores in Chicago. One of Dusty Groove's cofounders developed proprietary software to coordinate inventory and sales, customized to account for records' condition among other features unique to the format. As business has grown, the software has allowed Dusty to sell exclusively through its own website and avoid the costs—and data sharing—of partnering with Amazon or even Discogs.[17] Dusty Groove now maintains a staff of twenty-five, several of whom are assigned to aspects of their online traffic, and the cofounder who developed the software works full-time on maintaining and updating it. Most smaller merchants of vintage goods cannot afford the labor and other costs of developing and maintaining their own software, and they are forced to "partner" with Amazon, Discogs, and other platforms that drive internet traffic, in the process sharing their data as well as profits.

Online record sales provide a rich example of postdigital commerce as well as culture, and one whose materiality exceeds the goods for sale. The online vinyl marketplace is sustainable only through the use of logistical media such as shipping boxes built specially for records alongside the tracking numbers used by buyers to remotely monitor those boxes in transit. The labor of selling records has been logistically remediated, and the internet is a vital means of promotion and communication even for shops that don't sell online. Online sales can subsidize brick-and-mortar shops, and it has become a successful strategy for new record stores to establish their business online and then open a shop once sales reach a consistent level that can sustain the added costs. In addition to the visibility and prestige that comes with a desirable address, for merchants of bulky and breakable goods like records, a shop also functions as valuable storage capacity, even if the majority of sales continue to occur online.

The utilization of digital technology by distributors, merchants, and especially online storefronts has delocalized vinyl sales and dramatically increased the resources consumed for trafficking. Once records leave the pressing plant, minimizing the distance they travel is the only remaining way to temper vinyl's ecological impact. The next section provides a capsule account of the vinyl supply chain and describes how digital logistical media are reorganizing records' production as well as their distribution and sales. The same technology catalyzing vinyl traffic today is being utilized to help reduce or even eliminate the need for some materials and workers to travel, and these efforts underscore the limits of digital logistical media along any supply chain for goods whose manufacture entails parts and assembly. Vinyl is culturally noteworthy as an analog alternative amid digital ubiquity, but its production provides a model case for critical logistics studies that demonstrates how digital and nondigital media connect any supply chain today. The complexity of vinyl's supply chain and the vital role that shipping plays in coordinating it also underscore the necessity of holistic rather than isolated analyses when it comes to assessing the ecological contexts of logistical media.

Vinyl Stays Plastic

Vinyl's supply chain is complex mechanically and chemically, as well as logistically, and the production process is resource-intensive. Record presses are hydraulic and pneumatic and require massive amounts of electricity. Making records requires several pieces of intricate machinery and collaboration among discrete sets of technicians with rarified skills. Several suppliers and support services are also essential, such as the handful of companies globally that process the polymer we colloquially call "vinyl," not to mention the shipping firms that deliver it to pressing plants. A single company, Thai Plastics and Chemicals (TPC), was credited as recently as 2015 with supplying upward of 90 percent of the vinyl used to make records.[18] In their factory on the outskirts of Bangkok, TPC synthesizes polyvinyl chloride (PVC), a compound of "particles, fillers, lubricants, stabilizers and plasticizers," and manufactures it into pellets the size, shape, and weight of lentils; it is then shipped in this form to a warehouse in Long Beach, California, where a three-person staff distributes it to plants across the United States.[19] So before any vinyl has been melted into the hockey-puck-size "biscuits" that are loaded into a press, most of it has traveled over 8,000 miles. For plants on the east coast, add another 2,000 or 3,000 miles.

Any accounting of vinyl's ecological context must start and end with the material itself: vinyl is made from petroleum and qualifies as a "hyperobject" whose biodegradation occurs on "an 'almost unthinkable' timescale."[20] Vinyl in any form, including PVC, "requires hazardous chemicals for production, releases harmful additives and creates toxic wastes," earning it the distinction of being "the most environmentally damaging" among all plastics, according to Greenpeace.[21] A focus on vinyl's logistics helps emphasize how moving vinyl once it is manufactured compounds the damage done.

The fabrication of vinyl records entails three distinct steps: mastering, electroplating, and pressing. Ideally the decision to release a song or album on vinyl has been made before anyone enters the studio, because the same recording will sound different emanating from a record's grooves than it will on tape or transposed into binary code. (Not necessarily better, but different.) Virtually all professional recordings undergo mastering, or "the process of transferring audio . . . to a medium that can be used for mass duplication."[22] So mastering is the point at which a recording begins to undergo preparation for a particular format, any format, and often more than one in today's music business. For recordings slated for a vinyl release, the first transfer is almost always onto a lacquer disc. Music recorded in a professional studio used to be committed to reels of analog tape, and a fraction still is, but now most mastering engineers expect to receive high-resolution digital files. For instance, Masterdisk Studios in Peekskill, New York, handles everything from the avant-garde (e.g., Laurie Anderson, John Zorn) to the ubiquitous (e.g., Sting, Steely Dan), and they encourage clients to use a dedicated Dropbox folder that "puts your mixes right onto our servers."[23] PVC may travel halfway around the world before it arrives at a pressing plant, but for most music that will end up on vinyl, its first relocation—from the recording studio to the mastering studio—happens over the internet. Once a recording is transferred onto a lacquer disc, however, no amount of digital technology will suffice for moving it to the next stage. Furthermore, lacquers begin to degrade after forty-eight hours; in order to avoid the added costs of expedited weekend shipping, mastering studios avoid cutting lacquers on Fridays.

Some recording studios are equipped to handle mastering in-house, and a few can even master for vinyl, but studio recordings bound for any format are usually sent to another facility for mastering. And while there is no shortage of mastering studios out there, only a small fraction of them are equipped to cut lacquers. The reason for this has less to do with the technical proficiency required to skillfully cut a lacquer, which is substantial, than with a physical lack of functional lathes left in the world. Any functional or salvageable lathe is increasingly hard to come by (rumor has it the Scientologists are hoarding them!), while the lacquer discs themselves are only being manufactured by two companies worldwide, one in California and the other in Japan.[24] The styluses used to cut lacquers are also only made by two companies globally. This dearth of supplies means that most mastering studios have them delivered from far away, and the paucity of available lathes worldwide means that these same studios in turn ship mastered lacquers long distances as well.

The situation at the middle stage of vinyl's three-part production process is even more precarious. Lacquer masters can be played on a turntable, but they're soft enough that they'll degrade each time, so they are reproduced in a more durable form for replication, in a procedure known as electroplating. Vinyl's revived popularity led to a backlog in pressing plants, which has largely been addressed by new openings in the past decade, but "the real problem is not in the pressing—the bottleneck is in the electroplating."[25] A handful of high-end mastering studios handle plating in-house, as do a few of the largest pressing plants, but in the United States there are only two dedicated facilities for electroplating: Mastercraft Inc., in Elizabeth, New Jersey, and the recently opened NiPro Records in Irvine, California. It is no coincidence that Mastercraft and NiPro set up shop about an hour from New York City and Los Angeles, respectively, where they are close enough to minimize transit costs to and from music industry hubs, yet beyond the environmental codes of both cities as well as Los Angeles County and New York State. (Federal EPA inspectors visit regularly.) During the Making Vinyl session about new plants, several panelists stressed the importance of healthy relationships with local communities, and they all reported that their municipal governments had been supportive and encouraging. None of the new proprietors had considered plating in-house, however, and one explained that local officials tend to "cringe" at even the mention of it. A new record plating facility will be virtually impossible to open, given the toxicity. A handful of new plants in cities including Cleveland and Chicago are exploring the possibility of partnering with an existing plating company in town, offering to fund and collaborate on their expansion into vinyl. Until that happens, plants across the United States will continue to receive most of their "stampers," as the electroplated metal discs are known, in the mail from one coast or the other.

The two most toxic aspects of vinyl manufacturing are the electroplating of stampers and the vinyl compound itself. Plating chemistry is essentially unchanged since vinyl replaced shellac as the music industry's go-to material after World World II. Shellac was used to make munitions, and shortages during both World Wars spurred record manufacturers to devise a "chemical substitute" for the renewable but now cost-prohibitive resource.[26] RCA-Victor won the race to market, and in 1945 unveiled the first iteration of what *Time* magazine hyped in a headline as "plastic music."[27] PVC has been the raw material for records ever since. Thai Plastics Company and its handful of competitors have recently "move[d] away from lead-based PVC to a more environmental friendly stabilizer in calcium," and a consortium of eight Dutch companies calling themselves the Green Vinyl Records project are "looking for a new material" that can replace PVC.[28] The consensus at Making Vinyl was that "green plating would be a miracle," but attendees did hear a presentation from Guenter Loibel, founder of HD Vinyl, an Austrian start-up promising to eliminate plating altogether from records' production process. Instead, a "hi-resolution audio file is converted into a topographic 3D map," which is then "engraved with a high precision laser onto a ceramic plate."[29] Simply put, "no more electroplating, no more toxic waste," but the advantages of ceramic stampers would be economical as well as ecological: HD Vinyl claims its ceramic stampers will suffer no wear and tear, unlike the nickel stampers that have been used for more than sixty years. Nickel stampers are replaced after pressing roughly one thousand records, and each copy is technically less detailed than the one before. (Collectors and audiophiles pay exorbitant prices for records pressed with a "hot stamper.") For records that sell more than a thousand copies, new stampers are required. The Beatles' *Abbey Road* (Apple, 1968) has been pressed 350 times on five continents.[30] (I repurposed a McCartney ballad on side two for this chapter's title.) *Abbey Road* is the highest-selling album among new vinyl sales in the United States over the past decade, with seventeen pressings since 2009, despite there being more than 2,300 vinyl copies of *Abbey Road* for sale via Discogs alone, starting with one for $0.99 (plus $14.60 to ship to the United States from Canada).[31] In the next section, I suggest how the logistical media of vinyl's contemporary marketplace could be used to govern new pressings of already overproduced records that do not sell as well as *Abbey Road*.

First, it's worth noting that the spate of new plants opening in the United States are operating on a smaller, more localized scale and fostering a vinyl supply chain that is more ecologically as well as economically sustainable. A new record press has not been built in the United States since 1982, but Viryl Technologies, founded in 2015 and based in Toronto, is manufacturing new presses featuring several upgrades that increase speed, efficiency, and accuracy. For example, traditional presses require a boiler to melt PVC pellets into biscuits, but Viryl has patented a system for using electricity rather than gas to "achieve the necessary 285 degrees Fahrenheit without the use of steam or even a tank."[32] Smashed Plastic is the first record plant in Chicago since 1980, and their single press is the first of Viryl's steamless model to come online. Especially in a cold city like Chicago, steam boilers are heavily regulated, and to use an old-fashioned press Smashed Plastic "would've had to bring in a stationary engineer just to maintain one, and many landlords balked at the additional construction a boiler would've required."[33] Steamless record pressing lowers costs, increases speed and efficiency, and improves worker safety. The ecological advantages include minimizing water waste, eliminating the chemicals used to clean and treat boilers, and using less energy.

Viryl's steamless press still uses PVC pellets and nickel-plated stampers, but the company is utilizing digital technology to monitor its presses in ways that may "reduce carbon footprint, shipping and duty costs, and annoying logistics delays."[34] Viryl's new presses are equipped with sensors that continuously upload data to their A.D.A.P.T.™ platform and PhonoHive® network, which allows plant managers to monitor and adjust production remotely. This responsiveness can reduce downtime, and it means that Viryl's engineers can track in real-time all of their presses in plants around the world, reducing the need for site visits for maintenance and repair. Along a supply chain as convoluted and shipping-intensive as vinyl's, any potential to replace transportation with telecommunication should be seized for the sake of ecology as well as efficiency. No company has done more to revitalize vinyl's supply chain than Viryl, and its innovations are helping foster a vinyl supply chain that is more ecologically as well as economically sustainable.

Many of the new plants installing Viryl's presses are following suit. Chicago had not housed a (legally) functioning commercial record press for nearly three decades when Smashed Plastic opened, and its owners explicitly set out to fill the void. To date they are accepting orders exclusively from local bands and labels, and as a result they've yet to mail any fulfilled orders, instead delivering the records in person or arranging for pickup. In the back of their shop, Smashed Plastic's owners have also a built a listening room, cozily furnished with a stocked bar, where customers can hear test pressings on site rather than shipping them back and forth. The advantages of minimizing shipping are ecological and economic as well as ethical and interpersonal—it saves customers time and money while conserving energy and other resources. The flowering of smaller plants like Smashed Plastic, especially in cities like Chicago with thriving music scenes and vibrant vinyl cultures, allows for a more localized and sustainable supply chain for new records, which is as ecologically urgent as it can be economically advantageous and experientially enriching.

Reissue Fewer Records, Recycle More Vinyl!

The first chapter of *Eco-Sonic Media*, Jacob Smith's resourceful 2015 book, is devoted to imagining "a more convivial phonography."[35] Smith looks to the past for guidance, noting the biodegradability of shellac, PVC's predecessor as records' raw material, and chronicling the sustainability of its human and nonhuman production. He also draws inspiration from the earliest record players, which were powered by hand cranks rather than electricity, in order to pursue a "minimal phonography." In this brief section I follow Smith's lead and suggest how to mitigate vinyl's footprint by utilizing the same digital logistical media facilitating the format's booming sales to help govern the amount of new PVC entering the supply chain. Then, I conclude with a note about applying insights from this chapter's account of shipping along vinyl's supply chains to a more ecologically oriented logistical media studies.

Unsurprisingly, record manufacturers are more environmentally (self-) conscious today than their predecessors were during the format's heyday. Burlington Record Plant in Vermont ("family owned and operated since 2014") is exemplary but not unusual in its commitment to "energy efficient manufacturing processes, clean vinyl recycling practices, and recyclable shipping materials."[36] No one along the vinyl supply chain is resistant to enhancing efficiency or reducing waste, and several recycling practices have always been standard operating procedure in plants, even if it's only recently that they have begun to be touted as such. For instance, each record pressed is individually inspected by human ears and eyes, same as it ever was, and the rejects (as many as one out of every five in some plants) have always been melted and mixed in with "virgin vinyl" to be pressed again. Efforts to recycle records already in circulation are hamstrung by the fact that vinyl needs to be pristine in order to still sound good after being ground, melted again, and repressed. Still-sealed records in stores could be more aggressively targeted for recycling, while most used records would not work. Until a less toxic, more biodegradable material for records is developed, logistical media could be utilized to help govern the amount of new PVC entering the supply chain in the first place.

Sites like Discogs could be utilized to restrict needless reissues and to identify albums with an excess of copies still in circulation, some of which could be recycled. Not all vinyl recycling needs to lead to repressing, and logistical media could help recycle old as well as new records after they've left the plant. For example, *Whipped Cream and Other Delights* by Herb Alpert and the Tijuana Brass (A&M, 1965) is a pleasant and historically significant record with (in)famous cover art, but it's no *Abbey Road*; there are already more copies in circulation, still sealed as well as used, than will likely ever be sought. Discogs lists 141 different releases, including a remastered version in 2015 released on 180g vinyl as well as CD and a FLAC file, and a limited-edition picture disc in 2009, copies of which list on the site for $25–50. Furthermore, among Discogs' half-million users (a sizable but far from comprehensive or even representative pool of vinyl listeners), more than 18,000 report having a copy, while 735 copies are currently for sale via the site, several dozens of which cost $2 or less—before shipping of course. Discogs' user-maintained database could help determine whether a reissue is "worth it," based on the number of copies still in circulation rather than the calculations of a major label's marketing staff, and also whether or how many copies of an overproduced staple like *Whipped Cream* merit recycling. Before a label reissues a record with a critical mass still in circulation, they should collect some of the old ones. That vinyl could be recycled, if possible; if not, then the records themselves could be repackaged with updated or expanded liner notes and ephemera. Sound quality has never been vinyl's primary appeal anyway, and on the other side of digitization, some listeners (especially younger listeners) may be even more charmed by the sound of an old record than a new one.

Follow the Mail, or Post-Digital Media Logistics

In their 2012 book *Greening the Media*, Richard Maxwell and Toby Miller call for an ecological turn within media and cultural studies; since then it has become only more urgent to at least consider, if not center, environmental costs in any critical study of technology, logistical or otherwise. The analysis of vinyl's supply chains in this chapter provides a possible model of ecologically-oriented logistical media studies. Vinyl's marketplace has gone digital, but its blatant materiality requires logistical media that can connect buyers and sellers offline as well as on. Similarly, despite ongoing upgrades along new vinyl's supply chain, the role of shipping and delivery remains essential. Digital media facilitate both the fabrication and the trafficking of vinyl records, but digitization has seen nondigital logistical media become more vital to vinyl's economy rather than less. In this chapter I have emphasized the centrality of shipping for vinyl's revival, and the same "postdigital" logistical media utilized by the people making and moving vinyl records abound in other culture industries and sectors of the global economy. For instance, the tracking number strikes me as a postdigital technology par excellence that could help organize critical logistics studies focused on any number of subjects and sectors. If the digitization of logistical media requires critical scholars to follow the data as well as the money, then it follows that logistical media studies will have to account for the energy and other resources consumed by streaming and cloud storage. The significance of shipping in vinyl's revived economy suggests that critical studies of media logistics will be well served by continuing to follow the mail as well.

NOTES

1. Making Vinyl conference program, Detroit, MI, November 6–7, 2018, p. 5. This quotation from the first Making Vinyl program applies to the second as well.

2. Nielsen Staff, "2017 Year-End Music Report, U.S.," *Nielsen Music*, January 3, 2018, https://www.nielsen.com/us/en/insights/reports/2018/2017-music-us-year-end-report.html.

3. Total Sonic Network, "Vinyl Record Pressing Plants," last updated October 25, 2018, http://www.totalsonic.net/vinylplants.htm.

4. Geert Lovink and Ned Rossiter, *Organization after Social Media* (New York: Minor Compositions, 2018), 7.

5. For exceptions, see Jacob Smith, *Eco-Sonic Media* (Berkeley: University of California Press, 2015); and Kyle Devine, *Decomposed: The Political Ecology of Music* (Cambridge, MA: MIT Press, 2019).

6. Richard Maxwell and Toby Miller, *Greening the Media* (Oxford: Oxford University Press, 2012), 43.

7. David Novak, *Japanoise: Music at the Edge of Circulation* (Durham, NC: Duke University Press, 2013), 222; on critical logistics studies, see Charmain Chua, Martin Danyluk, Deborah Cowen, and Laleh Khalili, "Introduction: Turbu-

lent Circulation: Building a Critical Engagement with Logistics," *Environment and Planning D: Society and Space* 36, no. 4 (2018): 617–29, https://doi.org/10.1177 /0263775818783101.

8. Ashley King, "The RIAA's Mid-Year Revenue Report: The Good (Streaming), The Bad (Downloads) and The Ugly (CDs)," *Digital Music News*, September 20, 2018, https://www.digitalmusicnews.com/2018/09/20/riaa-music-industry -report/. See also Steve Knopper, "The End of Owning Music: How CDs and Downloads Died," *Rolling Stone*, June 14, 2018, https://www.rollingstone.com /music/news/owning-music-buying-vinyl-cds-downloads-streaming-w521504.

9. David Berry and Michael Dieter, eds., *Post-digital Aesthetics: Art, Computation, and Design* (London: Palgrave-Macmillan, 2015); and Ewa Mazierska, Les Gillon, and Tony Rigg, eds., *Popular Music in the Post-Digital Age: Politics, Economy, Culture and Technology* (New York: Bloomsbury Academic, 2019).

10. David Sax, *The Revenge of Analog: Real Things and Why They Matter* (Philadelphia: Public Affairs Books, 2016), 11.

11. The exceptions are records sold to buyers who pick them up from sellers locally.

12. Sax, *The Revenge of Analog*, 20.

13. Discogs, "About Discogs," accessed December 2, 2020, https://www.discogs .com/about.

14. Nick Srnicek, *Platform Capitalism* (Cambridge: Polity, 2017), 92.

15. *You ask me why I carry cash around with me all the time. / Don't you see all these yard sale signs? / When I flip this first edition for a cool grand, / Then maybe you'll understand.*" Wooden Wand, "Mexican Coke," *Clipper Ship* (High Point, NC: Three Lobed Recordings, 2017).

16. David Nieborg and Thomas Poell, "The Platformization of Cultural Production: Theorizing the Contingent Cultural Commodity," *New Media and Society* 20, no. 11 (2018): 4275–92, http://journals.sagepub.com/doi/10.1177/1461444818769694. See also Tamara Kneese and Michael Palm, "Brick-and-Platform: Listing Labor in the Digital Vintage Economy," *Social Media + Society* 6, no. 3 (2020): 1–11, https:// journals.sagepub.com/doi/pdf/10.1177/2056305120933299.

17. For a revealing account of Dusty Groove focused on their offline procurement of inventory, see Danielle Beverly's 2019 award-winning documentary, *Dusty Groove: The Sound of Transition* (Chicago: Petunia Productions).

18. *Fact* Staff, "US Vinyl Suppliers Struggling to Keep Up with Demand from Pressing Plants," *Fact*, December 14, 2015, https://www.factmag.com/2014/12/15 /us-vinyl-suppliers-struggling-to-keep-up-with-demand-from-pressing-plants/.

19. Matthew Jaehrling, "Welcome Back, Vinyl Records," *ThermoFisher Scientific*, April 19, 2016, https://www.thermofisher.com/blog/materials/welcome-back -vinyl-records/.

20. Jacob Smith, *Eco-Sonic Media* (Berkeley: University of California Press, 2015), 7, quoting Timothy Morton, *The Ecological Thought* (Cambridge, MA: Harvard University Press, 2012), 28.

21. Smith, *Eco-Sonic Media*, 190n121.

22. Saff Mastering, "What Is Mastering," accessed December 2, 2020, http://www.saffmastering.com/_site/main.html.

23. Masterdisk, "FAQ," accessed December 2, 2020, https://masterdisk.com/faq#send-files.

24. On February 6, 2020, the Banning, California, factory of Apollo Master Audiodiscs was destroyed in a fire, leaving one supplier of blank lacquers globally. A month later, the fire's impact on new vinyl production was overshadowed—and delayed—by pandemic lockdowns. See Noah Yoo, "'Devastating' Manufacturing Plant Fire Threatens Worldwide Vinyl Record Supply," *Pitchfork*, February 7, 2020, https://pitchfork.com/news/devastating-manufacturing-plant-fire-threatens-worldwide-vinyl-record-supply/.

25. Thaddeus Herrmann, "Pressed to the Edge: Why Vinyl Hype Is Destroying the Record," *Fact*, May 7, 2015, https://www.factmag.com/2015/05/07/pressed-to-the-edge-vinyl/.

26. "Records without Shellac," *Newsweek*, August 17, 1942, 73–74, quoted in Smith, *Eco-Sonic Media*, 34.

27. "Plastic Music," *Time* 46, no. 17 (1945): 86, quoted in Smith, *Eco-Sonic Media*, 34.

28. Barbie Bertisch, "Making Music Sustainable: How to Solve the Vinyl Industry's Sustainability Problems," *Medium*, April 22, 2018, https://medium.com/novation-notes/making-music-sustainable-d700b034a3ab; the Green Vinyl Records Project, http://greenvinylrecords.com/het-project-en-us/.

29. HD Vinyl brochure booklet, distributed at Making Vinyl, Detroit, MI, October 1–2, 2018.

30. Discogs, "The Beatles—Abbey Road," accessed May 7, 2019, https://www.discogs.com/The-Beatles-Abbey-Road/master/24047?filter=true&format=Vinyl.

31. Discogs, "Marketplace: Shop Vinyl Records," accessed May 7, 2019, https://www.discogs.com/sell/list?sort=price%2Casc&limit=250&master_id=24047&ev=mb&format=Vinyl.

32. Leor Galil, "Chicago Gets Its First Vinyl Record Pressing Plant in Decades," *Chicago Reader*, November 14, 2018, https://www.chicagoreader.com/chicago/smashed-plastic-vinyl-pressing-plant-record-chirp-viryl-technologies/Content?oid=62708778.

33. Galil, "Chicago Gets."

34. Viryl Technologies, "Introducing PhonoHive—The Global Pressing Plant," https://www.viryltech.com/phonohive/.

35. Smith, *Eco-Sonic Media*, 17, 38.

36. Burlington Record Plant, "About Us," accessed December 2, 2020, http://burlingtonrecordplant.com/about/.

SOUND FROM
A MUSIC CONTAINER

The materiality of media shapes its meaning. In recorded sound, logistical limitations on the size and shape of media containers have defined the very structure of modern music. The length of a symphony's movements waxed and waned, but they were rarely shorter than ten or fifteen minutes. Wax cylinders permitted only two minutes. While the introduction of shellac records brought greater temporal possibilities, most songs rarely exceeded the lowest common denominator. Albums became a unit of organization because books were used to package collections of records, a logistical lesson copied from photography. When double-sided records were first introduced in the early twentieth century, there was no distinction between each side. But the confluence of stereo sound, the use of records on the radio, and other operative practices soon made one side better than the other. The B side became home to the weird and sometimes wondrous music that didn't always belong on the airwaves. Special tracks, instrumentals, and other unexpected recordings made efficient use of a more commercially irrelevant space. For every "Hello, Goodbye," there might be an "I Am the Walrus" waiting on the other side.

"Hello, Goodbye" / "I Am the Walrus," first issue (1967).

9

Supply Chain Cinema, Supply Chain Education

Training Creative Wizardry for Offshored Exploitation

ON NOVEMBER 1, 2016, I received an email from a close friend, a British film industry professional who had dropped out of his usual levels of communication. My prior message had simply read, "Alive?" Days later than is typical, to excuse his silence, he joked, "No, I'm an automated bot, a courtesy service from Warner Bros. for the friends and family of those who have sold their souls to us." Alongside many other British crew members, this friend is regularly hired by the American-headquartered entertainment company (as well as other global media conglomerates), who now shoot the larger part of their movies in the United Kingdom. His quip divulges draining labor conditions that are actualized by a battery of variegated yet tightly synchronized managerial practices, technologies, governmental policies, and employee acclimatization whose interconnection this essay hopes to illuminate. Our exchange (between a film worker and an academic) invites us to question the role higher education adopts within this circuitry.

In the languages of film scholarship, the offshoring practices that bring Warner Bros. to Britain have come to be known as split location production, the scattering of portions of manufacturing to wherever is cheapest, most convenient, most efficient, or most appropriately skilled.[1] To readers of this volume, the process will immediately figure as a supply chain: capital homing in on optimal production conditions that can be seamlessly marshalled into a more embracing and regulated sequence. While movies have long been shot, in part or whole, away from established production bases, recent affordances provoke me to renew our customary terminology and instead label what is happening here *supply chain cinema*. With logistics at the analytical forefront, the systemic nature of labor exploitation becomes all the more conspicuous.

Big-budget filmmaking, of course, lends itself comfortably to the ways and means of the supply chain. Diverted from factory-like assembly since the disintegration of the studio system in the 1950s, the industry now turns out movies on a project-by-project basis. Each venture contracts a unique cast and crew solely for the required duration and often on extremely short notice. These preferences for flexibility and disposability, principal feeders to the supply chain's supremacy, have themselves been nourished (as in so many other sectors) by advances in telecommunications, digitization, and transnational financial mobility. Cumulatively, they have eased the modularization and dispersal of production to wherever emerges as most cost-effective by diminishing time, risk, and unpredictability. As the platform economy with its over-the-top video-streaming services escalates, decentralized custom viewing and the demand for copious content prompt more responsive feedback loops and a faster-than-ever pace to market. In its service, specially designed logistical software integrates traditionally siloed phases of a film's journey from ideation to consumption, guaranteeing greater potential to oversee, quicken, and economize. On the ground, production logistics companies promise to arrange travel, obtain shooting permits, and lock down locations; job descriptions for production planners increasingly request expertise in supply chain management. And, frequently, such innovations are abetted by locally tailored, often purpose-built, outward-looking infrastructures fashioned to support offshored production.

So far, so typical of any given supply chain's immediate management of capacity and flow. But the film industry remains an unusual beast, still heavily reliant on the input of a sizable human workforce whose ingenuity is as crucial to its success as it is tricky to bend to the shapes of logistics. The courtesy bot, after all, can only be envisioned to cope with the mundane task of excusing employees from foregone sociality; current automated capacities fall a long way short of the creative demands of these jobs. Supply chain cinema therefore also hinges on sensitizing film personnel and their artistic predispositions to logistical principles.

Formal training emerges here as a crucial element and is, I argue, engineered accordingly. Education does not simply endow specialist technical skills; it simultaneously strives to inure the current and would-be worker to the rationalities of the supply chain, including its inevitable and systemic future of insecurity and debt. The conscious crafting of this worker subjectivity has led Stefano Harney and Fred Moten to project that "logistical populations will be created to do without thinking, to feel without emotion, to move without friction, to adapt without question, to translate without pause, to connect without interruption."[2] Harney and Moten's turn to the future tense stresses the deliberate design of a longer timeline, the kind familiar to educational expectations. My film worker friend's casual, dystopian reference to an imagined technology, one that exculpates what is lost through labor exploitation, also firmly lodges these conditions in the here and now.

The United Kingdom currently ranks third of all the world's countries in terms of film production spending. The lion's share (over 80 percent, and worth £1.9 billion in 2017) derives from overseas interests, almost exclusively offshored Hollywood filmmaking.[3] The question thus arises: How do film personnel drawn mainly from London—a city with one of the planet's highest costs of living—now register as a viable, globally competitive workforce? Interviewed for a House of Lords report on the industry in 2010, Roy Button, managing director of Warner Bros., cataloged the draws: a highly skilled *but casualized* English-speaking workforce, the ease of bringing equipment and workers into and out of the country (a basic logistical advantage), the lubricated mobility of capital through of its financial infrastructures, favorable exchange rates, and tax breaks that push toward 25 percent (with lax impulsions to apportion spending locally), rendering it, in Button's words, "fiscally irresponsible" to shoot in places less accommodating.[4] Research conducted by the now-defunct UK Film Council in the first decade of the millennium concluded that Britain placed second only after Hungary among a host of viable places to shoot, hampered merely by high construction costs and limited soundstage space.[5] The latter impediment was soon to be overcome.

So alluring were Britain's assets and assistance, so seemingly *constant*, that Warner Bros. began to convert Leavesden, a former aerodrome then Rolls-Royce factory, from a once makeshift studio servicing the Harry Potter franchise into a permanent large-scale base.[6] The complex comprises nine soundstages, a 102-acre backlot overlooking protected greenbelt land (thereby providing clear horizons for shooting), workshops, Europe's largest dive tank, a capacious commissary, and office buildings, with the potential to hire up to eight hundred people on a raft of different productions, including, to date, *Paddington* (dir., Paul King, 2014), *Mission: Impossible—Rogue Nation* (dir. Christopher McQuarrie, 2015), and *Wonder Woman* (dir. Patty Jenkins, 2017).[7]

Leavesden realizes a dream initiated at the turn of this century as part and parcel of the government's creation of the UK Film Council, whose first chairman, the movie director Alan Parker, urged the country away from "parochial British films" to instead strive to become "a natural destination for international investment . . . a natural supplier of skills and services to the global film market."[8] Duncan Petrie observes how this reorientation, stage-managed through policy, has instigated a state of affairs whereby British "cultural pluralism loses out to the powerful monopoly interests."[9] His comment speaks to how, at sites like Leavesden, an international division of creative labor becomes normalized, British crews supplying competitive technical services to an outside market arriving with its own vision, one that may well work at odds with the needs or priorities of the offshored support team.

Beyond just being a studio complex, Leavesden is also home to one of Britain's most trafficked visitor attractions, the Warner Bros. Studio Tour—The Making of Harry Potter. Significantly, the tour consolidates Parker's insistence on the country's "natural" (indeed "magical") propensities, trading, as much British tourism does, on unique heritage. The tour, as will become clear, aligns these attributes to a "competitiveness" afforded by the United Kingdom's education economy.

Anna Tsing's article "Supply Chains and the Human Condition" proves instructive for apprehending what happens at Leavesden. Tsing defines supply chain capitalism—from which I extrapolate supply chain cinema (Tsing herself never incorporates media industry examples)—as a web of specifically and differentially disciplined contributors, subcontracted and outsourced, embroiled in commodity production and distribution with ever-expanding global reach.[10] What she most adamantly stresses is how globalization, beyond also proliferating via processes of homogenization, characterizes itself by choreographing the world's varied economic and legislative *differences* (as just presented for Britain) to the benefit of capitalist enterprise. She is joined in this line of thinking by Sandro Mezzadra and Brett Neilson, who note how the types of spatial diffusion supporting supply chain exploitation create "gaps, discrepancies, conflicts, and encounters as well as borders [that should be] understood not as obstacles but as parameters from which efficiencies can be produced."[11] Tsing continues:

Supply chains offer a model for thinking simultaneously about global integration, on the one hand, and the formation of diverse niches, on the other. Supply chains stimulate both global standardization and growing gaps between rich and poor, across lines of color and culture, and between North and South. Supply chains refocus critical analysis of diversity in relation to local and global capitalist developments. . . . [They] link up dissimilar firms . . . diversity forms a part of the *structure* of capitalism rather than an inessential appendage . . . diversity conditions the responses of both capital and labor to the problems of cutting labor costs and disciplining the workforce.[12]

Globalized ascendency both plays nationally or regionally bounded particularities against each other and conjures a specific worker subjectivity: One that can compete, as highly skilled British film professionals must, on the basis of niche specialisms. One that complies with the flexible, modular, ever-shifting conditions of production demanded by employers constantly on the lookout for cheaper manufacturing possibilities.

These circumstances oblige a cunning balance of fitting in and standing out, something also hardwired into, as I shall later assert, the rapid "adjunctification" of employment in the very higher education institutions that train these workers accordingly. University education, I insist, is centrally implicated in the creation of exactly these sorts of capitalist ways of thinking, being, and working. My objective with this essay, therefore, is not so much to exercise academic analytical technique from a comfortable remove in order to pinpoint Britain's exact position in some global film industry race to the bottom. Rather, I would like to gauge higher education's conformity to the supply chain as a means of searching out what can be done, from within, to disturb it. To begin to grasp these imbrications, "Supply Chains and the Human Condition" petitions us to look beyond pay scale toward a more complex understanding of the attitudes and skills, consummate yet acquiescent, that render a country like the United Kingdom competitive. Higher education plays a central role here. But first I will provide a sense of the broader picture.

The United Kingdom has one of the world's largest percentages of creative-sector contributions to gross domestic product. Phil Ramsey and Andrew White, who have plotted out the economic policies the Labour government (in office from 1997 to 2010) implemented to shape this situation, also indicate that "the desire to raise the awareness of these industries was largely political, in that it served to provide justification for the Labour Party's decision not to reverse the long-term decline in manufacturing industries to which, through its traditional supporters and links with the trades unions, it still had a nominal attachment."[13] Gutted by forty years of economic and antiunion policy, formerly industrial spaces, factories, and hangars like Leavesden, have been converted into film studios, the rights of the workforce retrofitted in tandem. As suggested by my friend's comment about selling his soul, the labor protections furnished by the United Kingdom's traditional manufacturing unions do not extend nearly as far into the creative industries. British film industry crews are regularly obligated to sign waivers refusing EU provisions and regulations on maximum working hours, and seventy hours per week has been fairly average over this period.[14] Here we witness the machinations of what Ned Rossiter classifies as the "logistical state": national capacities (people, spaces, legislation) modeled to the needs of supranational marketplaces, vaunted as particular, unparalleled, and thus competitive via this very patterning.[15] Amid these coordinations, the distance separating business from university training came under sustained scrutiny.

Commencing in the 1990s and accelerated by New Labour throughout the 2000s, universities have been exponentially compelled, through any number of policy reforms, to "produce" graduates attuned to the knowledge and creative economies. In exact historical parallel, succeeding governments cast higher education further and further adrift from public funding (introducing tuition fees, replacing grants with loans), obliging the sector to search for its own means of staying afloat. One such strategy was to tender catchy and employment-oriented courses, including those assuring a grounding in media production. More than half of the film industry professionals who hold bachelor's degrees, which is two-thirds of them, studied a media-related subject, and 21 percent continued into postgraduate study.[16]

This media education now falls increasingly under the dominion of a training body called ScreenSkills, launched as Creative Skillset in 2007 and rebranded under its current name in 2018, which ratifies qualifications and those fit to award them. Only a few exclusive institutions have met the ScreenSkills standards. Doing so remains a costly endeavor (necessitating professional equipment as well as ongoing accreditation fees) for institutions that have weathered plummeting state support over the same period. ScreenSkills stipulates high levels of vocational training as determined by industry needs, responsive to these over and above other ideals of liberal, critical, or politicized education. The agency underscores that courses and programs looking for a spot under its umbrella "must have a particular focus on graduate employment rates, high standards of student work, a focus on professional preparation of students including teamwork, soft skills and business skills, relations with employers and an industry focus."[17] Its literature strikes "a clear distinction . . . between academic studies and vocational provision," unequivocally privileging the former.[18] Almost all educators within the arts will recognize this entanglement of the university and industry through a rise in placements and formalized, in-course internships, the kind that ScreenSkills compels and are sold on prospectuses as a "foot in the door," unique and prized openings afforded lucky graduates in an aggressive sectorial job market. The university thus becomes a potential site of struggle against both the tightening links to industry *under industry's own terms of exploitation* and the honing of a particular worker subjectivity that accepts, even relishes, extremely tough (read: competitive) conditions.

As a clear indicator of its industry logics, ScreenSkills awards its chosen educational partners with a TICK (trusted information creator) quality mark. In so doing, it borrows connotations from the British Standards Kitemark, now more than a century old and a respected endorsement for shoppers of rigorously regulated safety and manufacturing quality.[19] ScreenSkills thereby squarely frames distinction in consumerist terms that identify education as a product, boasting, "Courses awarded the Tick quality mark can use it to differentiate themselves in a crowded marketplace, delivering a distinct market advantage."[20] If the Harry Potter franchise works internationally to showcase a hallowed British education, all uniforms, boarding school houses, and Gothic architecture, it finds its counterpart in the Tick for university courses that match ScreenSkills' exacting criteria. Or, to put it more bluntly, standardizations (as required by a supply chain mode of production) are determined not by the education sector but by industry evaluators and utterly in line with their own needs. Time and time again, reports and executive interviews flag that Britain's advantage to the global supply chain is its *talent* and, more so, the *training* that nurtures it.[21] It is this education—once primarily state sponsored, now increasingly and expeditiously privatized— that is currently being traded.

Tellingly, an emphasis on the skills acquired also drives the narrative of the Harry Potter Studio Tour attraction at Leavesden. *Variety* journalist Adam Dawtrey reviews the experience as "[not] so much a theme park, as an exhibit paying homage to the craftspeople who built the franchise. Its purpose is not to create illusions but to strip them away and reveal the skill behind them." For him, "There's no better advertisement for what the British film industry can achieve than the Warner Bros. Studio Tour."[22] The tour's fastidious engrossment in how-to descriptions both entices visitors into this economy (hands-on, immersive, "you too can") and congratulates British creative exceptionalism. Copious labeling explains each filmmaking department's role and takes pains to acknowledge, often by name, the "more than 4,000 talented, passionate and dedicated people who worked on the *Harry Potter* motion pictures." Ticket buyers are encouraged not simply to marvel at the wizardry, but to appreciate how, latent within British ordinariness (the kind architecturally expressed by some of the film sets on view, such as the humdrum British cul-de-sac where Harry Potter lives), the nation, like Harry Potter, might also possess extraordinary faculties. Matthew Freeman, a media scholar who has analyzed the tour, defines this as a balance of "behind-the-scenes" and "into-the-scenes," one that creates both an illusion of entry into the fictional world and, I contend, an identification with the process of film manufacture itself.[23] Swept up in the faraway exoticism of technical expertise, fantastical film narrative, and theme-park marvel—the "difference" that Tsing flags as crucial to viable market placement—is the visitor's own enticement toward this sort of work. Freeman undertook interviews with people leaving the attraction and concludes that their first pronouncements about their time at Leavesden revealed how much they had learned about filmmaking there.[24]

Moreover, the means by which creativity is presented throughout trumpets the team's resourceful perseverance. One banner, for instance, quotes construction manager Paul Hayes: "Every day was a different challenge, but everything the art department came up with, we achieved. It was just brilliant." Such statements comingle with the neoliberal mainstay values of self-sufficiency and entrepreneurialism, exactly the qualities meant to replace the union protections from which government had concurrently been trying to distance the country. The ethos engendered is not solely of the crews' own making; it has not (only) been ingeniously generated from below. Policy drives British creativity, as I shall further extrapolate, into a casualization of the workforce, applauded at sites like Leavesden (and far beyond) as tenacity. Coextensive to and aligned with the government strategies already detailed, the withdrawal of student grants and the escalation of tuition fees have metamorphosed university degrees according to these tenets and into commodities promising individual human capital, labor power as personal investment. The bill for this training lands increasingly on the doorstop of the self-reliant trainee, not the nation-state or employer. The United Kingdom's "competitive advantage" lies in its blend of skills and assumption of grueling, deferential, and insecure employment conditions.

These shifts have helped maneuver into place a culture where long peri-ods of unpaid work, the kinds that nominate Britain's film industry as cost-effective to offshore production, are now considered a prerequisite for "mak-ing it" in film. It should be stressed how quickly the unpaid internship has been normalized as a career stage in the past twenty years. An entry-level employee now pays for their own training, including, most likely, shelling out fees to a university to work gratis in the industry (a work placement or internship). A question persists as to why so many tolerate a product (film) generated through this much free labor, when we might otherwise take an ethical stance on such practices. Partly, it is the fantastical obfuscation of the places and modes of production generated by the very mechanisms of cinematic rendition that make us love it so. But it is also the magnetism of the narrative that any of us would be fortunate to "follow our dreams" into a job in film, something that the university system may not necessarily find much time to interrogate.

Let us consider this situation, instead, in Marxian terms, where labor power comprises not a direct exchange of money for hours, but, primarily, the skills and experience we bring to a job. Through this lens, such training amounts to a clear ideological expression of how a population is recomposed politically and economically. As interns work for free, generating surplus, or profit, for the employer, the implication is that they contribute to their own personal labor power repertoire. Yet that possibility remains speculative at best, reinforcing all the while the "competitive self," an offloading to individ-ualism of employer exploitation. When the industry sets the terms of these "opportunities" for students, as ScreenSkills would have it through partner-ships with university courses, the supply chain lengthens further than the tax breaks and government incentives into pursuits that undermine orga-nized labor and multiply student debt. The risk and gamble involved mate-rialize and intensify precarious life as normative. Even the House of Lords Select Committee on Communications's 2010 report on Britain's film and television industries notes the decline of paid apprenticeships in the wake of a less-formalized entry-level structure that prefers selection through contacts: who a graduate knows but also a hand-in-glove relationship with educational institutions.[25] Differentiation, systematized as advantage, draws boundaries here according to the cost of access, gendering and racializing as it does so.

At this point, we could find succor in the academy's own endeavors to confront how prejudice and inequality take root as difference. But to what extent might the cosmopolitan ideals ballasting the curricula of the arts and humanities actually feed the supply chain? Thinkers like Gayatri Spivak and Aihwa Ong look closely and critically at our standard (and egalitarian in intent) multicultural pedagogies.[26] Both propose that objectives of inclusion, without a deep acknowledgement of the brutal injustices ruling the transnational flows of labor and finance, can, paradoxically, serve as handmaidens to capital. For these two writers, a liberal openness might slip into exactly the sort of preparation of future workers, who are, in Ong's words, "biopolitically and spatially attuned to the workings of global markets."[27] Their (paid-for) openness to the world's diversity, for Ong, eases in large part the "transnational linkage of sites."[28] They help render southern England, for instance, and zones of production like Leavesden still more familiar and desirable to visiting workers from the upper echelons of the pay scale. Britain's appealing touristic image, also promoted by the Harry Potter franchise, contributes in no small part. All the while, through technical fluency under ScreenSkills' insistence, British worker training converges on global industrial norms, which buttress these more social and cultural incarnations of the standardization logistics requires for ease of movement. Within the realms of the university, with its sensitivities to pluralism, we might press for a greater awareness of how instead to strike meaningful allegiances with others under the thumb of globally mobile commerce, rather than greasing its wheels through more elite cross-border affinities.

Similar but smaller scale and more realizable alliances could also be cultivated through a break from the university's habitual and habituating modes of assessment. The privileging of individualism necessary for competition and division propagates, for example, in how students are evaluated largely in singular terms, and in how universities' courses and programs vie against others to strive for "excellence," each with their own range of commodities, including the free labor opportunities rolled into their golden ticket enticements. These structures, and many more, comply closely with the neoliberal values of independently driven motivation, entrepreneurialism, and self-sufficiency that are also the bastions of the creative economy and that sustain the global supply chain Tsing has exposed. None of these relations, incentives, or propensities do much to foster solidarity or collective struggle against free labor.

The same could be said of life within the university's own crowded labor markets, determined, as they now largely are in the United Kingdom, by commodified doctoral preparation. Both sectors profit from a populous reserve army of willingly available graduates whose constitution abets a more competitive arena filled with exploitable trained personnel, more voluntarily accepting of casualization. Ballooning student debt plays a significant role here: in England, most drastically, tuition fees largely tripled in 2012. These two factors—aggressive labor markets and debt—prompt what Gigi Roggero pithily summarizes as "risk upstream and . . . capture downstream."[29] Debt, for Maurizio Lazzarato, one of its most comprehensive theorists, accelerates exactly the same sorts of disciplining to the regimes of capital that Tsing imputes to the supply chain. It compels the debtor not so much "to reimburse in actual money but rather in conduct, attitudes, ways of behaving, plans, subjective commitments, the time devoted to finding a job, the time used for conforming oneself to the criteria dictated by the market and business, etc. . . . In other words, debt reconfigures biopolitical power by demanding a production of subjectivity."[30] Through debt, risk is absorbed not by the state or the employer but rather right into the emotional and fiscal life of the student. In the industries of film and education, the financial reality that disposes a graduate to take on "whatever" job is bolstered according to an opportunistic illusion of their own further indebtedness. Entrants are asked to shoulder often unfeasibly taxing junior-level openings that are concomitantly framed as "lucky breaks" and (note the language of debt here) "paying one's dues."

At the same time as a professoriate is progressively enforced by agencies like ScreenSkills to understand and frame a degree as a job qualification—its customers' best attempt at self-commodification—its own composition suffers the insecurities and exploitation of expanded casualization. Given these shared conditions and the advancing proximity of the two sectors, how, within the practices of work itself, might we unite politically? I speak here mostly in and to my own role certainly as a researcher but more urgently and indivisibly as an educator in the university sector. To the mind of Charles Burnetts, here talking about adjunctification within higher education, but with ready applicability to the creative industries, "CMS [Cinema and media studies] is tainted by the contingent labor problem, which it sees as incidental to its modes of discourse, and it must be made visible through a self-reflexive reimagining of who we are and what we, as professionals, have to say."[31] Writers like Burnetts spur us not to stop short at the mere factual relaying of these difficult circumstances but to militate against their systemic aggressions in how we structure thought and theory. In sum, the imperative is to grasp and change—in form as well as content—our own imbrication in the systems of biopolitical preparation for capital's abuses, including through how the university becomes a node in the provision of workers for spaces like Leavesden, as well as its own casualized labor pools.

Concurrently, what potential resides within the actual *training*, so valued by and crucial to the supply chain, so explicitly commodified and individualized, yet still not utterly controlled by industry, for radical refusal and renegotiation? In the United Kingdom (and regularly working beyond its borders), a collective by the name of the Precarious Workers Brigade directly intends to intervene in this way, inspiring me to lay out their strategies here in some detail. One of their many aims is to transfigure an increasing emphasis on "employability" within university programs into something other than the subordination of students, through professionalization and work placement courses, to the norms and disciplines of precarious, individualized, competitive compliance. The Precarious Workers Brigade strives to imbue such curricular requirements with the critical or political ideals students might be developing elsewhere but from which such job skills instruction is almost uniformly cut loose. The collective comprises salaried academics who benefit from the potential to address such concerns in their daily praxis; they also regularly convene workshops in universities and other spaces, undoing the typical expert-consultant visitor relationship.

In 2017, the Precarious Workers Brigade published its free-to-download *Training for Exploitation? Politicising Employability and Reclaiming Education*, a tool kit for those requested to oversee such professionalization, often themselves either career advisors detached from the daily unfurling of critical scholarship, or colleagues in the most casualized and vulnerable positions within their departments and consequently in serious need of shared materials to lessen their own heavy workloads. Stressing the unevenness of access to employment, disabusing the promise that such training safeguards against joblessness, and exposing the lack of "neutrality" of the attributes ascribed to being "employable," the resources collected within include bibliographies and statistics that support the critique of the current engineering of the labor force. Drawing on a host of radical pedagogies, *Training for Exploitation?* provides ready-made possible templates and exercises that range from manifesto writing, forum theater, and photo romance creation to how to devise open letters and "ethical internship" contracts or convert industry placements into militant worker inquiry. These activities invite students to question their positions as laborers, past, present, and future. The publication provides advice on how to involve oneself in or initiate worker cooperatives and time banks, alerting students to genuine economic alternatives.

Throughout *Training for Exploitation?* solidarity takes center stage. The Precarious Workers Brigade's stance is worth quoting at length:

To re-introduce solidarity into educational conversations about work is to offer an alternative that does not otherwise seem to exist. Under the neoliberal logic, anyone you meet, including a co-worker, is largely understood as another networking opportunity. Yet, it should be clear that competition is not the only way of us relating to each other; self-reliance is neither something desirable, nor possible to achieve. . . . Solidarity is a very different kind of relating to and helping one another, of improving one's work and life. It is fundamentally linked to justice and ethics. It calls for standing together with other people. Solidarity becomes concrete when we consider how we think about our career dreams. How can we "get there" differently? Do we actually like the way the "there" operates? Since competition produces anxiety and stress, it can be a relief when the classroom becomes a space where it is possible to deconstruct this narrative and make room to explore more co-operative economies and goals. This process of addressing individualised competitiveness builds solidarities between students—and opens teaching to collective transformation.[32]

Paradoxically, and generatively, such solidarity might now seem more obtainable, given that the division between an "us" (in education) and a "them" (in the creative industries) no longer remains so clear-cut. As an academic, I too convince myself into intensive work schedules that a similarly compromised "commitment" persuades me to tolerate. I too could joke about needing a courtesy bot to sustain my friendships or ask myself the question, "Alive?" But to connect beyond simply commiserating? To start, it would be beholden on all of us not to convert the animosity generated by one side dictating the terms the other must follow into a breach that segregates workers. For certain, both sectors are independently arranged in ways that complicate collectivism. Each film project contracts a different composition of crew members; workers are fragmented through casualization. Academics tend toward lone, often competitive research ventures; they often study contexts with a projected objectivity that can preclude them from horizontal political organizing. Nonetheless, we carry distinct skills and tactics to offer each other within an ultimately shared struggle against how transnationalized, competitive capitalism drives down wages, conditions, and securities. If the supply chain capitalizes on the fleet flow between our sectors, then we must try to move through our circuitries differently.

For this, we might take some cues from the tradition of *conricerca*, co- or militant research.[33] *Conricerca* derives from deep alliances between community members, who need not all be researchers in the textbook sense, working together to realize radical and situated change. Militant research is expressly motivated by the needs and priorities of those involved and looks to acknowledge their labor and ideas squarely. It does not apologize for its partiality, amass research to then transfer it out of the immediate, or pass on the baton of responsibility. Unlike much conventional academic research, *conricerca* refuses the extractive impulse. Rather, it interrogates, often upends, its conditions and prejudices of production, here offering something closer to political transformation than a reinvestment back into human capital for the researcher. In all this, *conricerca* seeks to take seriously the restrictions encircling its communities, along with broader political and social ones, to better enact whatever action is deemed necessary. The work conducted aspires to communality rather than stratified pecking orders of labor or outcome and, in so doing, contravenes the weighted priorities of interaction insisted by the likes of ScreenSkills.

As the global supply chain and its governmental agents close the gap between academy and industry for their own ends, the resulting proximity renders *conricerca* more possible. The supply chain has forced us to learn each other's languages, through which we might now communicate and invent better idioms and praxes. Our shared encounters—the work placements, internships, guest visits to professionalization seminars, the growing trend in universities to hire practitioner-theorists (admittedly to save money), as well as the continuities fostered through the application of training—offer sustained potential for co-research and collective struggle. To do so, they must be redirected away from hierarchized master classes, tips on how to succeed, unique salable insight, a foot in the door, or an individualized yet highly ideologically confected "lucky break." Rather than peddling "professionalization," these congregations bear the potential to undo that very notion and its biopolitical lockstep with the supply chain's demands. There is scope to transform the wonder at expertise into a "you too can" (as the Harry Potter Studio Tour does for other ends) that assumes a much more politically emancipating application of creativity.

NOTES

1. Ben Goldsmith, Susan Ward, and Tom O'Regan, *Local Hollywood: Global Film Production and the Gold Coast* (St Lucia: University of Queensland Press, 2010), 87.
2. Stefano Harney and Fred Moten, *The Undercommons: Fugitive Planning and Black Study* (Wivenhoe, UK: Minor Compositions, 2013), 91.

3. Tom Grater, "Creative Skillset Rebrands as ScreenSkills, Urges Increased Training to Support Production Boom," *Screen Daily*, October 4, 2018, https://www.screendaily.com/news/creative-skillset-rebrands-as-screenskills-urges-increased-training-to-support-production-boom/5133241.article (figures on global ranking supplied by "research company IHS"); and Diana Lodderhose, "Mighty Blighty," *Variety* 325, no. 1, August 12, 2014, 128.

4. Reported speech of Roy Button, managing director of Warner Bros., cited in House of Lords Select Committee on Communications, *The British Film and Television Industries—Decline or Opportunity? Volume I: Report* (London: Authority of the House of Lords, 2010), 95.

5. House of Lords Select Committee on Communications, *The British Film and Television Industries*, 96.

6. It should be noted that this is not by far the United Kingdom's first such development. Foreign investment in built film-industry assets dates back to the 1920s, meaning that, for around a century, the fortunes of British cinema and its manufacture have been driven by, dependent on, and tightly interwoven with those of other national and transnational enterprises. For fuller descriptions of this history, see Ben Goldsmith and Tom O'Regan, "Still Exceptional? London's Film Studios," in *The Film Studio: Film Production in the Global Economy* (Oxford: Rowman and Littlefield, 2005), 135–49; Paul McDonald, "Britain: Hollywood UK," in *The Contemporary Hollywood Film Industry*, ed. Paul McDonald and Janet Wasko (Oxford: Blackwell, 2008), 220–31; and Behlil Melis, *Hollywood Is Everywhere: Global Directors in the Blockbuster Era* (Amsterdam: Amsterdam University Press, 2016), 69.

7. House of Lords Select Committee on Communications, *The British Film and Television Industries*, 95; and Adam Dawtrey, "Studio Schools Visitors on 'Potter,'" *Variety* 426, no. 8, April 2–8, 2012, 11.

8. Alan Parker, *Building a Sustainable UK Film Industry: A Presentation to the UK Film Industry* (London: UKFC, 2002), 8–9.

9. Duncan Petrie, "Creative Industries and Skills: Film Education and Training in the Era of New Labour," *Journal of British Cinema and Television* 9, no 3 (2012): 357–76, 369.

10. Anna Tsing, "Supply Chains and the Human Condition," *Rethinking Marxism* 21, no. 2 (2009): 148–76, 148–49.

11. Sandro Mezzadra and Brett Neilson, *Border as Method, or, the Multiplication of Labor* (Durham, NC: Duke University Press, 2013), 206.

12. Tsing, "Supply Chains and the Human Condition," 150.

13. Phil Ramsey and Andrew White, "Art for Art's Sake? A Critique of the Instrumentalist Turn in the Teaching of Media and Communications in UK Universities," *International Journal of Cultural Policy* 21, no. 1 (2015): 78–96, 79.

14. BECTU, the Media and Entertainment Union, "How Many Hours Are You Doing Today?" February 24, 2005, http://www.bectu.org.uk/news/gen/ng0217.html.

15. Ned Rossiter, *Software, Infrastructure, Labor: A Media Theory of Logistical Nightmares* (New York: Routledge, 2016), 173.

16. House of Lords Select Committee on Communications, *The British Film and Television Industries*, 70–71.

17. ScreenSkills, "How to Get Tick Accreditation," accessed January 31, 2019, https://www.screenskills.com/education-training/tick/how-to-get-tick-accreditation/ (URL no longer functional).

18. Cited as "SkillSet/UK Film Council 2013: 17," in Yael Friedman and Steve Whitford, "On the Edge of Practice: Reflections on Filmmaking Pedagogy in the Age of the Creative Industries," *Cinema Journal* 5, no. 1 (2018), http://www.teachingmedia.org/on-the-edge-practice-reflections-on-filmmaking-pedagogy-in-the-age-of-the-creative-industries/.

19. Ramsey and White, "Art for Art's Sake?," 87–88, remarks on the allusions to Kitemarking in SkillSet's promotional literature.

20. ScreenSkills, "How to Get Tick Accreditation."

21. See, for example, House of Lords Select Committee on Communications, *The British Film and Television Industries*, 70; Dawtrey, "Studio Schools Visitors," 11; and Adam McNary, "House That Harry Built," *Variety* 426, no. 8, April 2–8, 2012, 11.

22. Dawtrey, "Studio Schools Visitors," 11.

23. Matthew Freeman, "Transmedia Attractions: The Case of *Warner Bros. Studio Tour—The Making of Harry Potter*," in *The Routledge Companion to Transmedia Studies*, ed. Matthew Freeman and Renira Rampazzo Gambarato (New York: Routledge, 2019), 126.

24. Freeman, "Transmedia Attractions," 128.

25. House of Lords Select Committee on Communications, *The British Film and Television Industries*, 74.

26. See Gayatri Chakravorty Spivak, *An Aesthetic Education in the Era of Globalization* (Cambridge, MA: Harvard University Press, 2012), 137–57; and Aihwa Ong, *Neoliberalism as Exception: Mutations in Citizenship and Sovereignty* (Durham, NC: Duke University Press, 2006), 139–56.

27. Ong, *Neoliberalism as Exception*, 141.

28. Ong, *Neoliberalism as Exception*, 88.

29. Gigi Roggero, *The Production of Living Knowledge: The Crisis of the University and the Transformation of Labor in Europe and North America*, trans. Enda Brophy (Philadelphia: Temple University Press, 2011), 78.

30. Maurizio Lazzarato, *The Making of the Indebted Man: An Essay on the Neoliberal Condition*, trans. Joshua David Jordan (Los Angeles: Semiotext(e), 2012), 104.

31. Charles Burnetts, "'New Weapons' for the Precariat in Film and Media Studies," *Cinema Journal Teaching Dossier* 4, no. 2 (2016), http://www.teachingmedia.org/new-weapons-precariat-film-media-studies/.

32. Precarious Workers Brigade, *Training for Exploitation? Politicising Employability and Reclaiming Education* (London: Journal of Aesthetics and Protest Press, 2017), 16–17, https://joaap.org/press/trainingforexploitation.htm.

33. For a fuller description of *conricerca*, see Guido Borio, Francesca Pozzi, and Gigi Roggero, *"Conricerca as Political Action,"* in *Utopian Pedagogy: Radical Experiments against Neoliberal Globalization*, eds. Mark Coté, Mark, Richard J. F Day, and Greig De Peuter (Toronto: University of Toronto Press, 2007), 163–85; and Colectivo Situaciones, "On the Researcher-Militant," translated by Sebastian Touza, *Transversal Texts*, September 2003, https://transversal.at/transversal/0406/colectivo-situaciones/en.

FORKLIFT CINEMA

In 1952, the film *Denver and Rio Grande* sensationalized a nineteenth-century infrastructure expansion: the railroad that transformed Colorado mining towns into suppliers for American production. While the narrative focused on the logistical difficulty of construction in the mountains, the film's producers depended on a new logistical technology to navigate this rough terrain themselves. In the years prior, the forklift had spread from industrial plants to film studios, where it was used to move scenery and equipment, raise and lower lights, stretch wire, scaffold set construction, and support cameras when cranes were infeasible or too expensive. For *Denver and Rio Grande*, shooting in the very canyons the railroad had struggled to overcome, a modified forklift truck named the Blue Goose supported the bulky Technicolor camera and its cameramen, enabling the capture of wide-ranging aerial shots. On-location shots had always depended on the ability to get the camera into position as quickly as possible. Now, a technology that had been largely confined to the factories became an invisible support for the production of a roaming, expansive visuality. In this other kind of factory, the hydraulic forklift became part of the logistical network of cinematic production.

This image, documenting the logistical transformation of cinematic production, features a cameraman atop a forklift and surrounded by the film crew. From Arthur Rowan, "Universal-International Introduces New Camera and Location Truck," *American Cinematographer* (July 1955), 405.

The Politics of Cable Supply from the British Empire to Huawei Marine

SINCE THE EARLY EXPOSÉS OF WORKING CONDITIONS at the Apple supplier Foxconn in 2006, the supply chains of digital consumer devices have become an object of public scrutiny.[1] Critics have repeatedly pointed out that the disconnect between technology companies and their expansive and intricate networks of production makes it difficult to ensure ethics and accountability in digital media's assembly. As a way to put pressure on the tech industry, investigative journalism and documentary films, such as *Blood in the Mobile* (dir. Frank Piasecki Poulsen; 2010), revealed the industry's reliance on conflict minerals, ecologically devastating practices, and worker exploitation. Capitalizing on this attention, some companies tinkered with their supply chains and promised increased transparency through corporate social responsibility programs, while others, such as the creators of Fairphone, developed new technologies that were marketed as ethical alternatives. Throughout this struggle over digital media's sourcing, critics and corporations alike commented on the way that the production of digital devices is made possible by a globalized economic landscape, a series of complex logistical links, and the speed of digital networks themselves.

Counter to the mass production of digital consumer devices, the manu-facturing, installation, and operation of global internet infrastructure, es-pecially the undersea cables that carry almost 100 percent of transoceanic data traffic, have little in common with the digital culture they support. The cable supply chain embeds a different form of historical politics, one that re-sembles that of the nineteenth- and twentieth-century colonial cable system more than the contemporary network society. Undersea cable systems are pressure points in the global network. There are relatively few systems that carry almost all internet traffic across the oceans. In some locations, such as Cambodia and Greenland, there are just a few cables that connect the coun-try to the rest of the internet. And in other locations, even with multiple sys-tems in operation, traffic is funneled through only a handful of coastal land-ing zones. It is because of these systems' extraordinary capacity, expense, and longevity (they will operate for decades without being retrieved from the seafloor) that, counter to the planned obsolescence of many consumer digital technologies, long-term reliability is an essential component. Every part of the undersea network's production is known and documented. In turn, the intense dependence on cable systems and the need for reliability bind these systems up in a set of national anxieties.

This chapter examines the ongoing influence of national politics on the development of network infrastructure and particularly on the installation of undersea cable systems that constitute the backbone of the global inter-net. In the first section, I briefly describe the historical and contemporary suppliers of transoceanic cables. In contrast to the flexibility and modularity of many global supply chains, the manufacture of submarine cable has re-mained relatively fixed in a small set of locations and companies. The major suppliers of long-haul submarine cables are SubCom (United States), Alcatel Submarine Networks (France), and NEC (Japan). Even as these companies have been bought and sold over the past decades, all three originate in the late nineteenth or early twentieth centuries. Today, they remain a point of tension in digital networks in part because of their historical connections with state-owned or -affiliated telecommunications companies. Narratives about national security and these companies' ties to governments play a key role in their centrality to the global internet. In the second section of the chapter, I describe how rumors about hidden spying equipment in cable sys-tems, alongside backlash from the US and Australian governments, made it difficult for the Chinese cable supplier Huawei Marine to break into the transoceanic market. This means that most of the cables that connect con-tinents continue to be installed by companies that are based in the United

States, Europe, and Japan and that have been in operation since the telegraph era. This structure may function to delay, capsize, or redirect interest in cable projects that deviate from existing network formations.

Through an examination of cable manufacturing and installation, this chapter offers an approach to internet operations that reveals the global network's continued dependence on restricted supply chains and its imbrication within existing political regimes. The centralization of supply is a significant component of the cable industry's and internet infrastructures' conservatism. In turn, such politics also play a critical role today as the industry is shifting, with the OTTs (over-the-top providers, including Google and Facebook) reshaping the terrain of cable laying. The demand of the OTTs, coupled with narrow supply chains, means that the major cable suppliers are all currently running at capacity and yet their margins are not increasing—there is less and less money for research and development. This situation in turn helps to scaffold the OTTs' influence in the industry and potentially keeps smaller or regional projects from cable supply. As a result, the OTTs are not simply expanding cable ownership, but shifting the politics and paths of cable construction. While Huawei Marine developed projects that diversified the geopolitical landscape of the network (even while tying new territories directly into Chinese expansion), the moves by Facebook and Google could set the stage for a shift into a new vertically integrated model, with some speculating that either the OTTs or one of the telecommunications carriers will eventually purchase one of the cable suppliers and take over the supply chain itself, returning to a model reminiscent of the British monopoly of the nineteenth-century cable system.

Sourcing the Network

The sourcing of materials has long been a political component of networked communications. In the nineteenth century, gutta-percha, which was derived from the sap of trees in Southeast Asia, was an ideal cable insulator and critical to the production of undersea telegraph cables. As Bruce Hunt unequivocally states in his study of the natural plastic, "British firms' effective control of the Singapore-based gutta percha trade reinforced Britain's nearly total domination of the cable industry."[2] In turn, British cable companies laid lines to Singapore and around Southeast Asia that helped to solidify regional and global trade. While the French and Dutch both established gutta-percha plantations, these efforts ultimately failed, and John Pender's Telegraph Construction and Maintenance Company (Telcon) continued to control submarine cable construction. It was not until the 1950s, when polyethylene replaced gutta-percha as the insulation material for new transoceanic telephone cables, that it became much easier for non-British companies to take a significant role in cable manufacturing.

While the actual supply of gutta-percha helped to solidify the British domination of construction and installation, the sourcing of materials also helped to solidify ideologies of connection. For example, in the 1950s and 1960s, as coaxial cables were being laid across the oceans, telecommunications companies and consortia made films that foregrounded their multinational supply. *Eighty Channels under the Sea* (1960) and *Ring around the Earth* (1964), two films about the first transpacific cable linking Australia, Fiji, New Zealand, and Canada, were as much an articulation of the unity of the Commonwealth as they were a description of network operations.[3] The narrator of *Eighty Channels under the Sea* tells the audience: "The spirit of partnership behind this vast project has been carried to the supply of raw material," including steel from Britain and polythene from Australia. Similarly, an AT&T film about a transatlantic telephone cable features images of workmen producing cable in factories in France, West Germany, England, and the United States.[4]

At the same time as they revealed their networks of supply—the fact that they were produced by the countries they connected—these films articulated the importance of cable systems and the telephone conversations they carried to trade. For *Ring around the Earth*, the cable's production committee planned scenes that focused explicitly on the telephone and telex communications that coordinated global trade. In the film, a Scottish shepherd, whose sheep provide carpet wool, calls a veterinarian in New Zealand. A buyer at a wool auction in Australia receives a telegram. Canadian lumber enterprises communicate via cable with Australian builders. In the film's planning, the cable production committee, reviewing the film's script, stated explicitly that the commentator "will say . . . that rapid and reliable communication is vital for world trade."[5] The locations included in this network were always a political matter. One set of notes on the film script details: "Mention of shipments of materials behind Iron Curtain likely offend sensitivities of viewers particularly if film reaches USA and must be avoided."[6] As Brian Larkin observes, provision of infrastructure itself is "a work of state representation," and infrastructure's grand openings are often a "visual spectacle and political ritual."[7] This is true even for global telecommunications infrastructure laid on the seafloor. In these cable films, which were circulated beyond the industry and in theaters, networks of communication were ideologically sutured to networks of trade.

The materials and supply of contemporary fiber-optic cables are no longer tied to the British Empire, nor are they as often made into a visual spectacle, but they continue to be a subject of state politics and a means of state representation. The supply of undersea cables has historically been limited to a few companies, given the rarity and expense of projects, support infrastructure, and research and development. During the telegraph era, there were four submarine cable manufacturers based in London: Telcon, Siemens Brothers, W. T. Henley Telegraph Works Company, and the India Rubber, Gutta Percha and Telegraph Works Company. By the late 1930s, following the expansion of wireless, there remained only one: Telcon and Siemens Brothers merged their submarine cable divisions to become Submarine Cables Ltd., then the sole manufacturer of undersea cable in the United Kingdom. Although the British company Standard Telephones and Cables Ltd. entered the subsea systems market fifteen years later, it eventually took over Submarine Cables Ltd. (becoming STC Submarine Systems), and yet again there was only one supplier of undersea cables in the United Kingdom. As the fiber-optic era began, although STC Submarine Systems was one of the primary suppliers of submarine cable, it no longer had the monopoly British firms once possessed.[8]

Although through the 1980s and early 1990s there were several critical transitions in ownership (including the sale of STC Submarine Systems to a Canadian company, Northern Telecom, in 1991), the historical concentration of cable manufacturing in the United Kingdom dissipated in the 1990s when Alcatel Submarcom bought STC Submarine Systems for $900 million in 1994. Prior to the sale, the British Monopolies and Mergers Commission produced a report that "noted some concern that STC's future as an important UK business might be jeopardized by the proposed merger" but ultimately concluded that despite "the dangers inherent in the further concentration of supply" the commission expected Alcatel to continue to manufacture submarine cable systems in the United Kingdom.[9] Two years later, Alcatel shut down the historic Southampton cable factory. Although cable design and development continue to occur at the company's former Greenwich site (and Global Marine continues as the contemporary iteration of Cable & Wireless), the headquarters of Alcatel Submarine Networks would be located near Paris, and cable manufacturing would take place in its Calais factory.

Alcatel Submarine Networks (ASN) today ties together the legacy of British networks with a long tradition of French cable laying. In 1891, a submarine cable manufacturing plant was set up in Calais by La Société

Générale des Téléphone.[10] Calais was chosen due to the area's new port facilities and proximity to mining regions.[11] As industry historian Stewart Ash documents, the motivation to build this factory was in part generated out of a desire to break the British monopoly over the global cable system. In 1938, following the expansion of wireless and just after the British merger of Telcon and Siemens Brothers, the submarine cable division merged with La Compagnie Generále d'Electricité and became part of Les Câbles de Lyon (initially a manufacturer of power cables that had since moved into submarine systems). From 1970 onward, Les Câbles de Lyon worked through Alcatel Submarcom. Today Alcatel Submarine Networks (ASN), although owned by the Finnish telecommunications company Nokia, remains fixed in these historical locations in France and the United Kingdom. Between 2013 and 2017, ASN installed eight systems and manufactured just under 40,000 kilometers of cable.[12]

Through the history of international cabling, the national origin of cable supply typically corresponded directly with the national affiliation of cable owners. Systems laid from the United Kingdom and its current and former colonies, or simply contracted by the British General Post Office/Cable & Wireless/British Telecom, chose a British supplier. French-led projects contracted Les Câbles de Lyon/Alcatel Submarcom/ASN for their systems. On projects such as TAT-2, a collaboration of AT&T, the French PTT (Posts, Telegraph, and Telephone Department), and the German PTT, cables were also sourced from each national supplier: Submarine Cable, Simplex Wire & Cable, Câbles de Lyon, and Norddeutsche Seekabelwerke. And, in turn, Simplex and Western Electric supplied cable for projects led or jointly partnered by AT&T and the US military. The British firms still supplied cable for some key American projects, but critical defense networks were sourced to a US supplier.

The genealogy of the other two major suppliers in the industry can be tracked back through American and Japanese corporate histories. In the United States, Simplex was taken over by Massachusetts-based firm Tyco in 1974 and continued to work closely with AT&T (Western Electric) into the early fiber-optic era. In 1997, Tyco International Ltd. took over AT&T Submarine Systems, and the company, after several transitions, is now known as SubCom. Although currently under Swiss ownership, SubCom is based in the United States, with its ships located in Baltimore, its offices in New Jersey, and its manufacturing facilities in New Hampshire. Between 2013 and 2017, SubCom installed nine systems and manufactured over 60,000 kilometers of cable.[13] The third large cable installer, NEC, is likewise the contemporary iteration of a long lineage of companies that have been based in Japan. Cable manufacturing began in Japan in the early 1910s, and since then a series of mergers and acquisitions transformed early telegraph cable companies into the Nippon Submarine Cable Company (1935), the Ocean Cable Company (1964), and then NEC. Between 2013 and 2017, NEC installed five systems and manufactured 18,000 kilometers of cable.[14]

I synopsize this history of corporate transitions and transactions in order to highlight several key features of submarine cable supply. First, as of 2020, three primary suppliers are responsible for manufacturing almost all of the deep-sea cable that carries close to 100 percent of all transoceanic internet traffic (they are also responsible for much of the installation, though here they are accompanied by other companies, such as Global Marine and Orange Marine). At various points in history, there have been a few more companies that have contributed to the construction of the global network's backbone, and today, there remain several smaller suppliers that produce cable for regional projects. As a whole, however, global network construction has been sourced to a very small set of players. This concentration is a direct result of the enormous expense of research and development, of establishing manufacturing facilities, and of cable production, coupled with the reliance of each of these companies on relatively few projects as a source of income even across the span of a decade. The expense is in part due to unique factors such as the cost of enormous cable ships, which can carry in their large tanks enough cable to cross the ocean. Since these ships aren't used often, the expense of building and maintaining them is folded into many cable projects, and in turn, the need to acquire ships is just one of the many things that prohibits new companies from entering the transoceanic market. These companies represent not only a concentration of knowledge but of resources. Since reliability is critical, a company's reputation and perceived experience weigh heavily in the decisions about who to choose for a project. Collectively, the supply chain for communications infrastructure—and the backbone for the internet—is relatively knowable and is still manufactured at locations that have been in operation for decades, if not over a century.

These histories of cable supply also indicate the long-standing connections between the national affiliation of the companies that design and develop networks and the national affiliation of the companies that supply systems. What might be sketched as state (and Commonwealth) representation in the films *Eighty Channels under the Sea* and *Cable to the Continent* is a guiding ideology within the industry: safety is generated by companies that have had a long history of experience in cable manufacture (stretching back to colonial projects) and implicitly by the state itself. In turn, these companies' work is a form of state representation—a means of representing what the state can do, as well as its investments and capacities. Even as Alcatel Submarine Networks has capitalized on a long history of British investment, and people from many countries work at each of these suppliers, governments and popular discourse describe ASN as the French supplier and SubCom as the US supplier. There is a tacit sense of these as national companies, an internal ideology that legitimates choices in network design and that likewise assures both customers and politicians of the safety of the internet.

Supply Chain Politics: The Case of Huawei Marine

The function of cable supply as state representation and its connections in national politics can be seen vividly in the case of the new industry entrant: Huawei Marine. But to characterize Huawei Marine as a new supplier is not entirely correct. Formed in 2008, Huawei Marine was a joint venture of United Kingdom–based cable maintenance company Global Marine Systems and the Chinese company Huawei Technologies. Global Marine Systems is itself the contemporary iteration of Cable & Wireless Marine/British Telecom Marine, the cable support and installation units of the United Kingdom's global telecommunications company. While Alcatel's purchase of STC Submarine Systems only strengthened the French tradition of cable laying, Huawei Marine is understood in the world of internet infrastructure and beyond as a Chinese company, detached from, if ever even affiliated with, the history of British cable installation.

Even though the cable landscape has opened up in recent years, with telecommunications networks and suppliers orienting along lines of national affiliation much less rigidly than in the past, Huawei Marine has had difficulty obtaining contracts to build any major transoceanic cables. Instead, the systems that Huawei Marine has installed often remain outside the domain of traditional cable companies and at the margins of the historical cable system. These included intranational systems in Libya (2010), the Philippines (2013), Portugal (2013), Indonesia (2016, 2018), the Maldives (2016), and Belize (2017), and systems connecting Tunisia and Italy (2009), Trinidad and Tobago, Guyana, and Suriname (2010), Libya and Greece (2012), China and Taiwan (2014), Nigeria and Cameroon (2015), Equatorial Guinea and Cameroon (2016), Oman and Somalia (2017), Greenland, Canada, and Iceland (2017), and Malaysia, Singapore, Cambodia, and Indonesia (2011, 2017).

Between 2013 and 2017, the company installed six systems, but manufactured under 10,000 kilometers of cable—many of these links were relatively short.

Moreover, the geographies that Huawei Marine connects are indicative of their relationship to the cable industry. Many of their existing systems have linked areas historically underrepresented in the global network: west Africa, Indonesia, South America, and small island chains. They also mirror the pattern of Chinese economic investment more broadly. In 2018, Huawei Marine completed its first major transoceanic cable: the South Atlantic Inter Link (SAIL) cable from Cameroon to Brazil. As a joint project of China Unicom, China Unicom do Brasil Telecomunicacoes Ltda., and Camtel, the project pioneered (along with a second cable system, SACS) a route that directly linked South America and Africa. What made the system innovative was also what made it possible: Huawei Marine's participation was enabled by the system's placement on the margins of the global cable system and its development outside of the historical centers of cable supply and carrier operation.

While Huawei Marine's dependence on others for the fabrication of the cable itself has hindered its ability to take on transoceanic projects, it has also been an object of national anxieties and a site of state representation. In 2011, Huawei Marine was set to break into several key markets in the Atlantic and Pacific. Hibernia Atlantic was building a new cable—Project Express—that would be the lowest latency system between New York City and London. A decade after the cable market crashed and since any transatlantic systems had gotten off the ground, Project Express was set to shift the terrain of internet infrastructure. In a press release in January 2011, Hibernia Atlantic announced that Huawei Marine had offered a financing commitment of US$250 million. "We are proud to be part of this historic cable build across the Atlantic," stated Nigel Bayliff, then CEO of Huawei Marine.[15] The following November, Hibernia Atlantic and Huawei Marine announced a successful test of the first 100 GB connection: the "highest capacity ever transmitted across the Atlantic Ocean."[16] The cable was set to be historic not only in speed, capacity, and in its revival of the transatlantic cable market, but in the company's selection of Huawei Marine as the supplier over ASN or SubCom, which had laid almost all of the transatlantic fiber optic cables.

In the year that followed, US and Australian politicians targeted Chinese suppliers, arguing that the company's equipment raised "security concerns."[17] In November 2011, the US House of Representatives' Permanent Select Committee on Intelligence launched an investigation into Huawei and another Chinese company, ZTE. In a widely circulated segment on Huawei on CBS

News's *60 Minutes*, Republican congressman Mike Rogers told audiences: "If I were an American company today . . . and you are looking at Huawei, I would find another vendor if you care about your intellectual property, if you care about your consumers' privacy, and you care about the national security of the United States of America."[18] The television segment played up a narrative that the Chinese government could exploit Huawei's communication infrastructure to wage cyberwar. The day after the segment aired, the committee released its report and "strongly encouraged" US network providers to seek other vendors for their projects.[19] Even though it did not specifically mention undersea cables or Huawei Marine, the report stated broadly that "United States' critical infrastructure, and in particular its telecommunications networks, depend on trust and reliability"—and articulated that Chinese providers were simply not to be trusted.[20] Following this, in February 2013, Hibernia Atlantic suspended work on the cable. Several "key US carriers" reportedly warned Hibernia that they "would not use the route, due to fears of losing lucrative contracts with US federal government agencies due to Huawei's involvement."[21] Hibernia ultimately switched to SubCom as its vendor.

The same tensions unraveled Huawei's aspirations in the Pacific. In 2011, a Chinese-backed consortium planned to build a new system between Sydney and Auckland, one that was positioned to break up the virtual monopoly of the Southern Cross Cable Network, which at that time controlled almost all traffic in and out of New Zealand. On the west coast of Australia, the ASSC-1 Communications Group was planning a cable from Perth to Singapore, diversifying what was then a single system stretching out from Australia's west coast. As in the case of Hibernia Atlantic, these were all private systems, not controlled or financed by the telecommunications companies that had long dominated the cable world. And each sought to break up what was a relatively static market. Huawei Marine was signed on as the supplier for each. In 2012, however, Australia's Attorney-General's Department barred Huawei from supplying infrastructure for the country's National Broadband Network, and the same "security concerns" that were raised in the Atlantic inhibited the network development around Australia. The Axin and Huawei cable across the Tasman Sea never materialized. In its place, Vodafone, Spark New Zealand, and Telstra contracted ASN to build the link between New Zealand and Australia. Likewise, instead of the ASSC-1 cable, a rival cable was built, also using ASN. Huawei was effectively blocked from entering both of these geopolitical zones because it was imagined as an extension of the Chinese government.

Such conflicts only continued in the increasingly nationalist US and UK landscapes related to the Trump presidency and Brexit, respectively. In 2017, Huawei Marine was appointed as the contractor to supply the Solomon Islands with its new cable. Shortly thereafter, the Australian government took issue with the project due to the involvement of Huawei. The Solomon Islands dropped Huawei Marine as a vendor, in part due to external pressure by Australia and allegations of corruption; ultimately the Australian government stepped in to fund two-thirds of the project. In the United States, security concerns continue to spark congressional conversation and public debate about Huawei's technologies. Take, for example, the congressional bill Defending US Government Communications Act (introduced in January 2018; HR 4747, 115th Congress [2017–18]), which cites the 2012 investigative report as one of many rationales for prohibiting government agencies from extending contracts to any entity that uses Huawei's equipment as an essential part of their system. The bill cites the US Federal Bureau of Investigation's statement that China's "cyber warfare strategy is predicated on controlling global communications network infrastructure."[22] And in May 2018, the US Federal Communications Commission (FCC) released a set of proposed rules for comment: "Protecting National Security through FCC Programs." The introduction of the document begins: "A critical element of our national security is the security of America's communications networks. Therefore, threats to the security of our nation's communications networks posed by certain communications equipment providers have long been a matter of concern. . . . And as the supply chain for our nation's communications networks increasingly reaches far beyond U.S. borders, the need to address these threats has become more pressing."[23] The FCC proposed that the Universal Service Fund would not be distributed to communications equipment or service providers that posed a national security risk either to communications networks or, vaguely, "to the communications supply chain."[24] Drawing on the former reports, the FCC specifically mentions Huawei as a potential threat to national security.

Despite such concerns, Huawei Technologies' share of the internet infrastructure market more broadly has grown, even if Huawei Marine has not captured the transatlantic and transpacific cable routes.[25] In 2019, however, the company sold its share of Huawei Marine to another Chinese company—Hengtong Optic-Electric Company, a Chinese cable manufacturer and vendor. The popular press and industry members speculated that the spying rumors and Huawei's reputation were in part the reason for the sale. Others believed that Hengtong bought Huawei Marine in order to make possible their own cable expansion given the lack of markets for Chinese cables in Western-led projects. Regardless of the intent, the move signals the ongoing presence of national politics in cable infrastructure as well as a transition to a vertically integrated model of cable supply.

Conclusion

The targeting of Huawei is not new—it activates anti-Chinese sentiment that has long circulated around the supply of digital media. This particular moment of opposition, however, is significant in several ways. First, as the US and Australian governments attempted to blacklist Huawei, they drew attention to the equipment and cables that support internet traffic and articulated cyberwar not merely as a project of remote attack via digital networks but as a process of invasion that could take place through hardware. As a result, the problem of communications security was framed as a problem of access to and participation in digital media's supply chain. The responses and resistance to these articulations involved counter-imaginations of the supply chain. As John Suffolk, the global cyber security and privacy officer for Huawei, argued: "The ICT supply chain is global," and because of this, "the risk is from the cumulative supply chain, not the vendor whose name happens to be on the 'box.'"[26] In the case of the thwarted undersea cable projects, this was a moment when whose name was on the "box" of the internet's backbone suddenly became a public political issue. As I have shown here, the installation of these systems has always been a political matter, especially the systems that form the pressure points for contemporary internet traffic, where information funnels through a tube the size of a garden hose. In other words, Huawei Marine's exclusion, despite the fact that it is a legacy of British telecommunications companies, does not represent the moment that politics enters the supply chain, it merely draws into relief the broader political matrix that has always shaped the installation of undersea cables.

For many global workers in the submarine cable industry, Huawei Marine's Chinese affiliation is seen as both stronger and more dangerous than their own political orientations. John Tibbles, an industry veteran, writes, "Huawei is effectively a state-owned enterprise," whereas "links between Government and the cable supplier in USA and the EU are at least one stage removed from the days of AT&T ownership in the USA and the Franco-British enterprises that ultimately combined into ASN."[27] Although an "oligopoly," Tibbles writes, it is "globally balanced," even if "US and EU politics mean it is highly unlikely Huawei could acquire a competitor or even be allowed to build a system that landed in the USA."[28] Others in the industry observe that even if they were allowed to land in the United States, building with Huawei would be "out of the question," because they wouldn't be able to attract US customers to purchase bandwidth "because of the security concerns."[29] Some also criticize these decisions, but point out that the constraints originate in the US government: it is "unfair to single out individual Chinese companies like Huawei Marine and ban them from doing business in Western nations," one builder writes.[30]

There are many implications of the current organization of cable supply and its political tensions. On the one hand, the consolidation of the system serves a fundamentally stabilizing function for the cable industry. Knowledge about past projects, past routes, and past conflicts is centralized. Given the need to maintain operational systems for decades, these companies provide assurance not simply for the nations they connect, but for banks that back smaller companies new to the subsea cable world. On the other hand, this supply chain, and its limited capacity and competition, can become a choke point if a project is not seen as viable or if there are too many proposed cables.

In recent years, Google and Facebook have begun to enter the cable market. Although the popular press often reports this as "Google builds its own undersea cable," like almost all cable systems, these companies contract with existing suppliers: SubCom or ASN. At times, Google and Facebook work with existing telecommunications carriers, but at other points, their cable plans end up disrupting the carrier-led initiatives. While there is suspicion about Huawei Marine in the industry, it tends to be that sourcing one's cable will lead to regulation or loss of financing. Suspicion about the OTTs stems from the concern that they are creating an alternate network or seeking control over the backbone of our global telecommunications infrastructure. They participate in and plan many projects, create demand for cable supply, and keep the suppliers booked. Some, such as entrepreneur Sunil Tagare, suspect that "all they are doing is getting all the cable supply held hostage so that the carriers have no more cables left to build."[31] As a result of this demand, suppliers may be unavailable for other companies' projects and would not be incentivized to take on "marginal" cables. Some members of the industry have speculated that Google or Facebook might even consider purchasing one of the cable suppliers, should their margins get any smaller. Although as John Tibbles writes, "it is hard to imagine the US or EU governments allowing sale of these entities to anyone outside their own sphere and certainly not to anyone outside of 'the West,'" it is certainly possible for one of the OTTs to purchase a supplier, ensuring a virtual monopoly over both supply and network construction.[32] Likewise, rumors about France's Orange taking over ASN indicated a similar imagination of returning to an earlier, vertically integrated model.[33]

In sum, while there has been some recognition of the importance of the supply chain in consumer electronics and digital devices, the public and political understanding of the supply of digital media infrastructure has lagged behind in both scholarly and popular discourse. Public discussions continue to be animated by fears of Chinese influence and by misunderstandings of how cable systems actually operate. Turning our attention to the supply of internet infrastructure and cable infrastructure in particular reveals a field of technology production that is uniquely installed in extraterritorial sites, deeply invested in ideologies of reliability and neutrality, and dependent on over a century's worth of accumulated expertise in a set of three companies. To politicize this field is to point out how the continued operation of the internet is largely reliant on these factors: reliability, proposed neutrality, and accumulated expertise. It is also to reveal how these operate as ideological orientations within politics, policy, and the industry itself to constrain competition and pre-empt opposition. Lastly, it means paying attention to emerging monopolies that are poised to capitalize on the narrowness of the supply chain and to transform how the internet operates.

NOTES

1. Raymond Li, "iPod Maker Sues over Labour Story," *South China Morning Post*, August 29, 2006, http://www.scmp.com/article/561980/ipod-maker-sues-over-labour-story; and "The Stark Reality of iPod's Chinese Factories," *Daily Mail*, August 18, 2006, http://www.dailymail.co.uk/news/article-401234/The-stark-reality-iPods-Chinese-factories.html.

2. Bruce J. Hunt, "Insulation for an Empire: Gutta-Percha and the Development of Electrical Measurement in Victorian Britain," in *Semaphores to Short Waves*, ed. Frank A. J. L. James (London: Royal Society of Arts), 85–104.

3. *Eighty Channels under the Sea* (Supreme Sound Studios, 1960); *Ring around the Earth* (dir. Stanley Willis, Eyeline Films, 1964).

4. *Cable to the Continent* (John Sutherland Productions, 1959).

5. *Ring around the Earth*.

6. Archives New Zealand, COMPAC [Commonwealth Pacific Cable—South East Asia Commonwealth Telephone Cable]—Film of Overall Project AAMF W3174 909 104, 43/7.

7. Brian Larkin, *Signal and Noise: Media, Infrastructure, and Urban Culture in Nigeria* (Durham, NC: Duke University Press, 2008), 19.

8. "Closure of STC Submarine Cable Factory, Southampton," Early Day Motions, House of Commons, tabled April 25, 1996, https://edm.parliament.uk /early-day-motion/12484/closure-of-stc-submarine-cable-factory-southampton.

9. Monopolies and Mergers Commission, *Alcatel Cable SA and STC Limited: A Report on the Proposed Acquisition by Alcatel Cable SA of STC Limited*, presented to Parliament by the secretary of state for trade and industry by command of Her Majesty (London: HMSO, February 1994).

10. Stewart Ash, "Back Reflection," *SubTel Forum* 47 (November 2009): 42–44, 43.

11. Ash, "Back Reflection."

12. Submarine Telecoms Forum, *STF 2017 Industry Report* (2017): 40.

13. Submarine Telecoms Forum, *STF 2017 Industry Report*, 40

14. Submarine Telecoms Forum, *STF 2017 Industry Report*, 40.

15. "Hibernia Atlantic Achieves an Important Milestone for Project Express," *Business Wire* (New York), January 5, 2011.

16. "Hibernia Atlantic and Huawei Complete First 100 Gbps Transatlantic Trial," *PR Newswire*, November 8, 2011.

17. Sean Buckley, "Hibernia Halts Cable Build with Huawei Due to US-China Cybersecurity Issues," FierceTelecom, February 11, 2013, https://www .fiercetelecom.com/telecom/hibernia-halts-cable-build-huawei-due-to-us-china -cybersecurity-issues.

18. "Huawei," *60 Minutes*, CBS News, produced by Graham Messick, October 7, 2012.

19. "Chairman Rogers and Ranking Member Ruppersberger Warn American Companies," US House of Representatives Permanent Select Committee on Intelligence, Washington, DC, October 8, 2012, https://intelligence.house.gov /news/documentsingle.aspx?DocumentID=95.

20. "Investigative Report on the U.S. National Security Issues Posed by Chinese Telecommunications Companies Huawei and ZTE," US House of Representatives 112th Congress, October 8, 2012, 1.

21. Kavit Majithia, "Hibernia Keeps Faith with Express Cable," *Capacity Magazine*, September 11, 2014.

22. "Defending U.S. Government Communications Act," 115th Congress, 2d Session, HR 4747, 4.

23. Federal Communications Commission, "Protecting against National Security Threats to the Communications Supply Chain through FCC Programs," *Federal Register* 83, no. 85 (May 2, 2018): 19197.

24. Federal Communications Commission, "Protecting against National Security Threats."

25. Drew FitzGerald, "Huawei's Role in Internet Traffic Grows; Despite Being Shunned in U.S., Huawei Increases Internet-Gear Sales Share," *Wall Street Journal*, March 24 2014.

26. Federal Communications Commission, "Exhibit A: Declaration of John Suffolk, before the Federal Communications Commission, Washington, DC 20554, in the Matter of Protecting against National Security," WC Docket No. 18–89, Threats to the Communications Supply Chain through FCC Programs, August 4, 2020, Comments of Huawei Technologies Co., Ltd., and Huawei Technologies USA.

27. John Tibbles, "Submarine Cables, Security and the State," *Submarine Telecoms Forum* 94 (May 2017), 28.

28. Tibbles, "Submarine Cables," 29.

29. FitzGerald, "Huawei's Role in Internet Traffic Grows."

30. Sunil Tagare, "Trade War with China," *BuySellBandwidth* (blog), October 16, 2018, http://blog.buysellbandwidth.com/ (URL no longer functional).

31. Sunil Tagare, "Maybe I Was Wrong about Facebook," *BuySellBandwidth* (blog), November 20, 2018, http://blog.buysellbandwidth.com/ (URL no longer functional).

32. Tibbles, "Submarine Cables," 28.

33. "Orange Ready to Discuss Acquisition of Alcatel Submarine Networks with Nokia and Bpifrance," *Telecom Paper*, May 3, 2019, www.telecompaper.com /news/orange-ready-to-discuss-acquisition-of-alcatel-submarine-networks-with -nokia-and-bpifrance—1291284.

WHO WATCHES THE WATCHERS?

Streaming video is an almost insurmountable logistical challenge. For a company like Netflix, high bandwidth content needs to be delivered in a fraction of a second to any of the service's 158 million subscribers in nearly two hundred countries. While the website is run using Amazon's "cloud" infrastructure, Netflix developed an original logistical product, "Open Connect," to meet the particular challenges of video delivery and further optimize its distribution. The core of this content delivery network is an "appliance" installed in network exchanges throughout the world. Here, Netflix's most recent videos—whether *Orange Is the New Black* or *Roma*—are localized. They are placed in locations as close as possible to their potential viewers, ready to be loaded, without having to cross oceans or continents. The sole responsibility of this appliance, Netflix reports, is to deliver playable bits as fast as possible. This logistical innovation underwrites the apparent seamlessness, instantaneity, and accessibility of the company's video service—approximately 15 percent of global internet traffic. But optimization isn't just about speed. It's about profit. By uploading its content to these remote appliances during off-peak hours, such as the middle of the night, the company avoids backbone transit on undersea cables or other expensive routes. This efficiency is predicated on prediction—Netflix watches its users watch, and this data determines which shows are kept in any given appliance, at any given location. Viewers' rhythms and habits are appropriated into logistical designs.

Laugh Out Loud

(Human) Robots

From across the Internet, it is not always easy to tell a human from a robot. After spammers outsmarted an earlier version of the reCAPTCHA test, which involved typing in the letters or numbers in an image, Google, its owner, now uses a secret algorithm that is based on how "human" your behavior is: how you move your mouse, if you always click in the same way, how quickly you react.[1] You invisibly cross over the human/robot line many times a day, and likely don't even know you are doing so—until you do something a little too mechanically, and a prompt pops up, asking you to prove you are human. Because these tests are behavioral, they are essentially arbitrary: how do you define what "human" behavior is? Search the web too quickly, and Google will challenge you to prove you are not scraping its results. Interact too slowly with a video—for example, by letting it autoplay in the background—and YouTube will ask you to show that you're still there. What is the "right" amount of interaction for a human? Worse, these definitions of "human" are often exclusionary: some algorithms look upon web browsers that don't load images with suspicion, reasoning that robots typically speed things up by requesting only a web page's text—but persons with visual disabilities may also forgo images.[2]

That tests for humans can be fraught with inequality is not surprising if we take a wider historical view: as critical race scholars point out, race was invented as a technology "for differentiating subjects from objects."[3] Sylvia

Wynter has shown that Eurocentric culture has repeatedly fashioned "humanity" in its image by distancing itself from what it imagined to be non-humans or subhumans.[4] In a previous moment of automation, for example, white Detroit auto workers blamed their Japanese counterparts for layoffs during the 1980s, and stereotyped Asians and Asian Americans as embodying the robotic. To take a closer look at the line between human and robot online, then, must be about more than detecting fraud.[5] In a logistical system that fuses together human and robotic work, and in a moment when the idea we typically most associate with humanness, emotion, is slowly being imitated and automated by artificial intelligence, examining the human/robot line is also to examine the uneasy junction of race, work, and emotion in our digital environment.

Consider this example: in 2018, thousands of fake accounts bearing gray, crudely drawn avatars suddenly appeared on Twitter. Though each account bore biographical descriptions, for instance about their aspirations for social justice, their creators—a group of alt-right trolls on boards such as Reddit—also gave them expressionless faces, and account names such as NPC4921337. NPC is an abbreviation for "non-player character," and it refers to computer-generated characters in video games that are pre-programmed to interact with human players in certain ways, such as saying canned lines about the weather. The trolls invoked the NPC's mechanical bearing and scripted responses to mock the supposed inability of liberals to think for themselves. In this rhetoric, NPC-like liberals are "completely dependent on their programming," spouting the same one-liners about deposing Trump or killing capitalists as a result.[6] Indeed, the profiles' "About Me" sections often contain pseudocode depicting their internal "programming"; referring to Trump, one typical profile reads "if(man.Color == Color.ORANGE) man.Bad = true."[7]

However gray and colorless, these avatars were typically intended to represent (and belittle) persons of color: one avatar evoked the football player and activist Colin Kaepernick, while other avatars tweeted about "graycism" and used the hashtag #GrayLivesMatter.[8] Several meme creators also used NPC avatars to illustrate and represent the conspiracy theory that African Americans have been "brainwashed" by the media to vote Democratic (or so people like Kanye West argue).[9] In this dismaying line of thought, so-called free thinkers see persons of color as lethargic drones who merely imitate the look of humanness but are unable to think for themselves.

While the NPC memes may represent an extremist worldview, the logic underlying them is in fact commonplace; that logic is what Sianne Ngai terms "animatedness," the old stereotype of racialized subjects as excessively or minimally emotional and expressive—and, simultaneously, puppetlike and lacking control over their own bodies, as if they had been animated by another.[10] Whether Asian Americans stereotyped as repressed and unfeeling robots that are emotionally inscrutable, Mexican migrants as automatons for manufacturing and construction, or African Americans as hypersexualized and overly emotional bodies that are always out of control, animatedness becomes a technology through which subjects are racialized. What's especially interesting for a discussion on bots is that Ngai's thinking links animatedness to a problem of media. Writing in 2005, she observes that the largest "live" events on television (OJ Simpson, Rodney King, 9/11) all transmit the spectacle of racialized bodies. Liveliness, spontaneity, and zeal, Ngai speculates, draw their force from the liveness of the medium, allowing television to become a device to display and train us in racial difference. Just as television teaches its viewers to appreciate the "spontaneous" and the "lively," digital platforms implant norms about animatedness in the very idea of the user, even if those norms refer now to acceptable amounts of sociality, interactivity, and expressivity.

Racial animatedness is readily visible in the world of gaming, where the NPC meme originated. Examining the multiplayer game World of Warcraft, Lisa Nakamura has demonstrated that many players profile certain styles of repetitive motion and stilted speech in gameplay as "Asian," due to the historical presence of other players based in China who engaged in a practice of mining virtual gold for sale offline—so-called gold farmers.[11] Likening the gameplay of asocial or noninteracting characters to NPCs or nonhumans opens the door for everyone else to target them with vitriol, violence, or in-game death. Nakamura's example shows how a crude racial logic is reinscribed onto data bodies, despite the absence of visible signs of race; after all, every actor is an arbitrary animation on-screen. To make this distinction between human and nonhuman therefore requires some fumbling about, since there is no "naturally" human state. As Wendy Chun writes, the idea of the human is instead "constantly created through the jettisoning of the Asian and Asian American other as robotic."[12]

There is some irony here. By focusing entirely on the work of making money, gold farmers anger other players who are attached to an idea about gaming and expressivity or "fun." Gold farmers aren't playing by the rules, paradoxically, because they are playing by the rules too well. In contrast, customers of gold farmers are wealthier players, often North American and European, who effectively outsource the repetitive work of mining gold to Asians so that they can focus on the more interesting or expressive parts of gameplay. This dynamic underscores a racialized system of labor that is at the heart of many digital platforms for "fun," sociality, or expressivity: liveliness is something that can be, and increasingly is, purchased from lower-wage microworkers elsewhere. More generally, microworkers quench the seemingly insatiable demand by persons and corporations—as well as the social algorithms that evaluate them—for popularity, for having an audience, for being liked. They can encompass thousands of computers or phones and laborers, and be employed to stream a song, watch a video, or click "like" on a post in the thousands and millions; they amount to a vast transfer of "likability" from the Global South to the Global North.

Yet the labor of human robots is imprecisely described by the metaphors we currently use to understand exploitation. Digital scholars often use the images of the "digital sweatshop" and the "maquiladora" to describe the labor system at the base of digital capitalism.[13] However sympathetic I am to those ideas, it's an open question of how the microworkers themselves might view and work within this labor system, or of how well those metaphors apply to the ordinary experience of digital environments. Mary L. Gray's interviews with the on-demand laborers, often pejoratively referred to as clickworkers, showed that her subjects understand their job as one that "takes quite a bit of creativity and insight and judgment," rather than as a series of menial, sweatshop-like tasks.[14] And while scholars of digital labor tend to think only of microwork as clicking on images, moderating content, cleaning datasets, or converting images to text, these same platforms for microwork are increasingly used for the assembly and recirculation of emotional labor and care. While journalists and scholars typically attempt to humanize microworkers by emphasizing their aspirations for better lives, or by describing them as individuals entitled to (but deprived of) the same forms of meaningful work as their peers in wealthier countries, they nevertheless position microworkers' lives just outside the category of the human; in the words of Kalindi Vora and Neda Atanasoski, they are surrogates for humanity.[15]

This precarious position—lacking agency and thus personhood—is a state that I call lethargy.[16] From the outside, a lethargic body is enframed in the supply chain; a lethargic body looks robotic. The lethargic body is either less animated than a "proper" human or, paradoxically, overly animated, because in the latter case, the suggestion is that it is an automaton controlled by someone else: as the deprecating Internet jargon *sock puppet* suggests, the animation comes from without. Rather than a condition to be cured, however, lethargy holds its own potential. As this essay explores, lethargy creates space for other forms of affective experience delinked from animatedness.

To help us think through the lethargy within microwork, I turn to an artwork, *Risas enlatadas,* or *Canned Laughter* (2009), by Mexico City–based artist Yoshua Okón, which depicts a fictitious maquiladora in Ciudad Juárez. Instead of processing textiles or electronics, however, it manufactures shiny red cans of laughter destined for US sitcoms—cans labeled evil laughter, manly laughter, and sexy laughter, among others. As we are learning, a dystopian world where low-wage workers across the border or around the world laugh, cry, or otherwise emote for white audiences is not as far away as we might think.

Canned Laughter

In *Canned Laughter,* you enter a concrete space that resembles a factory floor—indeed, in its first iteration, Okón rented a former assembly plant in Juárez—and come across a long table styled as an assembly line. On it, there are the cans, which you can listen to, and there are 1990s-style televisions playing a video loop of corporate propaganda stamped with the name of the fictitious factory ("Bergson," after the French philosopher who wrote about, among other things, laughter). Hung on racks are workers' uniforms, and on the wall, there is a video loop showing a German conductor coaxing a chorus of Mexican workers through various types of laughter. "This laugh, a witch's laugh, is from my home town, the Black Forest," he says at one point. A few minutes later, the video cuts to show workers at the assembly line, injecting sound in the cans by operating a machine that dips a rod into the metal, or testing quality by seeming to inspect the sound.

How are we to interpret this? We might begin with the artist himself, who writes that *Canned Laughter* shows the "impossibility [of] translat[ing] and reproduc[ing] true emotions through technological means."[17] While Okón is clearly taking a shot at the fakeness of canned laughter, this explanation feels inadequate; what, after all, is "true" emotion? To suggest that there is a "true emotion" in the body that technology then distorts is to ignore the ways that the body is itself physically and culturally technical: love letters are produced by hands grasping pens and alphabets and scripts for praising the beloved. Technologies mask, amplify, and convey emotion to us. And crucially, technologies shape the terms by which the emotion of others is registered, turning, for example, a nonresponse by a gold farmer into an example of a racialized threat to the rules of the game.

Rather than reading Okón's artwork as humanist satire, we might be better off taking the artwork seriously, that is, as a documentary on the very

11.1 Still from Yoshua Okón, *Canned Laughter*, 2009, projection video in installation. Courtesy of the artist.

immanence of "reproducing true emotions through technological means." If it seems counterintuitive to call this essentially arduous and manual work technological, the difference is that rather than work progressing from human to robot, as futurists might have expected, we have entered a phase where it's more cost-effective to hire human robots—what Amazon CEO Jeff Bezos terms "artificial artificial intelligence."

The artist's own description for it is the "infomaquila," which briefly flashes on screen during one of the inane corporate videos that loops on the television sets. This is a word that he likely borrowed from the filmmaker Alex Rivera, who in his contemporaneous film *Sleep Dealer* (2008) describes an info-maquiladora in Tijuana called Cybracero Systems Inc. A cybracero, in Rivera's description, is a cybernetic update of the 1950s Mexican guest worker, or *bracero*, tasked to pick crops for California's agriculture industry and then return home at the end of the picking season. The cybracero is "safely" contained behind a US-Mexico border wall; physically implanted with telepresence technologies, the cybracero animates robots north of the

11.2 Yoshua Okón, *Canned Laughter*, 2009, installation view, *Yoshua Okón: 2007–2010*, Yerba Buena Center for the Arts, 2010. Courtesy Yerba Buena Center for the Arts. Photograph by J. W. White.

border to water lawns or construct skyscrapers, or, in a different form of (re-)animation, provide "memories"—narrated feelings and impressions—to willing buyers. The cybracero helps to whitewash this future by moving colored bodies out of view, just as today's microwork platforms help to mask the identities of digital laborers from their employers, so that employers are executing a computer program, rather than employing individual bodies.[18] Exclaims one of *Sleep Dealer*'s characters, "They want work without the worker."

The laughter of Okón's own outsourcing firm similarly displaces the workers' national origin, and, in turn, the racial capitalism underpinning this strategy. Imagining the fictional world Okón creates, Anca Parvulescu writes that the workers' canned laughter is "exported to the rest of the world, including presumably back to Mexico . . . [and] likely to be consumed by the same workers who participated in Okón's installation, after their working hours in the maquiladora."[19] Parvulescu's suggestion is that the workers, if real, would be doubly exploited: they presumably do not recognize the sound

11.3 Still from Yoshua Okón, *Canned Laughter*, 2009, monitor video in installation. Courtesy of the artist.

of their own laughter on the sitcoms, even as they consume those shows to unwind after a day of work. They pay both times—with their body in the factory, and with their eyes at night—and thus they "express their gratitude for their chance at being oppressed."[20]

Again, however, I want to move beyond applying a one-size-fits-all model of oppression to either this artwork or to microwork. The artwork's reflexiveness pushes us to talk about the infomaquila model differently, for it stages a problem about critique by making its ostensible message a little *too* obvious. Witness *San Francisco Chronicle* art critic Kenneth Baker, who writes that there is "no doubt as to Okón's intervention. Intended as critical satire of the global corporate order, it feels forced in every respect, at best pleasing viewers with the thought of the artist having employed some needy people for a while."[21]

To be sure, the literalism of seeing former maquiladora workers mechanically performing maquiladora work does lead to a sense that something, in the critic's words, "feels forced," as if someone telling a joke had insisted

CYBRACERO
Systems

With workers available 24/7 for up to
12hr shifts, you can get your work done
on time and way under budget.

Stop

| Mission | Technology | Invest | Careers | Blog | Communicate | Contact |

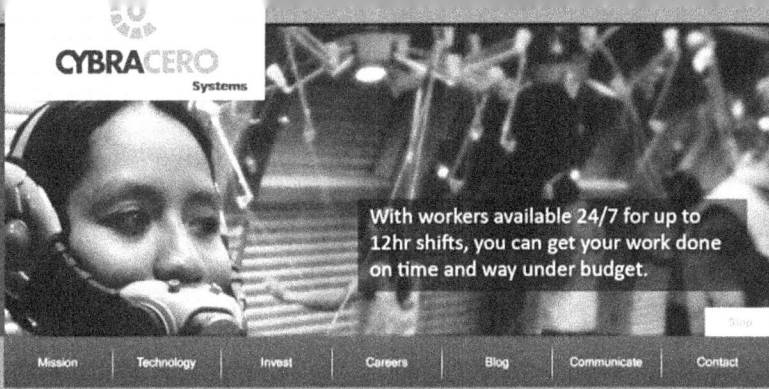

PLEASE NOTE: Cybracero wants people that the movie *Sleep Dealer* opening this weekend is an inaccurate and undeservedly critical portrait of our pioneering business model and is not representational of our business.

OPEN LETTER TO ALL AMERICANS

QUICK LINKS

Welcome to Cybracero Systems.

These days, it's hard to avoid the news: America is facing a crisis unlike any seen before. A combination of economic catastrophes and international security challenges threaten the very fabric of our nation.

Central to these challenges is one issue: Immigration.

Node Me To Innovation - Discover the missing link that makes this AMAZING technology possible!

A Stunted Leader - Cybracero Systems pioneers the merging of internet and robotics technologies.

11.4 Screenshot from Alex Rivera, Cybracero Systems (www.cybracero.com), 2009. Courtesy of the artist.

on asking "get it?" afterward. But what the critic misses is that the feeling of frustrated satire is part of the artwork's very design: the word *enlatada* means "canned," but as Amy Sara Carroll notes, it also means "canceled" or "put on ice," as in the English expression "the project got canned."[22] In other words, *Risas enlatadas* tells you, quite directly, that it won't succeed: laughter is cancelled here. If one of the contracts of performance is that a performer performs, and the audience reacts, here, Okón severely limits the audience's ability to react. The workers seem to laugh on our behalf, as if they were a reaction GIF, *our* reaction GIF. This interpassive use of laughter short-circuits our response, making it all but impossible to resolve our experience through aesthetic judgment. Consequently, the artwork doesn't feel like critique or satire, nor does it allow much unguarded pleasure or humor. Instead, it moves us toward something more ambivalent: perhaps a feeling of expecting laughter to happen and being disappointed, a feeling of things being "forced," somehow, whether the satire itself or the forced laughter the workers themselves perform.

And the critic's dismissal of the artwork as a vehicle for "pleasing viewers" by employing "needy workers for a while" inadvertently reveals one of the conceits of the project: if you are the viewer pleased, you are indirectly those workers' employer. As you look around, perhaps "sampling" a can of laughter or examining the rows of uniforms for their symmetry, are you not behaving like a factory supervisor? Perhaps you consider the assembly line, the ways workers are organized, and the logistics of the supply chain as if you were an administrator of a process or institution.[23] Or perhaps you focus on the glistening, almost bejeweled red cans (a clear reference to Warhol's soup cans), like a client coming to inspect their purchase. None of these positions allow for a straightforward position of opposition.

Similarly, there is a more ambivalent relationship between microwork and microworker than outsourcer and exploited victim. Referencing Payal Arora's critique of big data, Antonio Casilli argues that even those "'at the bottom of the data pyramid' are just about as involved in creativity, online recreation, and leisure—and just about as subject to mechanisms of data extraction" as users elsewhere.[24] And documentary filmmakers and ethnographers have shown that what most well-meaning scholars in the West might term "mindless" or "fraudulent" work may well be a source of pride. The interviewees in Garrett Bradley's short documentary about clickfarmers in Dhaka, *Like* (2016), for example, describe their work in terms of getting their foot in the door in the online marketing and the information technology sectors; clickfarming is a creative way of finding work in a constrained job market and of, in the words of one subject, "maintaining and surviving."[25] In a particularly thought-provoking sequence, one subject likens clickwork to sex work: Facebook sells the idea of romance, he says, but clever marketers such as himself sell "love" and "like." This is particularly trenchant, given how much of the exploitation in digital labor (indeed, as I have argued, the very subject position of the personal "user") has resulted out of the mystification of an economic framework as doing things "out of love." This is how online platforms convince us to give our time freely to write online reviews,[26] and how Facebook convinces us to "like" the advertising posts inadvertently promoted by our friends. And it is also the line of thinking that justifies the low wages paid to Amazon Mechanical Turk workers, who are—in this line of thinking—housewives doing microwork as a fun hobby, in their free time, for a few extra dollars. (The platform positions itself as an enjoyable alternative to "just sitting there," but the recruitment of couch potatoes into the ranks of the gig economy is another instance of digital capitalism's clawback of idleness.[27])

This is not to dismiss the fact that microworkers and "info-maquiladora" workers sometimes labor under terrible working conditions.[28] I simply mean that describing such work as inherently mindless or robotic is troublesome. We must be careful not to describe these workers as passive, robot-like laborers who could become *more human* by doing more dignified work—or, even worse, by receiving attention from Western saviors. Instead, to supplement traditional models of digital labor, we might try to offer finer-grained descriptions of how one makes do within a compromised (digital) environment—including how one "maintains" and "survives," to quote the worker whom Bradley interviewed. And here is where the ambiguities in *Canned Laughter* might point the way toward a different vocabulary. Even as its intensities (or lack thereof) of feeling are hard to parse into real or manufactured, human or robotic emotion, *Canned Laughter* seems to show us laughter uncoupled from the workers' affective states. They laugh to a rhythm demanded by a conductor, and it could be funny, or not. "Funny" may coincide with the sound of laughter, or it may lag. In a model of exploitation, we might equate performance with inauthenticity and assume that all the laughter Okón's workers produce is false. But a closer examination of the installation shows something else going on.

Performance under Working Conditions

Consider a moment from the longest sequence of Okón's video, when the maquiladora workers are performing as a chorus. They stand shoulder to shoulder in their uniforms and are orchestrated by a conductor, while a sound engineer records on the side. As they laugh, they are also listening to themselves laugh—and that laughter they produce seems to arrive a fraction of a second late. This causes a slight out-of-sync quality to the sound, an effect underscored by the camera panning over individual faces that react differently and move differently to form the sounds. The sounds coming out of their mouths are coded as laughter, but they aren't necessarily moved by it. Their faces articulate the canned phoniness of the performance. Which leads, at times, to moments of meta-laughter: there is a woman on the assembly line who begins laughing spontaneously at the men in the chorus, presumably in an off-script moment when she is supposed to be silent. And a few workers occasionally break character, as it were, and seem to guffaw at the ridiculousness of the sounds they are producing—even as they are producing them.

One way of describing this moment might be to say that the woman and the man are laughing authentically in the middle of the task of faking laughter. But rather than continually attempt to distinguish between authentic and fake, as the CAPTCHA test purports to do, consider that fake laughter can lead to real laughter and vice versa; indeed, laughter is inherently unstable.

Instead, the laughter indexes a state of emotional undecidability that occurs within this logistical system, where it is unclear what (or who) is feeling. Laughter, after all, is commonly produced in response to social and power dynamics. Particularly in the awkward encounters between two parties on opposite sides of a transaction—say, viewer and worker—one often laughs to cover over something else, over what we might call the friction in that difference. Indeed, we might conclude that laughter is not just the cover for that ambivalence but the very embodiment of that friction.[29]

What I am claiming is that the laughter in the video operates at the unstable border between emotion and affect. This is a fuzzy hinge that nearly every person who has written *LOL* in a text message understands intuitively. *LOL*, laugh out loud, is very likely written because the person is not laughing; it is a marker that simply acknowledges the genre of humor. As the most popular definition of *LOL* in Urban Dictionary puts it: "nobody laughs out loud when they say it. In fact, they probably don't even give a shit about what you just wrote. More accurately, the acronym 'lol' should be redefined as 'Lack of laughter.'"[30] The same thing goes for *haha*. Explains one commentator, *haha* "doesn't really reflect how much they are actually laughing/how much they actually thought something you said was funny."[31] Both words are phatic gestures, like *uh-huh*, meant simply to acknowledge that you are communicating—indeed, even a way of acknowledging the need for you to respond, to be just animated enough.

Thus LOL is not simply a masquerade, a way of cloaking one's identity from surveillance or data platforms, or pretending to be otherwise while maintaining a hidden inner life, all of which would require us to resurrect the distinction between fake (and therefore subversive and presumably agentive) and real (and therefore presumably not subversive and non-agentive). All laughter is at some level real. Instead, *LOL* is not the full feeling of humor but rather the space or hesitation of it, the attempt to express something while not yet being ready to commit to a specific emotional endpoint. It is not what we could call "live" laughter, but canned, underperformed laughter: laughter as deadvoice.[32] Thus *LOL* stands primarily for a moment of undecidability and *unresolved affect*: it asks for time to think or feel, akin to a "pause game" feature. In a moment when expression has become instrumentalized, such deferrals are what literary scholar Anne-Lise François describes as a "recessive action," something that works within the "productive" time of narrative to create a different temporal structure.[33] François focuses her study on moments of unfulfilled expectations, on actions not accomplished, and on things done with no consequence. For Okón's artwork, the momentary confusion in laughter that I have described as a LOL also mediates the anticipations of time differently. Even though the individual's laugh proceeds as expected, and even though the logistics of production continues to assemble each laugh into a larger, choral whole, such deferrals function not as ways of resisting the temporal impositions of digital capitalism, but rather as ways of buying time for oneself.

While failing as a productive mode of critique—indeed, it typically looks like a stale or "forced" critical move—lethargy may offer a new field of the political to explore. Scholars have ample tools to detect and valorize moments of resistance or refusal, and these keywords have become staples of humanistic inquiry, which tends to valorize the agentive and political outspokenness (rather than, say, passive actions such as listening or vacillating). Yet as Kevin Quashie points out, we often miss the quieter and more reticent forms of being within and adjacent to those political moments; after all, it is perhaps the ease by which *Canned Laughter* appears as an allegory for standing up against capitalism that makes it harder to see the current of underperformance that runs underneath.[34] And the role of agency itself seems to have changed. Digital platforms incentivize, nudge, prod, and even coerce users into producing a certain form of liberal subjectivity, where one "speaks up" and "takes a stand." Though digital capitalism bills this frenetic activity as a form of empowerment, it incorporates such forms of liberal agency into its system of control.[35] In this context, the decoupling of liveness or animatedness from the user, particularly for persons of color, can offer a means for temporarily setting that pressure aside.

I say decoupling because outright refusal may not be possible in the always-on world foreshadowed by *Canned Laughter*. Lethargy approaches but ultimately is not passivity, because passivity, like rest or downtime, is generally foreclosed to the lethargic subject. Consider a final sequence from the video, where the workers are shown in the rather un-Fordist position of standing in a circle outside, holding hands and taking a company-mandated meditation break. The workers Okón interviewed said these breaks were common inside real maquiladoras, which have begun to operationalize silence and mindfulness as a tool of productivity. This is arguably even more depressing than, say, simply overworking the workers. Capital metaphorically captures all expression, even the absence of expression. And this operationalizing of silence is increasingly common in digital culture. A variety of techniques such as "scroll tracking" captures what a user doesn't look at on a webpage, or what a user fails to click on in recommendation algorithms.

11.5 Yoshua Okón, *Canned Laughter*, 2009, three-channel video projection with audio. Courtesy of the artist and Sfeir-Semler Gallery Beirut/Hamburg.

Of course, persons of color—especially African Americans—were deprived of the ability to do nothing long before digital trackers existed. As Lauren Michele Jackson puts it, even "when we [Black people] do nothing, we're doing something."[36] The newspaper headlines about two Black men arrested for waiting in a Philadelphia Starbucks gave rise to a new phrase: "waiting while Black." Antiblackness means African American life is inextricable from policing affect in public—avoiding too much noise, or too much joy, as in Ralph Ellison's telling of the laughing barrels positioned in public places in the South, through which Black persons were obligated to shunt the sound of their laughter when they felt an urge to laugh come on.[37] But the Starbucks example reminds us, yet again, that even the opposite, the act of waiting and doing nothing in an environment *designed for waiting*, can be criminalized and read as "loitering." Scholars should analogously attend to the myriad of ways that a racialized environment polices the act of doing nothing, whether this is practical—for instance, prepaid debit cards primarily issued to the unbanked that charge exorbitant inactivity fees, or sit/lie laws that prevent people from remaining still on the sidewalk—or more metaphorical, as in the way persons of color are expected to perform the emotional labor of commenting and educating on social issues, rather than being allowed to remain silent.

While lethargy describes the state of being forced to constantly move and be animated, lethargy also acts by gradually spreading out, flattening, or detuning oneself from this regimen—allowing oneself to grow bored of it, be reticent, underperform. And by doing so, canned laughter shows us that the special privilege of being live or human is not particularly special after all. Canned laughter can make one laugh as much as live performance. Okón's choral performance is the performance of "staleness," after all, of pre-recorded emotion. The canned or lethargic qualities of this artwork invert this equation and put the "human" on lesser footing than the manufactured, object-like qualities of the robotic. After all, why should the highest aspiration for digital technology be to be more vital and more human (and why should that be our aspiration, too)? Lethargy is exhausting, but it also exhausts the oppressively live environment in which colored bodies are animated against their will.

In the end, lethargy is a kind of dwelling longer in the negative or ambivalent affect of a situation. We write *LOL* because we don't have anything else to say in the moment, because we are required to respond, but aren't sure how to feel. But that state of postponement is valuable, too. When an artwork doesn't produce the right reactions, and leaves us interpretively idle, with "dead time," as it were, it causes a decoupling of the subject from the media environment around them: bored, one begins to do the laundry list or begins to notice one's body cramp up.[38] This deferral might help us notice the mediation that occurs at the level of the phatic, the social, and the racialization of subjects within that environment. For that environment—how much someone laughs, or doesn't—is, like breath, something that can exhaust or enliven subjects unequally. If lethargy doesn't rise to the level of an intervention, it gets us one step closer to acknowledging the ordinary weight of each forced interaction, like a column of atmosphere that weighs on our shoulders, but that we have nonetheless become accustomed to enduring.

NOTES

1. Not so surprisingly, Google benefits when you "fail" its reCAPTCHA test, because then it forces you to teach its computers how to recognize cars, stop signs, and storefronts. For more on the initial shift away from traditional image-based CAPTCHAs, see Google Security Blog, "Are You a Robot? Introducing 'No

CAPTCHA reCAPTCHA,'" December 3, 2014, https://security.googleblog.com
/2014/12/are-you-robot-introducing-no-captcha.html.

2. Campaigners for accessibility further note that audio CAPTCHAs are
poorly executed and virtually incomprehensible, while those with dyslexia may
find blurry images impossible to solve. See "Captchas Suck," Axess Lab, November 2, 2017, https://axesslab.com/captchas-suck/.

3. Neda Atanasoski and Kalindi Vora, citing Wendy Chun, "Race and/as
Technology," in *Race after the Internet*, ed. Lisa Nakamura and Peter Chow-White
(New York: Routledge, 2012), 38–60; and Beth Coleman, "Race as Technology,"
Camera Obscura 24, no. 1 (2009): 177–207. In Kalindi Vora and Neda Atanasoski,
Surrogate Humanity: Race, Robots, and the Politics of Technological Futures (Durham,
NC: Duke University Press, 2019), 14.

4. Sylvia Wynter, "Unsettling the Coloniality of Being/Power/Truth/Free-
dom: Towards the Human, after Man, Its Overrepresentation—An Argument."
CR: The New Centennial Review 3, no. 3 (2003): 257–337.

5. *Robot*, after all, has always referred to labor: it originally designated a
certain number of days of unpaid labor that serfs were compelled to work in the
Habsburg monarchy.

6. BasedMedicalDoctor (Reddit user), as quoted by Kevin Roose, "What Is
NPC, the Pro-Trump Internet's New Favorite Insult?" *New York Times*, October 16, 2018, https://www.nytimes.com/2018/10/16/us/politics/npc-twitter-ban
.html.

7. Profile of NPC201620201337 (anonymous Twitter user), as archived by
Josh Emerson (@josh_emerson), "wow the trolls are taking this NPC thing so
seriously," Twitter, October 14, 2018, 9:13 a.m., https://twitter.com/josh_emerson
/status/1051461034433765376.

8. See, for example, @N83652574, "I just made a twitter accound like 10
minutes ago and already i am discriminated. I AM LITERALLY SHAKING RIGHT
NOW #NPC #GrayLivesMatter #NPCmeme," Twitter, November 1, 2018, 7:52
p.m., https://twitter.com/N83652574/status/1058144735838326785.

9. See Roose, "What Is NPC?"

10. Sianne Ngai, "Animatedness," in *Ugly Feelings* (Cambridge, MA: Harvard
University Press, 2005), 89–125.

11. Lisa Nakamura, "Don't Hate the Player, Hate the Game: The Racialization of Labor in World of Warcraft," *Critical Studies in Media Communication* 26,
no. 2 (2009): 128–44.

12. Chun, "Race and/as Technology," 51.

13. For examples, see Jonathan Zittrain, "The Internet Creates a New Kind of
Sweatshop," *Newsweek*, December 7, 2009, https://www.newsweek.com/internet
-creates-new-kind-sweatshop-75751; Lydia DePillis, "Click Farms Are the New
Sweatshops," *Washington Post*, January 6, 2014, https://www.washingtonpost
.com/news/wonk/wp/2014/01/06/click-farms-are-the-new-sweatshops/; and

Julian Dibbel, "The Life of the Chinese Gold Farmer," *New York Times Magazine*, June 17, 2007, 36–41.

14. Mary L. Gray, unpublished talk for "Labor in the Global Platform Economy," University of Michigan, June 1, 2019. Also see Mary L. Gray and Siddharth Suri, *Ghost Work: How to Stop Silicon Valley from Building a New Global Underclass* (Boston: Houghton Mifflin Harcourt, 2019).

15. Vora and Atanasoski, *Surrogate Humanity*.

16. See also Tung-Hui Hu, "Wait, then Give Up: Lethargy and the Reticence of Digital Art," *Journal of Visual Culture* 16, no. 3 (2017): 337–54.

17. Yoshua Okón, *Canned Laughter*, 2009, https://www.yoshuaokon.com/canned-laughter_text.html.

18. Lilly Irani, "The Cultural Work of Microwork," *New Media and Society* 17, no. 5 (2013): 720–39.

19. Anca Parvulescu, "Even Laughter? From Laughter in the Magic Theater to the Laughter Assembly Line," *Critical Inquiry* 43, no. 2 (2017): 506–27, 522.

20. Parvulescu, "Even Laughter?" 511.

21. Kenneth Baker, "'Yoshua Okón: 2007–2010' Review: Uneasy Video," *San Francisco Chronicle*, November 11, 2010, http://www.sfgate.com/entertainment/article/Yoshua-Ok-n-2007-2010-review-Uneasy-video-3166758.php.

22. Amy Sara Carroll, REMEX: *Toward an Art History of the* NAFTA *Era* (Austin: University of Texas Press, 2017), 94.

23. While not explicitly a work of institutional critique, *Canned Laughter* nonetheless references the art market and the art institutions that fuel it. See, for example, Benjamin Buchloh, "Conceptual Art 1962–1969: From the Aesthetic of Administration to the Critique of Institutions," *October*, no. 55 (1990): 105–43.

24. Antonio Casilli, "Digital Labor Studies Go Global: Toward a Digital Decolonial Turn," *International Journal of Communication* 11 (2017): 3934–54, 3946; Payal Arora, "The Bottom of the Data Pyramid: Big Data and the Global South," *International Journal of Communication* 10 (2016): 1681–99.

25. *Like*, directed by Garrett Bradley (New York: Field of Vision, 2016), at https://vimeo.com/160794617.

26. Tiziana Terranova, *Network Culture* (Ann Arbor, MI: Pluto Press, 2004).

27. Katharine Mieszkowski, "I Make $1.45 a Week and I Love It!" *Salon*, July 24, 2006, http://www.salon.com/2006/07/24/turks, as quoted by Vora and Atanasoski, *Surrogate Humanity*, 100.

28. Because "sweatshops" are typically closed to academic research, we tend to hear more in-depth studies of benign workplaces than not.

29. Anna Lowenhaupt Tsing, *Friction: An Ethnography of Global Connection* (Princeton, NJ: Princeton University Press, 2004).

30. Urban Dictionary, s.v. "lol," by no_one_2000, accessed March 19, 2021, https://www.urbandictionary.com/define.php?term=lol.

31. Urban Dictionary, s.v. "haha," by Entity1037, accessed March 19 2021, https://www.urbandictionary.com/define.php?term=haha.

32. Something similar occurs in Lauren Berlant's idea of underperformance or "flat affect" as a way of capturing the hesitation and unintelligibility of a subject's own desires to himself as he attempts to "allocate expressivity." See Lauren Berlant, "Structures of Unfeeling: Mysterious Skin," *International Journal of Politics, Culture, and Society* 28 (2015): 191–213.

33. Anne-Lise François, *Open Secrets: The Literature of Uncounted Experience* (Stanford, CA: Stanford University Press, 2007).

34. Kevin Quashie, *The Sovereignty of Quiet: Beyond Resistance in Black Culture* (New Brunswick, NJ: Rutgers University Press, 2012).

35. See Wendy Chun, *Control and Freedom: Power and Paranoia in the Age of Fiber Optics* (Cambridge, MA: MIT Press, 2005); and Hu, "Wait, then Give Up."

36. Lauren Michele Jackson, "We Need to Talk about Digital Blackface in Reaction GIFs," *Teen Vogue*, August 2, 2017, https://www.teenvogue.com/story/digital-blackface-reaction-gifs.

37. Ralph Ellison, "An Extravagance of Laughter," in *The Collected Essays of Ralph Ellison: Revised and Updated*, ed. John Callahan (New York: Modern Library, 2003), 617–62.

38. Scott Richmond, "Vulgar Boredom, or What Andy Warhol Can Teach Us about Candy Crush," *Journal of Visual Culture* 14, no. 1 (2015): 21–39.

SELECTED BIBLIOGRAPHY

Allen, W. Bruce. "The Logistics Revolution and Transportation." *Annals of the American Academy of Political and Social Science* 553 (1997): 106–16.

Aouragh, Miriyam, and Paula Chakravartty. "Infrastructures of Empire: Towards a Critical Geopolitics of Media and Information Studies." *Media, Culture and Society* 38, no. 4 (2016): 559–75.

Atanasoski, Neda, and Kalindi Vora. *Surrogate Humanity: Race, Robots, and the Politics of Technological Futures*. Durham, NC: Duke University Press, 2019.

Baran, Paul. "On Distributed Communications Networks." *IEEE Transactions* CS-12, no. 1 (1964): 1–9.

Baucom, Ian. *Spectres of the Atlantic: Finance Capital, Slavery, and the Philosophy of History*. Durham, NC: Duke University Press, 2005.

Berlant, Lauren. "Structures of Unfeeling: Mysterious Skin." *International Journal of Politics, Culture, and Society* 28, no. 3 (2015): 191–213.

Bernes, Jasper. "Logistics, Counterlogistics and the Communist Prospect." *Endnotes*, no. 3 (September 2013). https://endnotes.org.uk/issues/3/en/jasper -bernes-logistics-counterlogistics-and-the-communist-prospect.

Berry, David, and Michael Dieter, eds. *Post-digital Aesthetics: Art, Computation, and Design*. London: Palgrave-Macmillan, 2015.

Berry, Stephen. *A Path in the Mighty Waters*. New Haven, CT: Yale University Press, 2015.

Blackburn, Robin. *The Making of New World Slavery: From the Baroque to the Modern, 1492–1800*. London: Verso, 1997.

Blumenberg, Hans. *Shipwreck with Spectator: Paradigm of a Metaphor for Existence*. Translated by Steven Rendall. Cambridge, MA: MIT Press, 1985.

Bologna, Sergio. "L'undicesima tesi," in *Ceti medi senza futuro? Scritti, appunti sul lavoro e altro*. Rome: DeriveApprodi, 2007.

Bonacich, Edna, and Jake Wilson. *Getting the Goods: Ports, Labor, and the Logistics Revolution*. Ithaca, NY: Cornell University Press, 2008.

Borio, Guido, Francesca Pozzi, and Gigi Roggero, "*Conricerca* as Political Action." In *Utopian Pedagogy: Radical Experiments against Neoliberal Globalization*, edited by Mark Coté, Richard J. F. Day, and Greig De Peuter, 163–85. Toronto: University of Toronto Press, 2007.

Bratton, Benjamin. "Introduction: Logistics of Habitable Circulation." In Paul Virilio, *Speed and Politics*, 7–25. Los Angeles: Semiotext(e), 2006.

Bratton, Benjamin. *The Stack: On Software and Sovereignty*. Cambridge, MA: MIT Press, 2015.

Braudel, Fernand. *The Mediterranean and the Mediterranean World in the Age of Philip II*. Vol. 1. 1949. Reprint, Berkeley: University of California Press, 1996.

Brodie, Patrick, Lisa Han, and Weixian Pan. "Introduction: Becoming Environmental: Media, Logistics, and Ecological Change." *Synoptique* 8, no. 1 (2019): 6–13.

Browne, Simone. *Dark Matters: On the Surveillance of Blackness*. Durham, NC: Duke University Press, 2015.

Buchloh, Benjamin. "Conceptual Art, 1962–1969: From the Aesthetic of Administration to the Critique of Institutions." *October*, no. 55 (1990): 105–43.

Burnetts, Charles. "'New Weapons' for the Precariat in Film and Media Studies." *Cinema Journal Teaching Dossier* 4, no. 2 (2016).

Butel, Paul. *The Atlantic*. Translated by Iain Hamilton Grant. London: Routledge, 1999.

Carroll, Amy Sara. REMEX: *Toward an Art History of the* NAFTA *Era*. Austin: University of Texas Press, 2017.

Case, Judd. "Logistical Media: Fragments from Radar's Prehistory." *Canadian Journal of Communication* 38 (2013): 379–95.

Casilli, Antonio. "Digital Labor Studies Go Global: Toward a Digital Decolonial Turn." *International Journal of Communication* 11 (2017): 3934–54.

Chakrabarty, Dipesh. *Provincializing Europe: Postcolonial Thought and Historical Difference*. Princeton, NJ: Princeton University Press, 2000.

Chua, Charmaine. "The Quiet Port Is Logistics' Nightmare." *Empire Logistics*, September 21, 2015. http://www.empirelogistics.org/dispatches/the-quiet-port.

Chua, Charmaine, Martin Danyluk, Deborah Cowen, and Laleh Khalili, "Introduction: Turbulent Circulation: Building a Critical Engagement with Logistics." *Environment and Planning D: Society and Space* 36 no. 4 (2018): 617–29.

Chun, Wendy Hui Kyong. *Control and Freedom: Power and Paranoia in the Age of Fiber Optics*. Cambridge, MA: MIT Press, 2005.

Chun, Wendy Hui Kyong. "Race and/as Technology, or How to Do Things to Race." In *Race after the Internet*, edited by Lisa Nakamura and A. Peter Chow-White, 38–60. New York: Routledge, 2012.

Colectivo Situaciones. "On the Researcher-Militant." Translated by Sebastian Touza. *Transversal Texts*, September 2003. https://transversal.at/transversal /0406/colectivo-situaciones/en.

Coleman, Beth. "Race as Technology." *Camera Obscura* 24, no. 1 (2009): 177–207.

Coletu, Ebony. "Descendant Epistemology." *Ghana Studies* 22, no. 1 (2019): 150–72.

Cowen, Deborah. *The Deadly Life of Logistics*. Minneapolis: University of Minnesota Press, 2014.

Cuppini, Niccolò, Mattia Frapporti, Floriano Milesi, Luca Padova, and Maurilio Pirone. "Logistics and Crisis: The Supply Chain System in the Po Valley Region." Teaching the Crisis: Geographies, Methodologies, Perspectives, 2013. Accessed January 13, 2021, http://teachingthecrisis.net/logistics-and-crisis -the-supply-chain-system-in-the-po-valley-region-2/index.html.

Danyluk, Martin. "Capital's Logistical Fix: Accumulation, Globalization, and the Survival of Capitalism." *Environment and Planning D: Society and Space* 36, no. 4 (2018): 630–47.

Devine, Kyle. *Decomposed: The Political Ecology of Music*. Cambridge, MA: MIT Press, 2019.

Easterling, Keller. *Extrastatecraft: The Power of Infrastructure Space*. New York: Verso, 2014.

Ellison, Ralph. "An Extravagance of Laughter." In *The Collected Essays of Ralph Ellison: Revised and Updated*, edited by John Callahan, 617–62. New York: Modern Library, 2003.

Emerson, Harrington. *Efficiency as a Basis for Operation and Wages*. New York: Engineering Magazine, 1909.

Feigenbaum, Anna. "Resistant Matters: Tents, Tear Gas and the 'Other Media' of Occupy." *Communication and Critical/Cultural Studies* 11, no. 1 (2014): 15–24.

Ferreira da Silva, Denise "− 1 (life) ÷ 0 (blackness) = ∞ − ∞ or ∞ / ∞: On Matter Beyond the Equation of Value." *e-flux*, no. 79 (February 2017). https://www .e-flux.com/journal/79/94686/1-life-0-blackness-or-on-matter-beyond-the -equation-of-value/.

Field, Kendra Taira. *Growing Up with the Country: Family, Race, and Nation after the Civil War*. New Haven, CT: Yale University Press, 2018.

François, Anne-Lise. *Open Secrets: The Literature of Uncounted Experience*. Stanford, CA: Stanford University Press, 2007.

Friedman-Silver, Yael, and Steve Whitford. "On the Edge of Practice: Reflections on Filmmaking Pedagogy in the Age of the Creative Industries." *Cinema Journal* 5, no. 1 (2018).

Freeman, Matthew. "Transmedia Attractions: The Case of *Warner Bros. Studio Tour—The Making of Harry Potter*." In *The Routledge Companion to Transmedia Studies*, edited by Matthew Freeman and Renira Rampazzo Gambarato. New York: Routledge, 2019.

Frohmann, Bernd. "The Documentality of Mme. Briet's Antelope." In *Communication Matters: Materialist Approaches to Media, Mobility, and Networks*, edited by Jeremey Packer and Stephen B. Crofts Wiley, 173–82. London: Routledge, 2012.

Galloway, Alexander. *Laruelle: Against the Digital*. Minneapolis: University of Minnesota Press, 2014.

Gehl, Robert W. "(Critical) Reverse Engineering and Genealogy." *Le foucaldien* 3, no. 1 (2017): 1–14.

Geoghegan, Bernard Dionysius. "After Kittler: On the Cultural Techniques of Recent German Media Theory." *Theory, Culture and Society* 30, no. 6 (2013): 66–82.

Gillespie, Richard. *Manufacturing Knowledge: A History of the Hawthorne Experiments*. Cambridge: Cambridge University Press, 1993.

Gitelman, Lisa. *Always Already New: Media History and the Data of Culture*. Cambridge, MA: MIT Press, 2006.

Gitelman, Lisa. *Paper Knowledge: Toward a Media History of Documents*. Durham, NC: Duke University Press, 2014.

Goldsmith, Ben, and Tom O'Regan, "Still Exceptional? London's Film Studios." In *The Film Studio: Film Production in the Global Economy*, 135–49. Oxford: Rowman and Littlefield, 2005.

Goldsmith, Ben, Susan Ward, and Tom O'Regan. *Local Hollywood: Global Film Production and the Gold Coast*. St. Lucia: University of Queensland Press, 2010.

Gray, Mary L., and Siddharth Suri. *Ghost Work: How to Stop Silicon Valley from Building a New Global Underclass*. Boston: Houghton Mifflin Harcourt, 2019.

Guyer, Jane I. "Prophecy and the Near Future: Thoughts on Macroeconomic, Evangelical, and Punctuated Time." In *Legacies, Logics, Logistics: Essays in the Anthropology of the Platform Economy*, 89–109. Chicago: University of Chicago Press, 2016.

Harney, Stefano, with Niccolo Cuppini and Mattia Frapporti. "Logistics Genealogies: A Dialogue with Stefano Harney." *Social Text* 36, no. 3 (2018): 95–110.

Harney, Stefano, and Fred Moten. *The Undercommons: Fugitive Planning and Black Study*. Wivenhoe, UK: Minor Compositions, 2013.

Hartman, Saidiya. "Venus in Two Acts." *Small Axe*, no. 26 (2008): 1–14.

Heidegger, Martin. "The Question concerning Technology." In *Basic Writings*, edited by David Farrell Krell, 307–41. New York: HarperCollins, 1993.

Heidenreich, Stefan. "The Situation after Media." In *Media after Kittler*, edited by Eleni Ikoniadou and Scott Wilson, 135–53. London: Rowman and Littlefield, 2015.

Holt, Jennifer, and Alisa Perren, eds. *Media Industries: History, Theory, and Method*. Malden, MA: Wiley-Blackwell, 2009.

Hörl, Erich. "Introduction to General Ecology." In *General Ecology: A New Ecological Paradigm*, edited by Erich Hörl with James Burton, 1–73. London: Bloomsbury Academic, 2017.

Hu, Tung-Hui. *A Prehistory of the Cloud*. Cambridge, MA: MIT Press, 2015.

Hu, Tung-Hui. "Wait, then Give Up: Lethargy and the Reticence of Digital Art." *Journal of Visual Culture* 16, no. 3 (2017): 337–54.

Humes, Edward. *Door to Door: The Magnificent, Maddening, Mysterious World of Transportation*. New York: HarperCollins, 2016.

Hunt, Bruce J. "Insulation for an Empire: Gutta-Percha and the Development of Electrical Measurement in Victorian Britain." In *Semaphores to Short Waves*, edited by Frank A. J. L. James, 85–104. London: Royal Society of Arts, 1998.

Innis, Harold. *The Bias of Communication*. Toronto: University of Toronto Press, 1951.

Innis, Harold. *The Cod Fisheries*. 1940. Reprint, Toronto: University of Toronto Press, 1978.

Innis, Harold. *Empire and Communications*. Oxford: Clarendon Press, 1950.

Innis, Harold. *The Fur Trade in Canada*. 1930. Reprint, Toronto: University of Toronto Press, 1970.

Invisible Committee. *The Coming Insurrection*. Cambridge, MA: MIT Press / Semiotext(e), 2009.

Irani, Lilly. "The Cultural Work of Microwork." *New Media and Society* 17, no. 5 (2013): 720–39.

Jomini, Baron Antoine-Henri. *The Art of War*. Translated by G. H. Mendell. Kingston, ON: Legacy Books Press, 2008.

Joseph, May. *Nomadic Identities: The Performance of Citizenship*. Minneapolis: University of Minnesota Press, 1999.

Kanngieser, Anja. "Tracking and Tracing: Geographies of Logistical Governance and Labouring Bodies." *Environment and Planning D: Society and Space* 31, no. 4 (2013): 594–610.

Klose, Alexander. *The Container Principle*. Cambridge, MA: MIT Press, 2015.

Kneese, Tamara, and Michael Palm. "Brick-and-Platform: Listing Labor in the Digital Vintage Economy." *Social Media + Society* (July–September 2020): 1–11.

Larkin, Brian. *Signal and Noise: Media, Infrastructure, and Urban Culture in Nigeria*. Durham, NC: Duke University Press, 2008.

Latour, Bruno. *Science in Action: How to Follow Scientists and Engineers through Society*. Cambridge, MA: Harvard University Press, 1988.

Lazzarato, Maurizio. *The Making of the Indebted Man: An Essay on the Neoliberal Condition*. Translated by Joshua David Jordan. Los Angeles: Semiotext(e), 2012.

LeCavalier, Jesse. *The Rule of Logistics: Walmart and the Architecture of Fulfillment*. Minneapolis: University of Minnesota Press, 2016.

Levinson, Marc. *The Box: How the Shipping Container Made the World Smaller and the World Economy Bigger*. Princeton, NJ: Princeton University Press, 2006.

Lovink, Geert, and Ned Rossiter. *Organization after Social Media*. Colchester, UK: Minor Compositions, 2018.

Luhmann, Niklas. *Introduction to Systems Theory*. Translated by Peter Gilgen. Cambridge: Polity, 2013.

Martin, Craig. *Shipping Container*. London: Bloomsbury, 2016.

Mattelart, Armand. *The Invention of Communication*. Translated by Susan Emanuel. Minneapolis: University of Minnesota Press, 1996.

Mattern, Shannon. *Clay and Code, Data and Dirt: Five Thousand Years of Urban Media*. Minneapolis: University of Minnesota Press, 2017.

Mattern, Shannon. "Ear to the Wire: Listening to Historic Urban Infrastructures." *Amodern 2: Network Archaeology*, October 2013. http://amodern.net/article/ear-to-the-wire/.

Maxwell, Richard, and Toby Miller. *Greening the Media*. Oxford: Oxford University Press, 2012.

Mayer, Vicki. *Below the Line: Producers and Production Studies in the New Television Economy.* Durham, NC: Duke University Press, 2011.

Mayer, Vicki, Miranda Banks, and John Thornton Caldwell, eds. *Production Studies: Cultural Studies of Media Industries.* New York: Routledge, 2009.

Mazierska, Ewa, Les Gillon, and Tony Rigg, eds. *Popular Music in the Post-Digital Age: Politics, Economy, Culture and Technology.* New York: Bloomsbury Academic, 2019.

McDonald, Paul. "Britain: Hollywood UK." In *The Contemporary Hollywood Film Industry*, edited by Paul McDonald and Janet Wasko, 220–31. Oxford: Blackwell, 2008.

McKittrick, Katherine. "Mathematics Black Life." *Black Scholar* 44, no. 2 (2014): 16–28.

McLuhan, Marshall. *Understanding Media: The Extensions of Man.* New York: McGraw-Hill, 1964.

Melis, Behlil. *Hollywood Is Everywhere: Global Directors in the Blockbuster Era.* Amsterdam: Amsterdam University Press, 2016.

Mezzadra, Sandro, and Brett Neilson. *Border as Method, or, the Multiplication of Labor.* Durham, NC: Duke University Press, 2013.

Mezzadra, Sandro, and Brett Neilson. "Extraction, Logistics, Finance: Global Crisis and the Politics of Operations." *Radical Philosophy* 178 (2013): 8–18.

Mezzadra, Sandro, and Brett Neilson. *The Politics of Operations: Excavating Contemporary Capitalism.* Durham, NC: Duke University Press, 2019.

Moten, Fred. *Stolen Life.* Durham, NC: Duke University Press, 2018.

Mumford, Lewis. *The City in History.* New York: Harcourt, 1961.

Nakamura, Lisa. "Don't Hate the Player, Hate the Game: The Racialization of Labor in World of Warcraft." *Critical Studies in Media Communication* 26, no. 2 (2009): 128–44.

Neilson, Brett, and Ned Rossiter. "Still Waiting, Still Moving: On Migration, Logistics and Maritime Industries." In *Stillness in a Mobile World*, edited by David Bissell and Gillian Fuller, 51–68. London: Routledge, 2011.

Ngai, Sianne. "Animatedness." In *Ugly Feelings*, 89–125. Cambridge, MA: Harvard University Press, 2005.

Nieborg, David, and Thomas Poell. "The Platformization of Cultural Production: Theorizing the Contingent Cultural Commodity." *New Media and Society* 20, no. 11 (2018): 4275–92.

Novak, David. *Japanoise: Music at the Edge of Circulation.* Durham, NC: Duke University Press, 2013.

Okiji, Fumi. *Jazz as Critique: Adorno and Black Expression Revisited.* Stanford, CA: Stanford University Press, 2018.

Ong, Aihwa. *Neoliberalism as Exception: Mutations in Citizenship and Sovereignty.* Durham, NC: Duke University Press, 2006.

Orenstein, Dara. *Out of Stock: The Warehouse in the History of Capitalism.* Chicago: University of Chicago Press, 2019.

Parks, Lisa, and Nicole Starosielski, eds. *Signal Traffic: Critical Studies of Media Infrastructures*. Champaign: University of Illinois Press, 2015.

Parvulescu, Anca. "Even Laughter? From Laughter in the Magic Theater to the Laughter Assembly Line." *Critical Inquiry* 43, no. 2 (2017): 506–27.

Peters, John Durham. "Calendar, Clock, Tower." In *Deus in Machina*, edited by Jeremy Stolow, 25–42. New York: Fordham University Press, 2013.

Peters, John Durham. *The Marvelous Clouds: Toward a Philosophy of Elemental Media*. Chicago: University of Chicago Press, 2015.

Petrie, Duncan. "Creative Industries and Skills: Film Education and Training in the Era of New Labour." *Journal of British Cinema and Television* 9, no. 3 (2012): 357–76.

Precarious Workers Brigade. *Training for Exploitation? Politicising Employability and Reclaiming Education*. London: Journal of Aesthetics and Protest Press, 2017.

Prashad, Vijay. *Everybody Was Kung-Fu Fighting: Afro-Asian Connections and the Myth of Cultural Purity*. Boston: Beacon, 2002.

Quashie, Kevin. *The Sovereignty of Quiet: Beyond Resistance in Black Culture*. New Brunswick, NJ: Rutgers University Press, 2012.

Quayson, Ato. "'Still It Makes Me Laugh, No Time to Die': A Response." *PMLA* 131, no. 2 (2016): 528–39.

Ramsey, Phil, and Andrew White. "Art for Art's Sake? A Critique of the Instrumentalist Turn in the Teaching of Media and Communications in UK Universities." *International Journal of Cultural Policy* 21, no. 1 (2015): 78–96.

Ray, Carina E. *Crossing the Color Line: Race, Sex, and the Contested Politics of Colonialism in Ghana*. Athens: Ohio University Press, 2015.

Rediker, Marcus. *The Slave Ship: A Human History*. New York: Penguin, 2007.

Richmond, Scott. "Vulgar Boredom, or What Andy Warhol Can Teach Us about Candy Crush." *Journal of Visual Culture* 14, no. 1 (2015): 21–39.

Robinson, Cedric J. *Black Marxism: The Making of the Black Radical Tradition*. Chapel Hill: University of North Carolina Press, 1983.

Roethlisberger, Fritz Jules, and William J. Dickson. *Management and the Worker*. Cambridge, MA: Harvard University Press, 1939.

Roggero, Gigi. *The Production of Living Knowledge: The Crisis of the University and the Transformation of Labor in Europe and North America*. Translated by Enda Brophy. Philadelphia: Temple University Press, 2011.

Rosenthal, Caitlin. *Accounting for Slavery: Masters and Management*. Cambridge, MA: Harvard University Press, 2018.

Rossiter, Ned. "Copper." In *The Oxford Handbook of Media, Technology, and Organization Studies*, edited by Timon Beyes, Robin Holt, and Claus Pias, 160–71. Oxford: Oxford University Press, 2020.

Rossiter, Ned. "Imperial Infrastructures and Asia beyond Asia: Data Centres, State Formation and the Territoriality of Logistical Media." *Fibreculture Journal* 29 (2017): 1–20.

Rossiter, Ned. "Locative Media as Logistical Media: Situating Infrastructure and the Governance of Labor in Supply-Chain Capitalism." In *Locative Media*, edited by Gerard Goggin and Rowan Wilken, 208–23. New York: Routledge, 2014.

Rossiter, Ned. "Logistical Worlds." *Cultural Studies Review* 20, no. 1 (2014): 53–76.

Rossiter, Ned. *Software, Infrastructure, Labor: A Media Theory of Logistical Nightmares.* New York: Routledge, 2016.

Rossiter, Ned. "Translating the Indifference of Communication: Electronic Waste, Migrant Labour and the Informational Sovereignty of Logistics in China." *International Review of Information Ethics* 11 (2009): 36–44.

Rossiter, Ned, and Kenneth Tay. "Uneven Distribution: An Interview with Ned Rossiter on Logistics and Mediated Environments." *Public Seminar*, May 31, 2019. https://publicseminar.org/2019/05/uneven-distribution-an-interview-with-ned-rossiter/.

Rupprecht, Anita. "Excessive Memories: Slavery, Insurance, Resistance." *History Workshop Journal* 64, no. 1 (2007): 6–28.

Rowe, Aimee Carrillo, and Eve Tuck. "Settler Colonialism and Cultural Studies." *Cultural Studies ↔ Critical Methodologies* 17, no. 1 (2017): 3–13.

Sax, David. *The Revenge of Analog: Real Things and Why They Matter.* Philadelphia: Public Affairs Books, 2016.

Schanberg, Sydney H. "Six Cents an Hour." *Life*, June 1996: 38–48.

Schwoch, James. *Wired into Nature: The Telegraph and the North American Frontier.* Champaign: University of Illinois Press, 2018.

Sekula, Allan. *Fish Story.* Düsseldorf: Richter Verlag, 1995.

Sharpe, Christina. *In the Wake: On Blackness and Being.* Durham, NC: Duke University Press, 2016.

Siegert, Bernhard. "Cultural Techniques: Or the End of the Intellectual Postwar Era in German Media Theory." *Theory, Culture and Society* 30, no. 3 (2013): 48–65.

Siegert, Bernhard. *Cultural Techniques: Grids, Filters, Doors, and Other Articulations of the Real.* New York: Fordham University Press, 2015.

Simpson, Audra. *Mohawk Interruptus: Political Life across the Borders of Settler States.* Durham, NC: Duke University Press, 2014.

Smallwood, Stephanie. *Saltwater Slavery: A Middle Passage from African to American Diaspora.* Cambridge, MA: Harvard University Press, 2007.

Smith, George David. *The Anatomy of a Business Strategy: Bell, Western Electric, and the Origins of the American Telephone Industry.* Baltimore: Johns Hopkins University Press, 1985.

Smith, Jacob. *Eco-Sonic Media.* Berkeley: University of California Press, 2015.

Spillers, Hortense J. "Mama's Baby, Papa's Maybe: An American Grammar Book." *diacritics* 17, no. 2 (1987): 69–70.

Spivak, Gayatri Chakravorty. *An Aesthetic Education in the Era of Globalization.* Cambridge, MA: Harvard University Press, 2012.

Srnicek, Nick. *Platform Capitalism.* Cambridge: Polity, 2016.

Stamm, Michael. *Dead Tree Media: The Newspaper in Twentieth-Century North America.* Baltimore: Johns Hopkins University Press, 2018.

Starosielski, Nicole. *The Undersea Network*. Durham, NC: Duke University Press, 2015.

Stoever, Jennifer Lynn. *The Sonic Color Line: Race and the Cultural Politics of Listening*. New York: NYU Press, 2016.

Taylor, Frederick. *The Principles of Scientific Management*. New York: Harper and Row, 1911.

Taylor, Frederick. *Shop Management*. New York: Harper and Row, 1911.

Terranova, Tiziana. *Network Culture: Politics for the Information Age*. London: Pluto, 2004.

Toscano, Alberto. "Lineaments of the Logistical State." *Viewpoint Magazine*, September 28, 2014. https://www.viewpointmag.com/2014/09/28/lineaments-of -the-logistical-state/.

Toscano, Alberto. "Logistics and Opposition." *Mute* 3, no. 2 (2011).

Toscano, Alberto, and Jeff Kinkle. *Cartographies of the Absolute*. Winchester, UK: Zero Books, 2015.

Tsing, Anna Lowenhaupt. *Friction: An Ethnography of Global Connection*. Princeton, NJ: Princeton University Press, 2004.

Tsing, Anna Lowenhaupt. *The Mushroom at the End of the World: On the Possibility of Life in Capitalist Ruins*. Princeton, NJ: Princeton University Press, 2015.

Tsing, Anna Lowenhaupt. "On Non-Scalability." *Common Knowledge* 18, no. 3 (2012): 505–24.

Tsing, Anna Lowenhaupt. "Supply Chains and the Human Condition." *Rethinking Marxism* 21, no. 2 (2009): 148–76.

Tuck, Eve, and K. Wayne Yang. "Decolonization Is Not a Metaphor." *Decolonization: Indigeneity, Education and Society* 1, no. 1 (2012): 1–40.

van Creveld, Martin. *Supplying War: Logistics from Wallenstein to Patton*. Cambridge: Cambridge University Press, 1977.

van Wyck, Peter C. *The Highway of the Atom*. Montreal: McGill-Queen's University Press, 2010.

Virilio, Paul. *Polar Inertia*. Translated by Patrick Camiller. London: Sage, 2000.

Virilio, Paul. *Speed and Politics*. Translated by Mark Polizzotti. 1977. Reprint, Los Angeles: Semiotext(e), 2006.

Virilio, Paul. *War and Cinema: The Logistics of Perception*. London: Verso, 1989.

Vismann, Cornelia. *Files: Law and Media Technology*. Stanford, CA: Stanford University Press, 2008.

Walker, Jeremy, and Melinda Cooper. "Genealogies of Resilience: From Systems Ecology to the Political Economy of Crisis Adaptation." *Security Dialogue* 42, no. 2 (2011): 143–60.

Wallerstein, Immanuel. *Geopolitics and Geoculture: Essays on the Changing World System*. Cambridge: Cambridge University Press, 1991.

Winseck, Dwayne, and Robert Pike. *Communication and Empire: Media, Markets, and Globalization, 1860–1930*. Durham, NC: Duke University Press, 2007.

Winthrop-Young, Geoffrey. "Cultural Techniques: Preliminary Remarks." *Theory, Culture and Society* 30, no. 6 (2013): 3–19.

Wood, Marcus. *Blind Memory: Visual Representations of Slavery in England and America, 1780–1865*. New York: Routledge, 2000.

Wynter, Sylvia. "Unsettling the Coloniality of Being/Power/Truth/Freedom: Towards the Human, after Man, Its Overrepresentation—An Argument." *CR: The New Centennial Review* 3, no. 3 (2003): 257–337.

Young, Liam Cole. "Cultural Techniques and Logistical Media." *M/C Journal* 18, no. 2 (2015). https://doi.org/10.5204/mcj.961.

Young, Liam Cole. *List Cultures: Knowledge and Poetics from Mesopotamia to BuzzFeed*. Amsterdam: Amsterdam University Press, 2017.

Zieger, Susan. *The Mediated Mind: Affect, Ephemera, and Consumerism in the Nineteenth Century*. New York: Fordham University Press, 2018.

Zuboff, Shoshana. *The Age of Surveillance Capitalism: The Fight for a Human Future at the New Frontier of Power*. New York: Public Affairs, 2019.

CONTRIBUTORS

EBONY COLETU is an assistant professor of African American studies, English, and African studies at Pennsylvania State University. She received a Fulbright Scholar award to Ghana for 2018–2020, and her work has been published in *Ghana Studies*, *Transition*, *Comparative American Studies*, *Biography*, and *a/b: journal of auto/biographical studies*. She is currently working on a book about Chief Sam's African Movement and the origins of African American migration to Ghana.

KAY DICKINSON is professor of film studies at Concordia University, Montreal. She is the author of *Off Key: When Film and Music Won't Work Together* (2008), *Arab Cinema Travels: Transnational Syria, Palestine, Dubai and Beyond* (2016), and *Arab Film and Video Manifestos: Forty-Five Years of the Moving Image amid Revolution* (2018). She is currently working on a monograph project titled *Supply Chain Cinema*.

STEFANO HARNEY and FRED MOTEN are longtime friends and co-conspirators. They are authors of *The Undercommons: Fugitive Planning and Black Study* (2013) and *All Incomplete* (2020).

MATTHEW HOCKENBERRY is an assistant professor of communication and media studies at Fordham University. A media historian whose work examines the media of global production, his current project explores critical developments in the epistemology of assembly. He is particularly concerned with how transitional moments in the histories of paperwork, telecommunication, and computation shaped the emergence of logistics in the nineteenth and twentieth centuries. You can find him at supplystudies.com.

TUNG-HUI HU writes on media art and digital culture. He is the author of *A Prehistory of the Cloud* (2015) and *Digital Lethargy* (forthcoming), as well as three books of poetry, most recently *Greenhouses, Lighthouses* (2013). He has received fellowships from the National Endowment for the Arts and the American Academy in Berlin, and is an associate professor of English at the University of Michigan.

SHANNON MATTERN is a professor of anthropology at the New School for Social Research. Her writing and teaching focus on archives, libraries, and other media spaces; media infrastructures; spatial epistemologies; and mediated sensation and exhibition. She is the author of *The New Downtown Library: Designing with Communities* (2007), *Deep Mapping the Media City* (2015), *Code and Clay, Data and Dirt* (2017), and *The City Is Not a Computer: Other Urban Intelligences* (2021). She contributes a regular, long-form column about urban data and mediated infrastructures to *Places*, and she collaborates on public design and interactive projects and exhibitions. You can find her at wordsinspace.net.

MICHAEL PALM is an associate professor of media and technology studies and director of graduate studies in the Department of Communication at the University of North Carolina at Chapel Hill, and he is president of the UNC-Chapel Hill chapter of the American Association of University Professors. He is the author of *Technologies of Consumer Labor* (2017) and is writing a book about the contemporary economy of vinyl records. Articles based on his preliminary vinyl research have appeared in the *Journal of Popular Music Studies*, *Convergence: The International Journal of Research into New Media Technologies*, and *Social Media + Society* (with Tamara Kneese).

JOHN DURHAM PETERS is the María Rosa Menocal Professor of English and of Film and Media Studies at Yale University. He is the author of *Speaking into the Air: A History of the Idea of Communication* (1999), *Courting the Abyss: Free Speech and the Liberal Tradition* (2005), *The Marvelous Clouds: Toward a Philosophy of Elemental Media* (2015), and *Promiscuous Knowledge: Information, Image, and Other Truth Games in History* (2020), with the late Kenneth Cmiel.

NED ROSSITER is professor of communication and director of research at the Institute for Culture and Society, Western Sydney University, where he holds a joint appointment in the School of Humanities and Communication Arts. Rossiter is the author of *Organized Networks: Media Theory, Creative Labour, New Institutions* (2006), *Software, Infrastructure, Labor: A Media Theory of Logistical Nightmares* (2016), and (with Geert Lovink) *Organization after Social Media* (2018).

NICOLE STAROSIELSKI is an associate professor of Media, Culture, and Communication at New York University. Her research focuses on media, infrastructures, and environments. She is author of *The Undersea Network* (2015) and *Media Hot and Cold* (forthcoming), as well as coeditor of *Signal Traffic: Critical Studies of Media Infrastructure* (2015), *Sustainable Media: Critical Approaches to Media and Environment* (2016), and the Elements series at Duke University Press.

LIAM COLE YOUNG is a settler scholar living and working on unceded and unsurrendered territories of the Algonquin nation. He is an assistant professor in the

School of Journalism and Communication at Carleton University and the author of *List Cultures: Knowledge and Poetics from Mesopotamia to BuzzFeed* (2017).

SUSAN ZIEGER is a professor of English at the University of California, Riverside. Her research interests include nineteenth-century literature and culture, historical media studies, and the history of science, medicine, and technology. She is the author of *Inventing the Addict: Drugs, Race, and Sexuality in Nineteenth-Century British and American Literature* (2008) and *The Mediated Mind: Affect, Ephemera, and Consumerism in the Nineteenth Century* (2018). Her current project, *Logistical Life*, has been supported by the Max Planck Institute for the History of Science in Berlin and the Institute for Culture and Society at Western Sydney University.

INDEX

automation, 14, 208; geopolitics of, 12, 132, 134–35; technologies, 136, 140
autonomous vehicles, 135–36
avatars, 208

Baker, Kenneth, 214
Baldwin, James, 28
Beatles: *Abbey Road*, 162–63; "Hello, Goodbye" / "I Am the Walrus," 169, *170*
Bell, Alexander Graham, 125
Bell, Daniel, vii
Bell System, *114*, 119–20, 125
Benjamin, Walter, 156
Berlant, Lauren, 224n32
Bernes, Jasper, 5
Bestand concept, 95, 102, 107n4
Bezos, Jeff, 212
bills of lading, 8, 35, 36–41, 46, 48, 50n22
Bittle, William, 54–55, 64
blackness, 34, 44, 65, 220
Black studies, 7, 8, 34, 35–36, 45
body/bodies: enslaved, 10, 45, 46, 77; flesh and earth, 25–26; the heart, 26, 30–31; Indigenous, 98; laboring, 77–78, 213; lethargic, 210, 221; the mind and ownership of, 8, 24–25, 27; racialized, 17, 208–9; space and time and, 28
Bologna, Sergio, 11
Borrows, John, 105
Bradley, Garrett, 216, 217
Bratton, Benjamin, 11, 96
Brookes (ship), 41, *42*, 43–46
Browne, Simone, 10
Burlington Record Plant, 164
Burnetts, Charles, 181
Button, Roy, 173

cable systems: Huawei Marine and security concerns, 197–202; manufacturing and suppliers, 192–97; OTTs and, 202–3; overview of, 191–92
Cabot, John, 94, 96, 97
Calais, 194–95
Canada, 12, 109n16, 193; settler colonialism, 98, 104–7

cancellation, concept of, 12, 102–4, 106, 215
Canned Laughter (2009): description and critique, 17, 211–17, 223n23; fake and real laughter in, 217–18; images, *212*, *213*; lethargic quality of, 221; meditation break scene, 219, *220*
capital, 5, 48, 86, 172, 173, 219; accumulation, 140, 142, 149n25; diasporic, 55, 57, 58, 59, 63; efficiency and, 115; human, 178, 184; labor and, 29, 180
capitalism, 5, 14, 183; digital, 210, 216, 219; global, 11, 58, 75, 76, 86, 175; platform, 136, 157; racial, 45, 58, 213; supply chain, 4, 115, 141, 174–75; surveillance, 28–29; war and, viii, 2
cargo, x, 5; enslaved people as, 34–35, 37–40, 46, 52, *53*; private carriers of, 6; ships, 85, 100
Case, Judd, 3, 57, 75, 79
Casilli, Antonio, 216
Casson, Herbert, 117–18
casualization of labor, 178, 181, 183
Charles II, King, 102
China, 141–42, 209; cable companies, 197–201; Belt and Road initiative, 26, 95, 137
chronopolitics, 138, 140, 147
Chua, Charmaine, 81–82
Chun, Wendy, 209
cinematic production, 13, 185n6; forklift usage, 188, *189*; higher education and labor conditions, 175–77, 178–84; offshore practices, 171–72; studios, 173–74, 177–78; supply chain, 15, 172–73
circulation, 94–96; of culture, 1; mapping spaces of, 57–58; of paper materials, 7, 36, 41, 43, 45, 62; vinyl records in, 165
citizenship, 66, 71n25, 110n39
clickfarming, 216
clickworkers, 210, 216
clothing distribution, 153
cod fisheries, 94, 96, 100–101
Coletu, Ebony, 8

Incan Empire, 93

Indian Act (1876), 104, 109n16, 110n39

Indigenous peoples (North America), 108n16; colonial governance and documents and, 102–4; European traders and, 100–101; of New York, 93; wampum belts and treaty negotiations, 104–5, 110n39, 110n45

individualism, 5, 179, 180, 182

infomaquila, 212, *214*, 216

informal sector, 141

infrastructural sabotage, 140–41

Innis, Harold, viii, 8–9, 32, 100, 101, 103, 139

inscription (concept), 96, 102, 104, 106

instruments, logistical, 3, 8–13

Internet, 2, 16; bandwidth and speed, 206; CAPTCHA tests, 207, 217, 221n1, 222n2; human/robot distinction, 207–8; infrastructure, 191–92, 196–97, 201, 203. *See also* cable systems; online sales

internships, 179, 182, 184

interoperability, 2, 12, 97, 103, 137, 139, 140; definition, 95; of ships, 98, 101

interphone, 119–20, *121*, *122*

interval, the: decisionism and, 143–45; definition of, 17; digital logic of, 145, 146; multiplication of, 147; temporality of, 135, 139–40

Iroquois, 105, 110n39, 110n45

Jackson, Lauren Michele, 220

Jamaica, 30, 39

James, C. L. R., 36

Japan, 161, 195–96

Jomini, Antoine-Henri, 9, 78

Joseph Gathering Corn (c. 1275), 32, *33*

Kant, Immanuel, 25

Keynes, John Maynard, 124

Khalili, Laleh, 57

kin/kinship, 60–61, 68–69

Kittler, Friedrich, viii

knowledge production, 133, 146

Koerner, Brendan, 79

labor, 13, 29, 57, 138; casualized, 181; digital, 210, 213, 216–17; efficiency and, 117; exploitation, 2, 46, 173, 210, 213, 216; film workers, 171, 172–74, 176, 178–79; free, 35, 179, 180; logistical, 6, 113; maquiladora workers, 211–14; markets, 180–81; peasant, 140–41; power, 179–80; of selling records, 158–59; sounds and voices of, 77–78, 80–83; struggles and solidarity, 182–83. *See also* Atlantic slave trade

Labour Party (UK), 175–76

lac trade, 15

land claims, 65, 66, 102, 104–5

land transfers, 60, 61, 67–68

Langhorn, Peggy, 68–69

Langhorn, Webster, 68–69

Langley, J. Ayo, 55, 61, 70n6

Larkin, Brian, 193

laughter: African Americans and, 220; canned, 17, 211–15, 221; fake *vs.* real, 217–18

Law, John, 10

Lazzarato, Maurizio, 181

Leavesden studios, 16, 173–74, 176, 180, 181; Harry Potter Studio Tour, 177–78

LeCavalier, Jesse, 82–83

Les Câbles de Lyon, 195

lethargy, 210–11, 219, 221

Liberia, 61, 62, 64, 67, 68–69, 72n53

"likability," 210

Like (2016), 216

Lilly, Richard, 130

listening: distant and close, 78–79, 80–81, 82–83, 87n7; laboring bodies and, 77–78; logistical, 82, 86, 113, 126; overview of, 75–76; to signals and spectrum, 83–85; telephonic, 125; to vinyl records, 155

liveness, 209, 219

Locke, John, 8, 24–27

logic: digital, 17, 145, 146; economic, 28–29; logistics and, 27; operative, 3, 135; racial, 209

logistics revolution, 2, 79

LOL (laugh out loud), 218–19, 221

Lomas, Frank, 123

Longest Way Home, The (Bittle and Geis), 54–55, 64

Lopez, Aaron, 39

loss, prevention and sharing of, 24–27

Lovink, Geert, 140

Luhmann, Niklas, 139

magic, 52, *53*

mail orders, 7, 121

Making Vinyl (conference), 154–55, 162

Manchester, H. H., 32

Mannes, John, 84

maps/mapping, 57–58, 79, 86; flow, 73, 74; sounds, 84–85; supply chains, *112*

maquiladoras, 210, 219; in *Canned Laughter* (2009), 17, 211, 213–14, 217; info-, 212, 216

Marshall, Alfred, 117

Marx, Karl, vii, viii, 25, 179

mass production, 14–15, 156, 191

Masterdisk Studios, 160

mastering studios, 160–61

materiality, 111, 145–46, 157, 158, 166, 169

Mattern, Shannon, 8

Mayhew, Henry, 80

McKittrick, Katherine, 34

media industries, 13–15

media studies, viii, ix, 142; logistical, 3, 9, 156, 164, 166

media theory, 94, 142–43; colonial studies and, 96, 98, 106; of the digital, 146; equilibrium and, 139–40; logistical, 2, 12, 134, 136; provincial, 132–33

Mezzadra, Sandro, 2, 12, 174

microworkers, 210–11, 213–14, 216

Middle Passage, 7, 10, 35, 38–39, 41, 44, 46

military, viii, 8, 78–79; maps, 73, 74

Minard, Charles, 73, 74

missionary work, 59, 62

modernity, 97, 106, 148n22; electrical, 119; Paul Virilio on, 11, 115

monopolies, 194–95, 199, 203; King Charles II charter, 102

Moten, Fred, 8, 35, 45, 46, 173; on modern logistics, 10, 70n15, 77, 97

Mumford, Lewis, vii, 115

Nakamura, Lisa, 209

Napoleonic Wars, 9

national security, 191, 198–201

navigation technologies, 10, 83

NEC, 84, 195–96

Neilson, Brett, 2, 12, 174

neoliberalism, 2, 5, 59, 139, 178, 180, 183

Netflix, 16, 206

networks: African city, 59, 62; colonial, 15; digital, 16, 144–45, 190, 191, 201; distribution, 13, 95, 206; illegal e-waste, 141; inoperability of, 140; logistical, 16; of nonmovement, 125; rail, 85; road, 93; telecommunication, 14–15, 95, 123–24, 126. *See also* cable systems; telephone

New England, 100–101

Newfoundland, 94, 98, 100–101

newspaper business, 14

New Zealand, 193, 199

Ngai, Sianne, 208–9

Nike, 6

Nkrumah, Kwame, 54–56

noise pollution, 84

non-player character (NPC), 208, 209

North West Company (NWC), 103, 104

offshoring practices, 171, 172, 173–74, 179

Okón, Yoshua, 17, 211–19, 221

old media, 8–9

Ong, Aihwa, 180

online sales: clothing, 153; vinyl records, 16, 155, 157–59

orientation: of data, 146; listening and, 82; logistical, 3, 94, 95, 97, 106; points of, 9

origins of logistics: in the Atlantic slave trade, 10, 77, 97; in loss and emptiness, 26–27; multiplicity of, 57–58; in seafaring, 99; in warfare, viii, 9, 78

Osborne, Peter, 148n24

Tehanetorens, 104–5
telecommunication companies: history of global, 191, 192–95; Huawei Marine, 197–201; OTTs, 202–3. *See also* Western Electric
telegraph, 9, 14–15, 138, 192, 194, 196
telephone: advertisement for, *114*; cables, 193; efficiency and, 12, 116, 119–21; speech, 125; supply chain, 14, 123–24, 126
television, 209
template theory, 134
territoriality, 137–38
Thai Plastics and Chemicals (TPC), 160, 162
Tibbles, John, 201, 202
TICK (trusted information creator) quality mark, 177
timber trade, 14–15
time and space, viii, 2, 10, 12, 115, 148n22; capital accumulation and, 149n25; emplotment of, 26–28; listening across, 76, 82; of logistical and digital media, 135, 138–40, 142, 146–47; synchronization, 135; telephonic efficiency and, 119–20, 125
Toscano, Alberto, 7, 75, 85
tourism, 59, 61, 71n25, 174, 177, 180
tracking, 10, 12, 13, 29, 146, 220
trade flows, 73, *74*
training, 173, 176, 177, 178–80, 182, 184
Treaty of Fort Niagara, 105
truckstop network, 15
true emotions, 211–12
Tsing, Anna, 95, 141, 178, 180; on supply chain capitalism, 4, 16, 115, 174–75, 181
Tuck, Eve, 96, 107n8, 108n16
Twitter, 208

UK Film Council, 173–74
unions, 176, 178
United Kingdom: cable networks, 192, 194–95, 197; film industry and higher education, 171–81, 185n6; railway networks, 85

United States, 7, 14, 15, 137; cable suppliers, 195–96, 198–99; Civil War, 78, 79; national security, 199–201
universities, 175, 176–82, 184

van Creveld, Martin, 10
van Wyck, Peter, 99
video games, 208, 209
vinyl records: B sides, 169, *170*; ecological and economic sustainability, 155–56, 163–64; manufacturing and pressing plants, 159–64, 168n24; recycling and reissuing, 164–65; sales and online orders, 16, 154, 156–59; shift from shellac, 15, 162; shipping, 154–55, 166
Virilio, Paul, viii, 11, 95, 99–100, 140; chronopolitics of speed, 115, 138–39, 147
Viryl Technologies, 163
Vismann, Cornelia, 102–3, 104
voice-activated assistants, 113–14, 116
voice-picking software, 82–83
voices: of dockworkers, 80; of enslaved people, 77–78; Indigenous, 108n16; of ship crews, 82; telephone, 121, 124
Voss, Georgina, 84–85

waiting, act of, 220–21
wampum belts, 104–5, 110n45
warehouses, 37, 116; Alibaba and Amazon, 136–37; Egyptian, 32, *33*; Western Electric, 123
warfare, viii, 2, 9–10; listening practices, 78–79; propaganda, 11. *See also name of war*
Warner Bros., 171, 173–74, 177
Western Electric: efficiency and Interphones, 119–20, *121, 122*, 125; supply and distribution, *112*, 123–24, 195; "Supply Year Book," 120–21
Whipped Cream and Other Delights (Herb Alpert and the Tijuana Brass), 165
whiteness, 24, 25, 28
Wilderson, Frank, 10
Wood, Marcus, 41, 43

World War I, 37, 65, 67, 79
World War II, 11, 130, 162
writing, distribution of, 14, 15
Wynter, Sylvia, 207–8

Young, Liam Cole, 12

Zara, 153
Zen Buddhism, 26, 30–31
Zieger, Susan, 8
zines, 15
Zong (ship), 35
Zuboff, Shoshana, 28–29

www.ingramcontent.com/pod-product-compliance
Lightning Source LLC
Chambersburg PA
CBHW071102280326
41928CB00051B/2699